From N. Jablonski
M. Lenover

M000230267

Evan Pugh's Penn State

Evan Pugh's Penn State

AMERICA'S MODEL AGRICULTURAL COLLEGE

Roger L. Williams

The Pennsylvania State University Press

University Park, Pennsylvania

Library of Congress Cataloging-in-Publication Data

Names: Williams, Roger L. (Roger Lea), author.
Title: Evan Pugh's Penn State : America's model agri-
    cultural college / Roger L. Williams.
Description: University Park, Pennsylvania : The
    Pennsylvania State University Press, [2018] |
    Includes bibliographical references and index.
Summary: "Explores the contributions of Evan
    Pugh (1828–1864), founding president of today's
    Pennsylvania State University, in quickly building
    it into America's first scientifically based agricul-
    tural college"—Provided by publisher.
Identifiers: LCCN 2017047087 | ISBN 9780271080178
    (cloth : alk. paper)
Subjects: LCSH: Pugh, Evan, 1828–1864. |
    College presidents—Pennsylvania—Biography. |
    Agricultural chemists—Pennsylvania—Biography.
    | Agricultural College of Pennsylvania—History. |
    Farmers' High School of Pennsylvania—History.
    | Agricultural education—Pennsylvania—
    History—19th century.
Classification: LCC LD4481.P817 P84 2018 | DDC
    378.0092 [B] —dc23
LC record available at https://lccn.loc.gov/2017047087
Published by The Pennsylvania State University Press,
University Park, PA 16802-1003

The Pennsylvania State University Press is a member of
the Association of University Presses.

It is the policy of the Pennsylvania State University
Press to use acid-free paper. Publications on uncoated
stock satisfy the minimum requirements of American
National Standard for Information Sciences—
Permanence of Paper for Printed Library Material,
ANSI Z39.48–1992.

CONTENTS

On a snowy, blustery day in late October 1859, Evan Pugh, Ph.D., set foot for the first time on the grounds of the Farmers' High School in remote Centre County, Pennsylvania. After leaving his ancestral home in Oxford, Chester County, Pennsylvania, he had taken the train from Philadelphia to the depot at Spruce Creek, a whistle-stop hamlet twenty-two miles west of campus. There he was met by school trustee Hugh McAllister, an attorney from Bellefonte, and taken by buggy to his destination.

As they approached, Pugh saw a stark, stone building, only one-third finished, a tall tower dominating a barren landscape. There were a few ramshackle outbuildings, surrounded by muddy fields, including a gaping hole just to the southeast where limestone for the "college building" was being quarried. No amenities, no comforts. Only bone-hard work awaited.

School was already in session, having opened for instruction the previous February. Under the tutelage of four faculty members, some 119 young men and boys were enrolled during that first year, though not more than 100 were in residence at any one time. On the first day of classes, 69 students—nominated by their respective county agricultural societies—had shown up, with others filtering in (and out) as the academic year progressed.

One of those students, C. Alfred Smith, remembered the day as being filled with excitement and relief. As Pugh took his seat at the head table in the dining hall, there came a "genuine outburst of hearty welcome" as the students looked with anticipation at the imposing man "who would save the Farmers' High School of Pennsylvania from failure."[1]

On that day, Pugh had reached the great inflection point in his short but eventful life. Now the years of preparation were over, and Pugh at last could get on with his true purpose: "to develop upon the soil of Penna. the best Ag. College in the world for the ag. student of America."[2] In the four and one-half years remaining to him, Pugh would emerge as one of the most compelling

young leaders in American higher education, with particular influence upon the American land-grant college movement.

Pugh was a visionary with a driving sense of purpose—a man of unusually high educational attainment for his era who exuded extraordinary intellectual energy as well as physical and emotional stamina. In the mid-nineteenth century, a time when American agricultural interests were forging self-conscious political communities on the local, state, and national levels, Pugh was a forceful advocate for introducing scientifically based agricultural (and later industrial) education at the collegiate level. His larger goal was to harness science for the improvement of American agricultural productivity—a necessity not only for struggling farmers but also for the larger national agenda of growth, industrialization, and prosperity.

An inveterate planner, Pugh ordered his entire life in service to his vision. At age twenty-five, he left his home in southeastern Pennsylvania for Germany to pursue advanced study and, in 1856, secured a Ph.D. in chemistry from the University of Göttingen. Afterward, he went to England, where at the Rothamsted Experiment Station he conducted a revolutionary experiment that settled an international controversy on how plants absorb free nitrogen—and in so doing laid the foundation for the modern ammonium nitrate fertilizer industry.

Rather than continue his work as a researcher, Pugh turned his life to what he deemed to be its more urgent purpose: to establish a scientifically based American agricultural college that would serve as the national model for others to emulate. What Pugh really wanted, however, was a national system of state and federally sponsored agricultural colleges and subordinate schools, much like what had been developed in the German states, in which agricultural science could flourish and thus improve agricultural productivity across the nation. That system could best be developed, he maintained, through the establishment of a successful agricultural college at its apex.

Pugh quickly brought the fledgling school to life, graduating what he deemed to be the nation's first class of undergraduates trained in the agricultural sciences—eleven of whom in 1861 received the first Bachelor of Scientific Agriculture degrees granted in America. To accomplish this and set the stage for more success, he redesigned the curriculum, taught the students, promoted the school and the cause of scientific agriculture, fought for state funding, developed the campus's physical plant, and advocated for the Morrill Land-Grant College Act. Pugh believed that scientific institutions served both state and national interests, and thus needed to be amply funded by government, as was the case in Germany. The Morrill Act apportioned federal lands to the states for the purpose of establishing colleges in which agriculture and the mechanic arts (engineering) would be the "leading objects." Accordingly, the passage of the Morrill Act became a top priority for Pugh.

In the spring of 1862, as Congressman Morrill's bill was gathering a head of steam, Pugh renamed the school the Agricultural College of Pennsylvania to more accurately reflect its collegiate status and better position it to receive the funds the legislation promised. After the act's passage, he quickly secured the agreement of the state to accept the terms of the Morrill Act and designate the college as the sole beneficiary. The act of acceptance was passed by the Pennsylvania legislature and signed into law by Governor Andrew Curtin in April 1863.

Then things began to unravel. Pugh and his fiancée were injured in a buggy accident in June 1863. His broken arm required treatment in Philadelphia and took him away from the college for ten weeks of recuperation. At this same time, the college was nearly drained of students volunteering to defend Pennsylvania soil as the Confederate army invaded the Keystone state.

Returning to the college in October 1863, Pugh got the institution back on track. In early 1864, however, he was confronted by stiff political opposition in the form of legislation designed to repeal the state's acceptance act of 1863 and reapportion the Morrill Act proceeds to additional colleges. A few months later, as Pugh was writing an angry response to this legislation, he suddenly fell ill and died a week later, on April 29, 1864. He was thirty-six years old.

After Pugh's death, the Agricultural College of Pennsylvania descended into its dark age, eighteen years of retrogression in which it devolved into a backwoods classical college and was nearly closed for good. Pugh's foundational work might have been all for nothing had it not been for the contributions of the institution's "second founder," George W. Atherton (1882–1906), who reconciled the institution to its land-grant college mission and set it on a successful course.

Despite his brief life and unfinished work, Pugh has not gone unnoticed by scholars. Charles Rosenberg, in *No Other Gods: On Science and American Social Thought*, found Pugh to be a force of nature. Pugh and his lifelong friend and confidant Samuel W. Johnson, a Yale graduate who studied with him in Germany and later went on to found the first agricultural experiment station in America (1875), are described as "the most articulate and tenaciously entre-preneurial" of the handful of Americans taking advanced work in German laboratories in the 1850s. Upon his return to the United States, Rosenberg said, "Pugh guided the development of Pennsylvania's agricultural college into an early model for other such institutions before his premature death in 1864."[3]

Alan Marcus, in *Agricultural Science and the Quest for Legitimacy* (1985), observed that "figures most frequently identified as patriarchs of agricultural science in America included Evan Pugh, Eben Horsford, and John Addison Porter," with Samuel W. Johnson, who long outlived Pugh, being "acknowl-edged as the doyen of American agricultural science."[4]

Alfred Traverse, professor of palynology at Penn State and curator of the Pennsylvania Agricultural College (PAC) Herbarium, studied Pugh's nitrogen assimilation experiment at Rothamsted and concluded "that if research of such significance were published today, the author would likely get a Nobel prize or share one with the co-authors." This early scientific work, Traverse added, was "overshadowed by his accomplishment in turning 'Farmers' High School' into the forerunner of the great American Land Grant universities."[5]

Earlier scholars made similar assessments. Like Rosenberg, Charles A. Browne, chief chemist of the US Department of Agriculture, examined the correspondence of Pugh and Johnson in 1930 and concluded that Pugh's death "removed one of the most brilliant investigators in the field of agricultural chemistry. It is doubtful if any American chemist ever prepared himself so thoroughly for his future career as did young Pugh in the six years between 1853 and 1859 when he was occupied in studying chemistry at various institutions in Germany, France, and England." The letters Browne examined "show a remarkable keenness of observation, a delightful sense of humor, and a wonderful maturity of judgment for a man so young." Browne assessed Pugh as a man who was far ahead of his time. "Had his brilliant young life been spared we are confident that by the force of his leadership the great movement which began in the eighties for the promotion of agricultural chemistry and scientific agriculture, would have been advanced by at least a decade."[6]

And not long after Browne's assessment in 1930, the first historian of the land-grant college movement, Earle D. Ross, in *Democracy's College: The Land-Grant Movement in the Formative Stage* (1942), cited Pugh as one of four college presidents who worked vigorously for the passage of Morrill Act. Ross said Pugh "led the Pennsylvania group with characteristic zeal and with effective if not determining influence on the final result." Reading Ross, it is interesting to speculate how Pugh, "one of the ablest and most versatile science scholars and administrators of the time," might have influenced the land-grant college movement and the whole of American higher education had he lived to a ripe old age.[7]

While there have been articles, profiles, and a master's thesis written over the years, Pugh has never been the subject of a full biographical treatment. Although his early life is dealt with in some detail, this effort focuses more on Pugh's work in building the model agricultural college as the envisioned centerpiece of a larger national system of similar colleges. But there is much more to Pugh's vision. Years before the Morrill Act, Pugh envisioned a well-articulated national system—consisting not only of agricultural colleges but also of agricultural experiment stations, a strong federal department of agriculture, as well as national standards and reporting systems for all things agricultural. His models for the modern agricultural enterprise—encompassing education, research, and state support—were to be found in Europe, which he judged to be far ahead of America. Pugh wanted to borrow, adapt, and improve upon those European models for the benefit of American agriculture. To do so, one had to start somewhere, and for Pugh that meant building the model for scientific agriculture in American higher education.

Thus, the ultimate purpose of this work is to place Pugh in proper historical context. Somewhat obscured from higher education history because of his early death, he nonetheless merits attention for his foresight, influence, and accomplishments. To bring all of this to light, I have relied heavily on Pugh's voluminous writings—letters, articles, reports, catalogs, speeches, manifestos. Pugh was as gifted with the written word as he was with scientific apparatus. To the extent possible, I have tried to let Pugh tell his own story, in his own words, and in some depth and detail. Muted for more than a century and one half, his voice deserves a second hearing; with that, his vision and contributions will, I trust, become fully evident.

A work such as this requires the wisdom and perspective of many individuals. I am especially indebted to four early readers, whose guidance and critical remarks were indispensable to shaping the narrative. They are Roger L. Geiger, Emeritus Distinguished Professor of Higher Education at the Pennsylvania State University and author of numerous influential volumes on higher education history; Michael Bezilla, former director of research communications at Penn State and erstwhile institutional historian, having produced three volumes on the university's history; Leon J. Stout, emeritus head, Public Services and Outreach, Special Collections, and author of many articles on Penn State history; and Jacqueline R. Esposito, University Archivist and Head, Records Management Services, as well as her first-rate staff. Early inspiration was provided by Jerome K. Pasto, late associate dean in the College of Agricultural Sciences; throughout his career and retirement, Pasto kept Pugh's historical flame burning and passed on to me his collection of Pugh memorabilia.

I am also indebted to Barbara Dewey, dean of the University Libraries and Scholarly Publications at Penn State, for her early encouragement in this project. At Penn State University Press, I am especially grateful for the interest and support of director Patrick Alexander and acquisitions editor Kathryn Yahner, as well as Jennifer Norton, Laura Reed-Morrisson, Brendan Coyne, and Hannah Hebert. Copyeditor Therese Boyd was indispensable to the final product and a delight to work with. Sally Heffentreyer, retired assistant director of creative services at Penn State, provided invaluable assistance in reviewing drafts of the work and formatting the manuscript. And what a special thrill it was to have Chip Kidd, Penn State Distinguished Alumnus and world-renowned graphic artist, create the book cover design.

On the personal side, my wife, Karen Magnuson, created the comfortable conditions in our home and provided the love and support essential to this endeavor. My son Nathan Williams and daughter Andrea Weston, stepdaughter Jessica Yost and stepson Philip Horne, as well as my brother Keith

Williams and sister Melody Grubb, have been great cheerleaders throughout this project, as have other relatives and friends.

Finally, I wish to dedicate this volume to Roger L. Geiger, mentioned above. For thirty years, as a historian, teacher, mentor, dissertation advisor, editor, conference organizer, colleague, and friend, he has been a never-ending source of inspiration and encouragement to me. What a privilege it has been to witness his scholarly career as he profoundly influenced and reshaped the field of American higher education history.

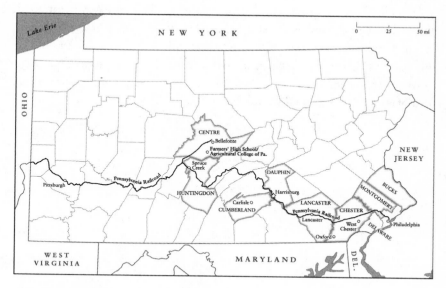

MAP 1 *Evan Pugh's Pennsylvania.*

MAP 2 *Evan Pugh's America.*

CHAPTER I

Evan Pugh

A Young Man Enamored of Science and Education

THE WORLD INTO WHICH Evan Pugh was born on February 29, 1828, was peaceable, well established, and relatively secure and stable, though life was far from easy. His ancestors, Welsh Quakers, had been in Pennsylvania for five generations, stretching back to the late 1600s when the Welsh immigrated to southeastern Pennsylvania in droves. They came mainly out of the desire for religious liberty and the prospect of establishing their own autonomous community within the larger confines of William Penn's Quaker (and thus exceptionally liberal and tolerant) proprietary colony. The Welsh settled to the west and north of Philadelphia, in what was called the Welsh Barony or Welsh Tract, located in the original Philadelphia and Chester counties and the later carve-outs of Montgomery and Delaware counties.[1]

According to family records, the first Pugh to settle in Pennsylvania was the Quaker Ellis Pugh, who arrived from Wales in the late 1680s, only a few years after Penn had established the colony in 1682. Beyond his work as a farmer and blacksmith, which for Pugh males became their two-pronged working tradition for generations, history provides no additional information about Ellis Pugh. John Pugh, Ellis's son, bought 500 acres near the village of Oxford, Chester County, and established the family homestead and farm for the ensuing generations.[2] Located in the extreme southwestern corner of

Chester County, Oxford is about twenty-seven miles southeast of Lancaster, sixty-five southwest of Philadelphia, and only a few miles north of the Mason-Dixon line.

John and his wife bore five children, one of whom was William, who married Mary Brown in 1742. They in turn bore six children, one of whom, Jesse, born in 1772, became Evan Pugh's paternal grandfather. Jesse married Elizabeth Hudson in 1795, a union that produced ten children, including Evan's father, Lewis Pugh, born in 1796. Lewis married Mary Hutton in 1822 and they begat six children: Rebecca, born in 1823 and dead a month later; Susannah, born in 1824; Elizabeth, Evan's closest sibling, who was born in 1826 and died in 1847; Evan, born in 1828, on February 29 in that leap year; Enoch, born in 1830; and John, born in 1832 and dying accidentally in childhood, in 1834.[3]

Upon their marriage, Lewis and Mary Pugh moved into a two-story farmhouse at Jordan Bank, near Oxford, on a tract of fifty-six acres that his father, Jesse, had carved out of the family homestead and deeded to Lewis. Having apprenticed as a blacksmith in the family tradition, Lewis quickly constructed a blacksmith shop on the property. To power the shop's tilt-hammer forge, he built a dam across nearby Jordan Creek. Between the farm and the smithy, Lewis and Mary prospered financially, and "life appeared happy and secure."[4]

But shortly after Evan's birth in 1828, the family suffered a reversal of fortune. In September 1830, Lewis was working in the shop, over the fire, "and had a fit and fell into the fire and was so badly burned before he was taken out that he lost his sight; but parcially [sic] got over the burn but could never see after."[5] Mary and her children took on increasing responsibilities as Lewis's health deteriorated. After his accident, the epileptic seizures continued every two to three weeks and eventually killed Lewis on July 20, 1840. Evan was twelve years old and, as the eldest son, suddenly became head of the household, but only for the moment. The family was forced to split apart. The two eldest children, Elizabeth and Evan, went to live at the neighboring farm with Jesse and his two unmarried daughters, Adrianna and Mary. The two daughters not only were Jesse's housekeepers but also conducted a small school for girls. Meanwhile, the two younger children, Susanna and Enoch, remained with their mother, Mary, at the family home.

The plan was for twelve-year-old Evan, obligated to carry on the family tradition, to follow in his father's footsteps and become a blacksmith's apprentice when he reached his sixteenth birthday. As he recounted it: "Considering the success of my father in the business, the prospect before him at the time and the lamentable sumination [sic] of all his hopes and prospects in the

FIGURE 2 *Grandfather Jesse Pugh's house, where Pugh lived after his father's death in 1840.*

accident of fifteen minutes—the gradual decline of everything he had erected to carry out his designs—the dependant [*sic*] state of my mother, it was natural that my friends should look to me as the eldest son, as one who should carry out the frustrated designs of my father."[6]

In the meantime, he continued his education in the township's elementary schools, and also accepted tutoring by his aunt, Adrianna Pugh, who taught him algebra, geometry, geography, history, Latin, and stenography. In addition, the Pugh family was always active in Quaker meeting, and Evan and his siblings were steeped in its religious training, supplemented by added religious instruction at home. Adrianna was a cut above the norm. Her wide-ranging studies and store of knowledge provided Evan with an early advantage, and she remained a strong proponent of his plans to acquire more education. Pugh attributed much of his success in life to the education he received at the hand of Adrianna.[7]

Evan had been imbued with a strong sense of obligation and duty to his family. But, at the threshold of puberty, his mind began to wander in different directions. He has been described as "reflective and even melancholy," given to daydreaming, and "inquisitive and adventuresome," and, though Quaker, not averse to looking elsewhere for religious inspiration. Not long after his father's death, Evan came into contact with some Mormons who had decamped in Chester County before traveling west to Ohio. When they left, Evan followed, but soon returned to his grandfather's home, confirming Jesse's faith in his "good sense and morality."[8] Jesse was a Quaker of the "more liberal school," his father being "not governed by their dogmas, yet approved of their principles." Still, he could not fathom Evan's attraction, however evanescent, to Mormonism.[9]

At an early age, Evan developed the lifelong habit of talking to himself. "Having passed my life from my 5th to my 15th year almost entirely without other associates of my own age except a sister, I embraced hours for this gratification," he said. He began reading at age seven, his first intellectual foray into the world beyond Oxford being *Sir William Wallace*, about the thirteenth-century leader of the Scottish Wars of Independence, from which he got his "first idea of heroism, of patriotic fire." Pugh read other books, from *Babes in the Woods*, his first and only novel, to antislavery tracts. He also began to imaginatively mount the rostrum and give public speeches: "They were always in defence [sic] of some unpopular, yet what I considered a just cause."[10]

When he was sixteen, however, his sense of familial duty and tradition reasserted itself. And so in 1844 Pugh entered into apprenticeship to become a blacksmith. It was not a happy episode. His apprenticeship lasted two years and ended in disaster. Pugh soon grew to hate his master, a certain Samuel Townsend, whom he deemed stupid and insensible. Pugh persevered, but later branded his apprenticeship an utter waste of time.[11] Still, the experience haunted him, the sense that he had deserted his post, abandoned his destiny, and failed in his responsibilities to his family. As Pugh later reflected, this "idea"—of taking his father's place as a blacksmith—"fought with me" for the seven years following his apprenticeship, not receiving its final "death blow" until the late summer of 1853, just before Pugh was to leave for Germany.[12]

In 1847, death came to those closest to Pugh—first, his beloved sister Elizabeth, followed three months later by his grandfather, Jesse. Dreaming of Elizabeth years later as he crossed the Atlantic, Pugh lamented that her "absence . . . has left a heavy vacuity in my lonely moments . . . which no living form can fill."[13]

This turn of events, coupled with Aunt Adrianna's encouragement, induced Pugh to leave Chester County and enroll at Whitestown Seminary near Utica, New York. Whitestown was a manual labor school where, among other things, Pugh evolved some of his later theories on the practical applications of science in education. At Whitestown he studied analytical geometry, differential and integral calculus, applied geometry, astronomy, botany, physics, geology, and chemistry.[14] He also studied Pitman shorthand, an arcane and nearly forgotten variant of standard shorthand, and in fact kept his journal for the entire Whitestown year in Pitman.

His Whitestown education, coupled with his wide-ranging intellect, childhood experiences, and natural curiosity, kindled an interest in scientific agriculture and teaching. Seeking to broaden his horizons, Pugh traveled to Utica, Albany, Niagara Falls, and New York City. He returned to the family farm in December 1848 with a new life's purpose. Thus, he began teaching during the spring of 1849 at an elementary school in nearby Blue Ball Tavern, Maryland, just across the Mason-Dixon Line.[15]

In the fall of 1849 Pugh took another leap and opened his own school—the Jordan Bank Academy for boys—on the family farm. He used the second floor of the blacksmith's shop for classrooms. His mother provided room and board at the farmhouse for some of his pupils. He taught the usual studies, with laboratory and fieldwork in botany, analytical chemistry, geology, and mineralogy. True to the Quaker ethos of gender equality, Pugh opened his lectures and demonstrations to his aunt's pupils in the "Misses Pughs' Pleasant Valley Seminary for Girls." Pugh's students could also learn the "art of photographic reporting," a combination of Pitman shorthand with some phonetically spelled longhand.[16] To the untutored eye, Pugh's writings in this style present an indecipherable communications code as esoteric as Runic or Sanskrit. But through this self-devised system, he was able to take notes copiously and accurately.

Pugh thrived as headmaster of Jordan Bank. For one thing, he got an early taste of the exhilaration of operating a school, whetting his appetite for what would come later, on a grander scale. He had time and equipment to experiment in chemistry, by now his greatest scientific passion. He also prospered financially and in the thrifty Quaker tradition salted away his profits for future needs. He fairly reveled in teaching and learning, composing a Jordan Bank ditty titled "Education," which exemplified the noble quest for knowledge on which he led his students:

> The elements that form our globe,
>   by chemistry we'll know,
> The truths this science will unfold,
>   Analysis will show;
> The soils and minerals of our globe,
>   beneath our eyes shall fall,
> And we will never stop to rest,
>   till we have learned them all.[17]

At Jordan Bank, Pugh's talent for versifying found larger and longer expression in "Osseology," a poem sung to the tune of "Auld Lang Syne" that covered the 208 bones in the human body. A sample:

'Tis of the human bones we'll sing, 208 we name,
   Which give us form, so neat, complete, and constitute our frame;
Of these, the Head has 26—the Teeth we don't include,
   Which, by themselves, will form a class, to which we must allude.
Eight bones in the skull we next will find, arch'd o'er the brain complete,
   And 'neath their concave tablets here, the mind has her retreat:
Occipital behind the head, where social feelings lie,
   And o'er it the parietal bones their tablets do apply.[18]

Jordan Bank Academy was successful on all counts, drawing students from well beyond Oxford. A roster from winter 1853 shows twenty-five enrollees. Of these, seventeen were boarding students and eight were day students. The seventeen boarding students included seven from Lancaster County, six from Chester County, two from Cecil County, Maryland, one from Wilmington, Delaware, and one from England. Of the eight day students, six came from Chester County, one from Baltimore, and one from Washington, D.C.[19] Much of the academy's allure lay in its scientific offerings. In February 1853 Pugh promoted the academy thus: "The summer term of this institution will open on the Fourth of the fourth month to continue twelve weeks. The course of instruction embraces all the branches of learning of a thorough English education, including the art of phonographic reporting and chemical analyses. Particular attention will be given to the sciences of Mineralogy, Geology and Botany which can be pursued successfully at no other season of the year. . . . Students in analytical chemistry are allowed the use of apparatus and reagents in analyzing soils, minerals . . . for an extra charge of $10.00."[20]

Pugh's years at Jordan Bank were happy ones, and his cast of mind turned optimistic. Pugh's younger cousin, Swithin C. Shortlidge, visited him for the first (and only) time in 1852. Shortlidge in old age recalled the twenty-four-year-old Pugh as "a handsome man with the school-boy flowing locks fancied at that period, enthusiastic, buoyant, alert and full of animation, and his conversation captivated my imagination."[21] Pugh characterized his Jordan Bank years as being of "great use. . . . It afforded me an opportunity for mental exercise and responsibility that I could not have had at any other place."[22]

FIGURE 3
*Evan Pugh in 1849, at age
twenty-one.*

In addition to teaching at Jordan Bank and conducting chemistry experiments, particularly as applied to plants and minerals, Pugh began to write.
Indeed, by his late teens he had become an inveterate journalist, contributing
articles and reports to county newspapers. Keenly observant with insatiable curiosity, he had an eye for detail, a penchant for elaborate description,
and abundant intellectual energy to go with it. He wrote reports of teachers' meetings, a trial of runaway slaves in Baltimore, and numerous travel
sketches—which he continued in great profusion from his peregrinations
during his study breaks in Europe. Indeed, his later journal entries and newspaper dispatches of German life and culture would rival Charles Dickens's
American Notes in astute commentary, sharp observations, and richness of
detail.

In June 1851 Pugh covered, in thirty-five pages, George Thompson's antislavery jeremiad. Thompson was an American who had returned after sixteen

years in England, decrying how rapidly slavery had grown and spread during his absence.[23] In August 1852 Pugh traveled to Newark, New Jersey, to cover the annual meeting of the National Association for the Formation of Education. The ten-page transcript, written as a recording secretary would render it, ends with Pugh's editorial comment lamenting that he was the only Chester Countian to attend. This disappointed him because "we can say we stand second to no county, of the same population, in the State in point of interest in the subject, as manifested by the number of public and private schools found all over the county." Pugh urged Chester Countians to have a meeting prior to the next year's convention and send more delegates.[24]

Pugh covered the trial of the Parker Girls at Baltimore, detailing the plight of two free African American girls who were kidnapped as runaway slaves, with the kidnapper, a Marylander, being found guilty. Turning to human interest, Pugh wrote about "Andy Job, the Hermit of West Nottingham," a "child of the forest" who lived in that fashion for fifty years: "He appears to have lost his comb and razor about forty years ago, and the consequence is his beard hangs down to his waste in matted knots that seem to be of half a century's standing."[25]

Through all of this, Pugh held fast to his Welsh Quaker principles. He abhorred smoking, alcohol, gambling, and idle pursuits. He hated slavery and championed gender equality. Indeed, the twenty-four-year-old Pugh spoke eloquently on the latter score at Pennsylvania's first Women's Rights Convention in 1852: "The question of women's rights affects the whole human race. We know from sad experience that man cannot rise while woman is degraded. . . . Who were the mothers of great men? Women of mind, of thought, of independence; not women degraded by men's tyranny, laboring in prescribed limits, thinking other people's thoughts."[26]

In addition, the Pennsylvania Quaker community in which Pugh grew up held a strong respect for science, particularly for science as it might be applied to agriculture, as did the wider Chester County intelligentsia.[27] As Pugh entered early manhood, Chester County was still largely agricultural. Its land was described as being unusually fertile, and early farmers did particularly well in raising Indian corn, barley, oats, rye, and wheat. As early as 1784 farms were large by the standards of the day, averaging 100–200 acres, with 4–9 percent of county land under cultivation. Toward the mid-nineteenth century, Chester County became a center of agricultural improvement and innovation, giving rise to some rudimentary attempts at inventing mechanized threshers and mowers. In 1838 the leading lights formed an agricultural society for Chester and Delaware counties. In 1845 or thereabouts, the Chester County Horticultural Society was formed. In 1853, Chester County formed its own Agricultural Society, appointing committees to study and report on "the prevalence and injurious effects of the fly on wheat; on the subject of deep plowing; on the potato plant and the best varieties and mode of cultures; on the culture of barley; and on the utility of guano or fertilizer."[28] In addition, the *Pennsylvania Farm Journal*, arguably the leading journal of its kind in the Commonwealth, was published in West Chester. Agriculture and its multifarious problems and concerns were always in the air, and Pugh breathed them in deeply.

In his early twenties, Pugh came in contact with local luminaries interested in promoting the application of science to agriculture and industry. Foremost among them was Dr. William Darlington (1782–1863), an eminent Chester County physician, politician, and renowned botanist. Until his death Darlington, also a Quaker, would remain a role model for, and champion of, Pugh. Darlington was the quintessential nineteenth-century man of affairs, with deep interests in agriculture, medicine, science, and politics. A Chester County native, he grew up on the family farm, hating the drudgery and resenting the way in which it prevented him from gaining an education. At age eighteen, he apprenticed to a physician from Wilmington, Delaware, after which he attended lectures in medicine at the University of Pennsylvania, receiving his M.D. in 1804. He then signed on as a ship's surgeon, after which he established a medical practice in West Chester. Darlington purchased a small farm and turned to public service of varying sorts, including three terms in Congress. He founded the Chester County Cabinet of Natural Science in 1826, which became for a time the most successful of the state's several natural history societies. In 1830 he was elected president of the Bank of Chester County and gave up his medical practice four years later.

As a physician, Darlington was described as a "medical innovator." He used the drug ergot for the "first time in obstetrics to stop a hemorrhage of childbirth." Under the tutelage of Dr. Benjamin Rush at the University of Pennsylvania, Darlington learned the dictum, "that as God put diseases on earth to plague man, He also placed nearby a plant which man could use to cure himself of a given disease if he had the sense to fund the plant and use it." It was this search for curative plants that led Darlington into botany.[29]

And it was in botany that Darlington made his most enduring mark. He edited and preserved the works of other noted botanists, including John Bartram and Humphry Marshall, also of Chester County. Darlington's first original work was a technical book, *Florula Cestrica* (1826), in which he gave

FIGURE 4
*William Darlington,
M.D., Pugh's early
mentor.*

brief descriptions of 735 native and naturalized plants in West Chester, work
that was later enlarged upon to encompass the whole of Chester County
(*Flora Cestrica*, 1837). His *Agricultural Botany: An enumeration of useful plants
and weeds* (1847) was written as a practical guide for the American farmer and
subsequently republished in a more useable format in 1859 as *American Weeds
and Useful Plants*. For his body of work Darlington was called the "Nestor of
American Botany" by no less a luminary than Asa Gray, professor of natural
history at Harvard.[30]

Darlington's son, J. Lacey Darlington (1809–93), also played a part in
Pugh's life. J. Lacey was editor of the *Pennsylvania Farm Journal* and a long-
term officer of the Chester County Agricultural Society.[31] He became well
acquainted with Pugh, and from his influential perch championed Pugh's
work and the Farmers' High School, always looking to nominate smart young
county boys for admission.

As a scientist of wide repute, Dr. Darlington (the elder) exerted a profound influence on young Pugh. As a result of his experiments, readings, and
conversations with Darlington, Pugh became a champion of the movement for

agricultural education.[32] In the spring and summer of 1853, with Darlington's encouragement, Pugh determined that he would go to Europe for advanced study in the sciences. Advanced study was largely unavailable in America and graduate study as yet unheard of. Germany—more accurately, the various German states, as opposed to the German nation that would be unified by Otto von Bismarck in 1871—was the leading scientific culture during the nineteenth century, being especially dominant in chemistry.

With the remaining members of his family having settled elsewhere, Pugh was now free to dispose of the family farm, which as the eldest son was his by inheritance. By the early summer of 1853, he closed his academy and sold the farm to his uncle Amos Pugh, who owned the adjoining farm, for $2,800 in cash.[33] With that sum and the savings from his five prosperous years as a schoolmaster, he was armed to finance his education in Europe and eventual return to the states. As an added resource, he took along some books, mineral specimens, and pressed flowers for exchange or sale.

At the age of twenty-five, as he prepared to leave for Germany, Pugh already had formed his agenda: to first master the science that should underpin the practice of agriculture, and then to use that knowledge to bring into being a new form of higher education that would transform American agriculture. His vision encompassed not only the urgent need for agricultural colleges but also a clear conception of what their curriculum ought to be. As he put it in a newspaper dispatch written upon his departure for Germany:

> To bring about a properly informed agricultural community, the subject of agricultural chemistry should be made an important item in the education of farmers' sons. We want agricultural schools where boys can get a thorough knowledge of the theory and practice of agriculture and the collateral branches of botany, geology and mineralogy; much of the time that is now spent in mathematics and the languages would be far more advantageously spent in becoming familiar with these sciences. . . .
>
> To accomplish what is suggested in the foregoing, we want what we have not yet, *vis.*, agricultural schools. First an agricultural college and model farm to give the first idea, then as a necessary consequence, smaller institutions of similar character, accessible to all would spring up all over the country.[34]

To establish the model college, Pugh first needed to prepare himself. He was determined to immerse himself in the most advanced scientific work that Europe had to offer and earn the necessary academic credentials. As he later wrote to his friend Samuel Johnson: "My plan was to remain 3 years in the German universities and *graduate*; then spend 6 or 8 months in Paris to study French and see the fashions and write (I shall not devote much time to chemistry in France). Then go to England and remain about one year looking around at the agricultural state of the country and working a little in their agricultural laboratories."[35] Remarkably, Pugh carried out this plan, almost to the letter.

Ever the observer and commentator of experiences, places, current events, travels, and of course people sublime and ridiculous, Pugh recorded his impressions in personal journals and lengthy letters sent home to friends or to newspapers. His detailed reports to the *West Chester Register and Examiner* describe his sailing from Philadelphia to New York, arriving August 25, 1853; his exploring the city while waiting for passage to Hamburg; and his visiting the World's Fair then under way at the replica of London's Crystal Palace near the old Croton Reservoir at 142nd Street. His subsequent reports described the twenty-one passengers and life in general aboard the ship *George Canning*, which sailed September 6 and arrived at Hamburg a month later.

It was Pugh's first foray on the high seas, and it wasn't particularly pleasant for him. The sailing went largely without incident, and it did provide some time for Pugh to study the German language and his chemistry books, and to write extensively in his journal. But the company was repulsive to him. He felt seasick initially, as did his fellow passengers, who "vomited without going to the window, until the floor was more like a swine pen than anything to stand on." His dislike soon grew to contempt: "About one half of them lie in bed all day—never get up to eat, wash, dress or anything. When the victuals come in, they rouse up like grunting swine and present their dirty, frowsy, uncombed heads and stick out their yellow, dingy forefeet and blubber out in Dutch for something to eat . . . then they commence smoking and spitting tobacco spit about." Pugh meticulously described the conditions of the weather and the seas, his musings at times philosophical or historical, at others nostalgic— "a rather motley group of ideas opinions, notions, dreams, descriptions, etc., all coming in as I felt inclined to write them."[36] At journey's end, Pugh waxed euphoric as the ship docked in Hamburg.

The question arises as to why Pugh, who lacked an undergraduate degree from an American college, opted for study in a foreign land as opposed to pursuing higher education in the United States, particularly at its leading scientific institutions of the day such as Yale, Harvard, Union, and Rensselaer.

There is no evidence in the Pugh Papers that he ever considered an American option. He was, however, most interested in agricultural chemistry, and knew that there was very little of that going on in the United States.

Agricultural Science and Education as Pugh Left for Germany

Early on, Pugh had developed an impressive knowledge of agricultural education and research in both Europe and the United States. As he described it, agricultural education and experimentation had their origins in eighteenth-century Europe. In Sweden Johan Gottschalk Wallerius conducted chemical-agricultural experiments, publishing in 1761 *Agriculturae Fundamenta Chemica*, in which he tried to develop a system of manuring based on the examination of the ashes of plants. In England Jethro Tull was developing his system of practical farming. In France, in 1747, Francois Quesnay founded the Physiocratic School, focused mainly on the dissemination of agricultural concepts.

But nowhere was this interest more pronounced than in the various German states. Agricultural professorships were established at the universities of Göttingen (1769), Giessen, Rostock, and Leipzig (1778). In addition, some agricultural instruction was made available in German high schools. The first school devoted to agricultural science and practice was founded by Albrecht Thaer, in 1807, near Berlin. Thaer soon after published his principles of agriculture (1809), advocating the application of science—chiefly botany, zoology, and chemistry—to agricultural practice. "It is evident that agriculture ought to borrow from every science the principles which she employs as the foundation of her own," Thaer presciently wrote. Over time, his enterprise grew to a model farm of 1,200 acres and a college for instruction. Thaer's success demonstrated the need for similar institutions, and several more sprang up, supported financially by the governments of their respective states.[37]

Two seminal books published in the first half of the nineteenth century were to form the theoretical underpinnings for agricultural science. Sir Humphrey Davy's lectures from 1802 to 1812 before Great Britain's Board of Agriculture were published as *Elements of Agricultural Chemistry* and opened up a new method of soil management. More influential, especially in America, was the *Organic Chemistry in Its Application of Agriculture and Physiology* of Justus von Liebig of Germany. Before its publication in 1849, most people accepted the Aristotelian theory that plants obtained nourishment from soil in the form of humus. Liebig showed that the roots do not absorb humus or any other compound, but rather the ions of simple inorganic substances, such as the nitrate ion, the phosphate ion, and the potassium and calcium ions.[38]

The publication of Liebig's *Organic Chemistry*, Pugh observed, "astounded the reading world." It was immediately translated into various languages and inspired legions of scientists "to test the correctness of Liebig's views." While these experiments led to certain modifications of Liebig's work, "in the main they were found to be correct, and the necessity for agricultural schools in which to teach the newly developed science of agriculture, became more apparent everywhere."[39]

Most significantly, Leibig's work suggested that soil fertility could be maintained permanently by restoring the proper balance of nutrients. But his chemistry of soils went only so far. The conceptual frameworks for experimentation on the many other variables relating to agricultural productivity were yet to be devised. As science historian Margaret Rossiter explained it: "One reason why the diffusion of agricultural innovations went through a boom and bust cycle in the nineteenth century was that there was available no adequate experimentation including statistical controls and cost-benefit analysis to determine what was or what was not a useful innovation." In addition, the many variables such as climate, rainfall, soil porosity, and its previous uses were not easily measured or subject to controls. Thus, it was virtually "impossible to tell what constituted an improvement or really applicable 'useful knowledge' and even harder to tell if it was economic or transferable to other soils and localities."[40]

By 1845 only one leg of the triad of fundamental biological processes for crop plants—photosynthesis—was known to scientists. The precise role of the other two processes related to the crop yield—respiration and water absorption-transpiration—awaited illumination.[41] By the time Pugh was leaving for Germany, the aborning but inchoate agricultural sciences, especially in the United States, had a long, long way to go.

Although the locus of scientific advancement was Europe, there were early inklings of interest in America, where science assumed an eminently practical cast. Before 1850 most of the innovation that took place resulted more from the "empirical observations of practical men, most of them ignorant of contemporary science."[42] Exceptions to this observation, however, might include Benjamin Franklin, Benjamin Rush, David Rittenhouse, Thomas Jefferson, and others known for generating scientific knowledge with an eye to its useful applications.

Before 1820 the American scientific establishment, such as it was, existed not so much in the colleges, such as they were, as in the various learned societies formed for the promotion of knowledge. Aside from the two major learned societies of the day—the American Philosophical Society (1743) and the American Academy of Arts and Sciences (1780), Philadelphia—then the metropolis of America—also gave rise to the Philadelphia Society for Promoting Agriculture (1785), the Academy of Natural Sciences (1812), and the Franklin Institute (1824, emphasizing mechanical improvements). The other hub of learning, Boston, was home to the Massachusetts Society for Promoting Agriculture (1792), the Linnean Society of New England (1814), and the *New England Journal of Medicine and Surgery* (1812).

The scientific spirit, or at least the enthusiasm for empirical investigation, enjoyed a remarkable popularity in the 1830s and 1840s. Much of the interest was sparked by Benjamin Silliman Sr., who with his son would become an admirer and champion of Evan Pugh. Educated at Yale, in Philadelphia, and in Europe, Silliman lectured extensively across the nation on a variety of scientific subjects. In 1818 he founded the *American Journal of Science, More Especially of Mineralogy, Geology, and Other Branches of Natural History; Including Also Agriculture and the Ornamental as Well as the Useful Arts.* Silliman served as sole editor of the publication, popularly known as "Silliman's Journal," for twenty years, until his son, Benjamin Silliman Jr., succeeded him.

The public fascination with science held metaphysical implications as well. The unlimited potential of science and its potential for providing a cornucopia of practical benefits for a democratic society caught the fancy of the literary and transcendentalist communities. The 1840s brought more permanent avenues for disseminating scientific knowledge, notably the Smithsonian Institution and *Scientific American* magazine.[43]

And science did not go unnoticed by the American colleges of the day. Though the older historiography of American higher education held that the antebellum, denominational, classical, or "literary" colleges were highly resistant to admitting science into the curriculum, newer scholarship has shown that to be not quite the case. In all, the numbers of science and mathematics professors on college faculties grew from about 60 in 1828 to more than 300 in 1850, when Pugh was coming of age.[44] By mid-century, most practicing scientists in America were in fact on college faculties. In the main, however, they manned lonely outposts, isolated from one another, overburdened by the demands of teaching and student discipline, and heavily constrained to do any kind of research or otherwise keep up with advancements in their disciplines.

In the 1840s the two leading American colleges—Yale and Harvard—began to lay the groundwork for the establishment of scientific schools and quickly became "the outstanding centers of American science."[45] In 1846 the Yale Corporation established two new professorships—one in agricultural chemistry and animal and vegetable physiology and the other in practical chemistry. These became the foundation of the Sheffield Scientific School. In 1847, through a philanthropic gift, Abbott Lawrence established the Lawrence Scientific School at Harvard. The founding of the Lawrence School was closely associated with the 1846 arrival of Louis Agassiz in Boston to deliver a course of popular lectures. The agriculture historian Alfred C. True described Agassiz's visit as "an event of very great importance in the history of science teaching in this country."[46]

But there were no scientific facilities comparable to Europe's or provisions for formal graduate training, even at the leading colleges such as Yale and Harvard. And in those institutions, where there was experimentation and analysis, the profit motive often compromised the pursuit of pure science. Until the late 1840s, as Charles Rosenberg observed, advanced training in chemistry was to be "found only in a handful of private analytical laboratories, ad hoc, expensive, and often inadequate by contemporary European standards." Even Yale's Analytical Laboratory, opened in 1847 and providing a prototype for graduate training, "was in form not much different from competing private analytical laboratories; fees for analysis and the tuition of private students provided its only income." Finally, science as a professional field did not enjoy the prestige it was accorded in Europe. "Scientists complained again and again that material success alone seemed to determine such social acceptance. . . . Even the ordinarily sanguine Samuel W. Johnson could joke that a rich wife was a young chemist's only hope for success."[47]

Although some scholars have claimed, rightly so, that chemistry was "the first real science of the age," the natural sciences, particularly geology, commanded the greatest interest in the United States.[48] Most of the early learned societies were preoccupied with natural history—the distinctive plants, animals, fossils, and minerals of the North American continent. Jacksonian Democracy (1829–37) also spurred the rise of geology. Increasingly, influential manufacturers, businessmen, and farmers pressed state legislatures to survey natural resources. As early as 1830 the states were providing such a volume of surveys that geologists became more professionally organized and self-conscious of their status than any other scientific community in America.[49] In fact, the first true professional scientific organization was the American Association of Geologists and Naturalists, established by the leaders of state geological surveys. Seeking a broader field of inquiry, the organization transformed itself into the American

Association for the Advancement of Science (AAAS) in 1847. Populated by amateur and professional scientists, AAAS membership swelled to more than 2,000—including Evan Pugh—by the eve of the Civil War.[50]

Despite this growth in scientific interest, the United States lagged far behind Europe. As the historian Roger Geiger observed, "The United States in the first half of the nineteenth century was a provincial outpost in the world of science, and American scientists knew it too."[51] Certainly Evan Pugh knew it, and thus he arranged to travel to the epicenter of advanced science to study with its renowned practitioners.

CHAPTER 2

Study in Germany and France, Research in England

EXACTLY WHY OR HOW Pugh came to choose Leipzig University (or Leipsic as it was spelled in Pugh's day) in the German state of Saxony is unknown, but likely the choice was predicated on the international reputation of the school and its science faculty, particularly in chemistry.[1] Saxony was a center of science and royal patronage. Leipzig University was established in 1409 by a secession of students from the University of Prague. In 1778 a chair of agriculture had been set up. At the time of Pugh's arrival, about 900 to 1,000 students were enrolled, with roughly one-fourth of them being foreign students. In a few months Pugh had ascertained that there were between fifteen and twenty Americans in Leipzig, though not all were enrolled at the university. He had made no previous arrangements for admission to the university. Carrying his vitae in Latin, he showed up unannounced and petitioned for admission, which, after an interview and examination, was granted.[2] His experience was unusual; German universities typically required a bachelor's degree from Americans wishing to enroll.

But if Pugh was determined to study the science of agriculture before establishing his own agricultural college in America, he had come in the right place. In the nineteenth century, the German states were the Mecca for advanced scientific studies. The first Americans to seek higher learning in Germany began in 1816. By the 1850s, the decade of Pugh's experience,

American interest in European institutions had built considerably. And as the historian of the modern American university, Laurence Veysey, put it, German institutions were recognized as being "without doubt pre-eminent in the world."[3]

It is difficult to get the precise number of Americans studying in German universities before the American Civil War, but the best estimate is about 640 discrete Americans between 1810 and 1870. The two most popular universities were Göttingen and Berlin. Americans had the choice of enrolling in one of four "faculties" or schools—law, medicine, theology, and philosophy. The philosophy faculty consisted of the humanities and the natural sciences and was the most heavily subscribed, far outdistancing law, medicine, and theology combined.

Carl Diehl's analysis of American students in German universities from 1810 to 1870 found that a total of 264 U.S. students matriculated at four leading German institutions—Göttingen, Berlin, Heidelberg, and Halle—during those six decades. Some 158 of them were enrolled in philosophy—89 in the humanities and 69 in the natural sciences. The number of 264 students attempts to exclude multiple registrations, as American students were likely, in the fashion of the day, to enroll at multiple German universities to complete their course of study. Such would be the case with Pugh, who would study successively at Leipzig, Göttingen, and Heidelberg, with brief visits to Munich and Berlin in between.

For the decade of the 1850s, some 54 Americans were enrolled in the philosophy faculty at the four aforementioned universities—31 in the humanities and 23 in the natural sciences.[4] Thus Pugh was among a handful of Americans taking advanced study in the sciences at German universities during that decade. The number pales further within the larger context. Pugh sought out overall matriculation numbers for the twenty-eight German universities, reporting in the spring of 1854 that the aggregate number was 18,201 students.[5]

Studies in Germany

Pugh's enrollment at Leipzig University was serendipitous for another reason besides its high standing in science. It was there, at the beginning of the 1853 fall session, that he met Samuel W. Johnson, a recent Yale graduate who would long outlive Pugh and become, by the mid-1870s, the most influential agricultural scientist in America. Pugh and Johnson began a lifelong friendship, each the other's confidante. Their relationship was based on personal traits and

WARREN   LOWELL.

FIGURE 5
*Samuel W. Johnson, Pugh's lifelong
friend and colleague.*

shared values, but more especially on their similar scientific and professional
ambitions. After Johnson returned to Yale in the spring of 1854, they would
share an active, and candid, personal correspondence for the rest of Pugh's life.

In Johnson, Pugh found a kindred spirit—"a strictly temperate student, as
regards the use of tobacco and intoxicating drinks . . . and I am very willing to
lose the honor of being the only temperate student . . . during the six months
that we shall be together."[6] But there was much more to the relationship.
According to Charles Rosenberg, Pugh and Johnson—and other Americans
who studied in Germany during this time—shared four main motivations: the
"fulfillment of individual aspirations" in an environment devoid of materialist
considerations; "evangelical pietism," a belief that inspired serious purpose and
high calling, a career in science being at the apex of human endeavor; "faith
in the virtue of progress," with scientific progress more than anything else
better able to improve the human condition; and a shared ambition to advance

the national interest, which to them hinged on significant improvements in agricultural science.[7]

Pugh's first order of business in Leipzig was to secure lodging. He found a "good size" room only a ten-minute walk from the university, for only $3 per month. Then he and Johnson visited Professor Otto Erdmann, head of the chemistry department, to arrange their studies.[8] Pugh had found Nirvana, at least for the time being. Erdmann had high standing as a chemist in Europe. The laboratory he had established at Leipzig in 1843 was regarded as a model for the new "laboratory technique" of teaching the science. Erdmann had published several books and founded a highly regarded journal for practical chemistry, which he edited from 1834 to 1869. He had also won fame for his collaborative work in measuring the atomic weights of carbon (C), hydrogen (H), calcium (Ca), copper (Cu), mercury (Hg), sulfur (S), and iron (Fe).[9] Pugh was elated with Erdmann's laboratory technique of teaching. He and Johnson also found Erdmann approachable—a man of science who could "enter into friendly chat, introducing the lively anecdote, and laughing over its peculiar phrases."[10]

Erdmann could speak a "little English" and Pugh and Johnson "a little German." Despite his shipboard studies of German grammar, Pugh knew he had to improve his language skills quickly, as he was having difficulty understanding the lectures. He hired a tutor, studied grammar in the mornings before going to the laboratory, and associated almost exclusively with speakers of German. Within a few months he had mastered the language to the point where he could expand upon his studies in chemistry. Erdmann's lab became the center of Pugh's life for the next three semesters, the first of which was devoted to applied chemistry—much of his work being devoted to plant nutrition—and later theoretical chemistry. Pugh also studied the allied agricultural subjects of botany and mineralogy. For the latter, he worked with Franz Neumann, one of the greatest mineralogists in the world, studying crystallography and physical geography with him as well.[11]

Near the end of his third semester at Leipzig in December 1854, Pugh was ready to move on. He had learned about all he could from Erdmann and had, in fact, become disenchanted with the famous professor. Erdmann had been elected rector of the university and his new duties were consuming him. "I have not heard Erdmann this semester, indeed I have hardly seen him," Pugh complained. "He is very little in the laboratory now."[12] Pugh was not, however, disenchanted with German universities. In his dispatches to the homefront, he wrote frequently, and favorably, about the German system of instruction. "If there is any one word that will characterize this system better than others, it is *thorough*; emphatically *thorough*. German professors present the most complete examples of walking dictionaries that I ever saw. . . . In some hundred lectures that I have heard on science, scarcely a single blunder at any time on the most complicated subject has occurred."[13]

Before transferring to Göttingen, Pugh wanted to explore the country—its cities, towns, facilities, and especially its inhabitants. His motive in part was a desire to see "German life . . . to see the homes of the old men and women who attended our markets,—to learn how that part of the German population lived that constitutes our emigrants to America."[14] During the interlude between universities, in late March and early April 1855, he began his peregrinations, on foot. After Altenburg he went on to Ywickau, where he visited the town's chemical plants: "Here I am at the termination of another day's walk of 30 miles through wet, mud, cold, wind and rain."[15] Then on to Chemnitz to visit its factories, castles, and prison, and then to Ocderan. Freiberg was a highlight, where he visited the Freiberg school of mines—"the most celebrated of the kind in Germany, if not the world." There he toured a silver mine, one of about 130 mines of copper, silver, lead, and arsenic in the region. Pugh donned the necessary oilcloth pants, coat, hat, and apron, and with candles and a German student guide to show him the way, descended 500 feet. After negotiating a narrow passageway, they heard the sound of miners' hammers and "a few faint lights glimmering in the smoke of the gunpowder of their last blast." Pugh came away amazed by the "expenditure of muscular effort required to descend a mine," and he was a strong, fit man.[16]

Leaving Freiberg, Pugh found a light of a different sort: Martin Luther's cells in the old cathedral at Erfurt: "I had the pleasure of writing my name in the book for strangers from the cup that once held the black fluid, which . . . conveyed tones of thundering rebuke to the church of Rome."[17] Finally, he traveled by train to Gotha and Wartburg, where in the old castle "Luther was conveyed to avoid the catholic vengeance after his excommunication" and where Luther completed his translation of the New Testament Bible from Latin to German.[18] After a few more stops—in Eisenach, Cassel, and Munden—Pugh arrived in Göttingen in mid-April 1855, "Once more at my journey's end and once more ready to enter upon a year's duties at my desk."[19]

That same month, Pugh entered the University of Göttingen, in the German state of Hanover. Founded in 1737, Göttingen was much newer than Leipzig, though Göttingen had established a chair in agriculture in 1769, a few years earlier than Leipzig. Göttingen had about 700 students and a strong reputation created by leading scientific investigators. Pugh would sit at the feet of one of its most eminent professors: Friedrich Wohler, a former associate of Erdmann, who would in fact come to be known as the "father of organic chemistry."[20] Wohler's lab was overcrowded with students, but Pugh was well satisfied with his new mentor. As a student at Leipzig, Pugh had become familiar with Wohler's reputation, describing him as "a most assiduous teacher, takes a *constant, deep interest* in all his students, and devotes his entire time and interest to their promotion, and as a chemist is thought not to be much inferior to Liebig."[21]

Pugh would remain at Göttingen for a year, hoping to concentrate more on agricultural science. Continuing his laboratory work in applied chemistry, Pugh also studied physics and veered into mathematics, taking differential and integral calculus. The experience with the latter left him exasperated. His mathematical studies, he believed, were of little use in his study of agricultural chemistry, which he believed needed to be developed quickly as a viable field of inquiry: "there is not so very much in this science [agriculture] to study. There is immense to do and after this is done there will be something to study about." Six months later, however, his estimation of mathematics had changed dramatically; he now considered it to be "the great level by which the facts of nature are thrown around into such order that nature's laws are written on them in terms intelligible to man."[22]

Pugh thrived at Göttingen. "It is almost proverbial that if a student comes to Göttingen he comes to study, but if he goes to Berlin, he goes to have a 'good time'—that is, to run about to the theatre, the opera, the dancing saloon, etc., at night and sleep during the day." As he devoted more of his time to analytical and organic chemistry in Wohler's laboratory, his estimation of the man grew stronger: "To no man living does the science of chemistry owe as much for the facts it embraces as to Prof. Wohler, and no man has a higher reputation amongst the students of chemical science as he. When one reads his chemical works and sees the immense labors that this man has performed, he is surprised to find it possible that so much can be done by one man in the ordinary period of life. As a teacher he is unsurpassed."[23]

Pugh's daily regimen at Göttingen was quite agreeable to him. He found a roommate and they secured lodging with ample space: Each had a separate bedroom and separate study room, fully furnished, for $26 for the entire term, including a servant to provide them meals in their room. They rose at 7:00 a.m., ate a light breakfast, and then walked to the laboratory. They worked at their benches until 2:00 p.m., returning to their room, where a lunch of "bread and water and fruit" was provided. Then off they went to a lecture in natural philosophy and, later in the term, electricity, by Professor William Weber, whose course "is considered the best given in Germany." After the lecture, they returned to work in the laboratory until 5:00 p.m., then back to their rooms. They enjoyed a light supper, which for Pugh was mainly vegetarian, not as a matter of principle, but for "convenience and economy," not to mention mental alertness; Pugh found the typical German dinner of pork and potatoes to be stupefying. After dinner, they studied until midnight or 1:00 a.m. "Such is student life," Pugh said. "Who would not like to live it?"[24]

As spring 1855 gave way to summer, Pugh was thinking about the possibility of earning his doctoral degree, but remained ambivalent as to whether it was worth the effort. "I am determined that I will not be led from what I think is the most profitable course of study for me just to get something new to doctor on."[25] In September, before the start of the fall semester, Pugh embarked on a walking vacation through the Harz Mountains, the highest mountain range in northern Germany. He continued to think about a suitable dissertation topic, but his ambivalence remained. "I am very doubtful whether I should have gone to the expense of Doctoring (as we call it), but that some of my friends have expressed a desire that I should."[26] Pugh didn't arrive at a topic before he left, but the matter preyed on his mind during his walks through the mountains. Always the prolific writer, Pugh made daily entries in his journal. He had his month's worth of observations bound into a 407-page journal, "Göttingen and the Harts," which he sent to his family in Chester County.

Arriving in Göttingen, Pugh had still not found a dissertation topic. On September 25 he met with Professor Wohler to discuss the matter, but nothing definite came out of their conversation.[27] Shortly thereafter, Pugh selected a topic related to botanical chemistry, an interest that had germinated from his earlier interactions with William Darlington in Chester County. After investing eight weeks in research, Pugh found that his topic had been investigated and published by a Viennese chemist.[28] Instead, with Wohler's approval, Pugh moved on to the field of metallurgical chemistry. His dissertation was titled "On the Miscellaneous Analysis of Specimens of Meteoric Iron and Ores Found in Mexico and Other Parts of Central America."

His initial ambivalence aside, the conferral of his Ph.D. in March 1856 was the first great accomplishment in Pugh's master plan—"to remain 3 years in the German universities and to *graduate*," he had written to Samuel Johnson the year previous, although at that time there was no explicit

FIGURE 6
Evan Pugh, newly minted Ph.D., in 1856.

mention of what degree Pugh, who had no bachelor's degree, intended to pursue. Consistent with his values and temperament—to exceed expectations and take no shortcuts—Pugh not only completed the required dissertation but also insisted on sitting for the doctoral examination in chemistry and physics.[29] This was highly unusual. American students were generally excused from doctoral exams, needing only to complete a dissertation and nothing more. Apparently, a "custom" had developed whereby American students at German universities had only to give some plausible reason as to why they must be absent from the university at the time examinations were to be held, and the academic authorities routinely excused them from the exercise. That was not the case for German students, however. As the American chemistry professor George C. Caldwell, a fellow student with Pugh at Göttingen, later recalled: "Dr. Pugh would shirk no part of the requirement and he was the first one to make an attack on this 'bad method' by the force of his own example and to earn his degree by examination as well as by a thesis based on original work—and he took the highest grade of the degree 'summa cum laude.'"[30] Pugh dedicated his dissertation to his "Venerable Friend," William

Darlington, "in view of the valuable scientific services which he has rendered my native country." Darlington was pleased to be "thus remembered by a youthful countryman, while he is scaling the heights of science in a distant land."[31]

Pugh's next step was to move on to more advanced study in plant nutrition, extending his work learned in the laboratories of Erdmann and Wohler. With doctorate in hand, he now wanted to investigate the relation of gases, oxygen, and other components of the atmosphere to the nutrition of plants. And so he left Göttingen to study gas analysis under Robert Bunsen at the University of Heidelberg. He found, however, that getting to conduct the analyses was not so easy, as the number of students wanting to do likewise far outstripped the lab's capacity. Instead, Pugh attended lectures on geology, botany, and mineralogy.[32]

Looking to the day he would build his model agricultural college in America, Pugh used his time at Heidelberg in other constructive ways. One of those ways was to gather botanical specimens. Pugh spent many days during the summer of 1856 collecting plant specimens in parts of the Baden-Wurttemberg region near Heidelberg, embarking on professor-led scientific excursions at least once a week. "One can . . . collect in a single summer, some 600 different species of flowering plants," Pugh observed.[33] Then serendipity entered the picture. Pugh bought a large part of the herbarium that had been assembled by G. W. Bischoff, professor of botany at the University of Heidelberg and director of the Heidelberg Botanical Garden. Bischoff had died in 1854 and, as part of his estate, his herbarium was sold at auction on July 21, 1856. Pugh got himself to the right place at the right time and purchased it. Bischoff had been a prodigious collector of plants from 1820 to 1850 from various parts of the world, with some specimens coming from Pennsylvania and New Jersey. Thus, in a few short weeks, Pugh had managed to gather and purchase more than 3,000 specimens. More than 160 years later, what became the "Pugh Herbarium" still exists as the core of the 110,000-specimen Pennsylvania Agricultural College (PAC) Herbarium, located in a campus laboratory, where it remains in use. Despite their travels in Germany and England, the sea voyage across the Atlantic, and their storage and use during the rugged early days of the Farmers' High School, "most of the Pugh plants remain in excellent condition," according to their curator.[34]

Disillusioned with Heidelberg, Pugh wrote Darlington in August 1856, noting his intention to leave for Paris in his attempt "to make an arrangement for carrying on a scientific investigation in England next summer, that will be of importance in Agricultural Chemistry viz.—to ascertain whether or not plants can absorb nitrogen directly, as such from the air." Pugh revealed his desire "to devote my life to Agricultural Chemistry, as a teacher and investigator," and mentioned his interest in an eventual appointment to the Farmers' High School, chartered the year previous.[35]

Although soon to leave, Pugh had learned much about German life during his trips around the countryside over his three years, recording impressions that would stay with him the rest of his life. Germans, at least the hoi polloi, were veritable gluttons who ate too much, smoked too much, and drank too much. He observed that "the thought of drinking nothing but water is as absurd to a German as the supposition that the moon is made of green cheese is to an astronomer." He maintained, however, that his professors and university colleagues were far removed from the ordinary German. They lived disciplined lives, thought profound thoughts, and accomplished great things as a result. Pugh quickly discerned that men of science are not national citizens but "people of the world."[36] The quality of the educational systems within the German states produced some of the most thoroughly educated men in the world, and Pugh looked forward to the time when America would have a similar system in place.

The aspects of German life to which Pugh took particular umbrage, however, involved restrictions on freedom. As a student of science, he was free to express himself on scientific subjects without limitation. Beyond that, free expression and free association were limited by the various German states. At Leipzig he was forced to swear an oath forbidding any political association with students or townspeople. At Heidelberg he witnessed the suppression of student gatherings, which produced a chilling effect on student discussions regarding political, economic, or social topics.[37]

The mid-nineteenth-century Europe that Pugh encountered was, at root, he thought, republican, a sleeping giant needing to be reawakened to democratic reform through universal suffrage and the dissolution of monarchical or absolutist rule, as the largely unsuccessful revolutions of 1848 in Sicily, France, Germany, Italy, and the Austrian Empire had attempted to do. Republican thinking also opposed the Catholic Church, largely over its centuries of interference in matters of state. Pugh's Quaker and American principles hardened in Europe and his distaste for Catholicism—with the priesthood, with ritual, and with the art he encountered in museums and churches—thickened the more he came in contact with it, in Germany certainly, but especially in France.[38]

Experiences in France

Pugh left Heidelberg in late summer 1856, spent several weeks mountain climbing in Switzerland, and then made his way to the French border, where he "submitted to fourteen examinations for passport, political documents, and smuggled goods."[39] Hiking into the French countryside, he was repulsed by the French peasantry, whose farmhouses were "dirty hovels" and who appeared more "filthy" about their homes than the Germans.[40]

He was unimpressed with Paris, despite its reputation in mid-nineteenth-century Europe and America as the world capital of art, culture, medicine, and thought. "In this great city of fashion, of crime, of misery, licentiousness and degragation [sic]," Pugh said, "I don't like it."[41] As he stayed on, his disenchantment grew. He detested the Second Empire government of Emperor Louis-Napoleon (Bonaparte). Elected in 1848 as president of the Second Republic but limited to one four-year term, Louis-Napoleon seized dictatorial power, dissolved the Assembly, and declared a new constitution. In November 1852 he was confirmed as emperor. Pugh deemed it an illegitimate government, ruling without the consent of the people, though Louis-Napoleon, or Napoleon III, was wildly popular in his early years. To Pugh, however, he was a despot and an "unprincipled adventurer."[42]

Pugh had no particular object of study during his time in France. He deplored that the once-vibrant École Polytechnique had been shut down by Louis-Napoleon and turned into a military academy. Sitting in on lectures by eminent scientists at the University of Paris, Pugh concluded that "Paris is a fine school for medicine and the physio-mathematical sciences, though decidedly inferior to Germany in the chemical and electrical sciences."[43]

Nonetheless, Pugh's imagination was caught by a French agricultural chemist of "great reputation," Jean Baptiste Boussingault, and this fascination would soon lead him to England and Rothamsted. Boussingault, a professor at the University of Paris, was well known for his work on nitrogen fixation, work with high relevance for plant nutrition. He had analyzed carbon in plants deriving from carbon dioxide (CO_2) of the air and, in realms medical, had recommended iodized salt for goiters.[44] He was currently engaged in a controversy with another French agricultural chemist, Georges Ville. Both chemists had conducted experiments on the problem and arrived at antithetical conclusions. Boussingault found that plants do not assimilate free nitrogen from the air but rather from the soil. Ville maintained that plants took nitrogen from the atmosphere.[45]

This controversy was roiling chemists on the Continent. Actually, the roots of the issue stretched back into the eighteenth century, when Joseph Priestley suggested that the atmosphere was the source of the nitrogen in organic compounds in plants. In the nineteenth century, Liebig took up the mantle and proposed further that atmospheric ammonia was the nitrogen source. Then came Boussingault, who concluded that plant nitrogen was instead derived from soil nitrates and ammonia. His experimental data were faulty, however, and conflicting results (ultimately found to be flawed) were presented by Ville and popularized by Liebig.[46] Toward the end of 1856 and into 1857, Pugh would place himself at the epicenter of this controversy.

The issue had implications beyond the small community of European chemists. Scientists, farmers, politicians, and reformers were intensely interested in increasing agricultural productivity—the essential condition for the urbanizing and industrializing economies of Europe and America. Thus, people interested in crop improvement and fertilizers wanted to know conclusively how plants take in nitrogen—through the air or through the soil? If the latter, then how could the soil be augmented through chemical intervention to produce better crop yields? The question related not only to crop production but also indirectly to animal nutrition, as plants are the media through which nitrogen is made available for animal food.

The question of nitrogen fixation was of great interest to Pugh, who had done work on plant nutrition in Germany. In Paris he attended the lectures of both Boussingault and Ville. On first examination, Pugh found the quality of Ville's work to be sloppy and haphazard at best, disingenuous at worst. As he wrote to Johnson, by now professor of analytical chemistry at Yale: "Ville in Paris is a perfect humbug whose reports on the absorption of N by plants are not worthy of the least consideration—he is dishonest—holds his position by virtue of service rendered (to that vagabond on the throne of France) in the Coup d'Etat. I could tell you funny things about those experiments—Don't place one particle of reliance in them."[47]

Pugh suspected a case of egregious scientific fraud. He had an inside track to Ville's flawed methodology through a former colleague, Wunder, who in fact had worked with Pugh for three semesters at Leipzig as first assistant to Erdmann. Wunder was subsequently recommended for the position of Ville's assistant. In 1855 a commission of leading French scientists supervised a government-sponsored replication of Ville's experiment, soon after publishing a report confirming Ville's original results. During the replicative experiment, Ville had apparently tampered with the apparatus, the process, and subject of the experiment—the plants themselves. From Wunder, Pugh learned that Ville was found "washing his air for 'plant grown in ammonia free air' by passing a rapid stream of air through 1/2 an inch depth of Sulphuric Acid!" Further, on several occasions, "the pressure on his 'glass cage' broke the glass and 12 to 24 hours elapsed with the plant open to the air yet no mention of this in the report." Ville had also "evolved CO_2 by the action of nitric acid on limestone." And just before the Commission of the Paris Academy visited his laboratory, Ville noticed that his "healthy plant" was not growing in "Stagnant Air." Thus he "took out the 'healthy plant' (*which now looked quite sickly) and put in a Healthy One*!!!" as he didn't want the commissioners to see "an unhealthy plant." The report from Wunder further convinced Pugh that Ville had gained his post as a chemist "*only* by virtue of a certain part that he performed for Napoleon III in the disgraceful Coup d'Etat."[48]

The continued acceptance of Ville's work by the French scientific establishment, in addition to Boussingault's failure to secure support to verify his quite contradictory results, induced Pugh to make his own plan for the investigation of nitrogen fixation. While Pugh's original plan for his European studies, devised before he left for the Continent, had him in the last phase going to England for "general observation of its agriculture and to perhaps pursue something in its labs," he now was a man on a more pointed mission. Pugh was wise enough, however, to know that he could not directly accuse Ville of fraud in any public forum. He needed to expose him not through rhetoric but through science—through an elaborate experiment, meticulously constructed and freely accessible to the observations of visiting scientists. He thus made arrangements to conduct such work at Rothamsted.[49]

Research in England

Pugh arrived in England in July 1857, determined to settle the question of nitrogen fixation and, in the process, make an original contribution to the field. Pugh already was familiar with the experimental work being conducted in plant nutrition at Rothamsted. While in Paris, Pugh had written to Rothamsted's chief chemist, Joseph H. Gilbert, asking if the station would supply him with the equipment needed to investigate the Boussingault-Ville controversy. Pugh's inquiry met with success, and he wrote to Johnson that "they have supplied me with about $500 worth of apparatus and we have been doing up the subject on a scale unprecedented."[50]

Rothamsted was founded in 1838 by Sir John Bennet Lawes, when he began studying the effects of various substances on the growth of plants. Lawes invited Gilbert to join him in 1843 and brought in additional chemists as well. The Rothamsted experiments prompted scientific discussions and replicative experiments on the value of fertilizers; indeed, chemists such as Liebig tested their conclusions and, as they were found to be valid, conceded their results. The scientific prestige of Rothamsted grew accordingly. In fact, it served as the model for the U.S. agricultural experimental research stations, which came about decades later. Lawes's major contribution was his invention and patenting, in 1842, of "superphosphate," composed chiefly of super phosphate of lime, phosphate of ammonia, and silicate of potash, which yielded a phosphate source useful as a fertilizer. Then he went a step further, manufacturing and selling the compound, in the process beginning the development of the artificial fertilizer industry.[51]

Pugh was coming to Lawes and Gilbert at precisely the right time, during what has been termed "the Golden Age of Rothamsted," 1855–75. More to the point, their research interests on nitrogen coincided exactly. Lawes and Gilbert also had been involved in the nitrogen controversy with Liebig, who had stated that plants took from the soil only the mineral substances such as silica, phosphates and the alkalis—potassium, sodium, magnesium and calcium: Hence, only these substances needed to be supplied as fertilizers. Nitrogen, Liebig contended, came to plants from the ammonia in the air. Lawes and Gilbert disagreed, maintaining that atmospheric supplies of nitrogen were inadequate for plant growth and that nitrogen must be added as manure.[52]

Thus, Pugh was the perfect addition to Lawes and Gilbert's research program. Certainly Pugh was interested in exposing Ville as a fraud, but his main objective was to solve the problem scientifically and to do so with a research method that was unassailable. Ville's basic contention was not, after all, illogical on its face, but his approach was sloppy and, worse, dishonest. As Pugh outlined the issue for Frederick Watts, president of the Farmers' High School Board of Trustees: "Three-fourths of the air is nitrogen and the first question of an intelligent student after the above statement would undoubtedly be 'cannot plants assimilate this free gaseous nitrogen in the air?' Now this is a fundamental question staring us in the face."[53]

Although bankrolled at the outset with $500, Pugh's apparatus wound up costing $1,000—especially made for this experiment and nothing else. Thus he was exceedingly careful in his work. "Making combustions in which the breaking of a test tube would mean the loss of any experiment that had cost

FIGURE 7
*Interior and exterior
views of Pugh's laboratory
at Rothamsted.*

75 dollars is rather nervous work," he wrote Johnson.[54] George C. Caldwell, the former fellow Göttingen student with Pugh and later professor of chemistry at Penn State and Cornell, visited Pugh during his time at Rothamsted. Years later, Caldwell described Pugh's painstaking methods: "It was this very thoroughness, leading to such careful provision against all sources of error, that led the most renowned chemist of France [Boussingault], who also had investigated the question, to say on his visit there, while the work was in progress, that he would accept the results obtained whatever they might be."[55]

Pugh's research employed a double-pronged approach. First, he conducted a literature review, of sorts, examining more than a decade's worth of Lawes and Gilbert's experimental data already in existence at Rothamsted. For example, Pugh found that wheat crops, planted without manure, would double in output if the field lay fallow for a year after the harvest. The more surprising finding was that if, instead of lying fallow for a year, a bean crop had been planted, the crop alternating with the beans was just as productive as the crop alternating with a fallow year. The practical benefit for the farmer was that, if he could find some fertilizer with the same nutrients as beans, he would not have to forgo a year of "resting" his wheat crop in fallow field to regenerate the nutrients. This and other findings enabled Pugh to forgo years of additional field trials and held the added advantage of buttressing his laboratory experiments.[56]

Then there was Pugh's work in the laboratory. To ensure valid results, Pugh used different varieties of plants but limited them to two classes—*Graminacae*, which are grasses such as wheat and other cereal plants; and *Leguminosae*, which are plants such as peas and beans. To isolate the plants from atmospheric nitrogen, the specimens were grown under glass cylinders blown in a single piece. The open end of the cylinder, or bell jar, was provided with a foot filled with mercury, so that an airtight seal could be formed between glass and foot. Air and water of known composition were fed to the plants through control outlets at the base of the bell jars. The seeds from which the plants were grown were analyzed to determine their chemical composition. In this way, conditions were so tightly controlled that every particle of combined nitrogen available to a plant had been measured. Thus, if any larger quantity of nitrogen was found in the plant when it was removed from the sealed bell jar and analyzed, it could have happened only because nitrogen had been taken in the free state from the air that filled the glass cylinders at the time of their sealing.[57]

Pugh's experiments, not without an occasional accident or blunder on the part of an assistant, took longer than expected: about twenty months, rather than the six months originally contemplated. And scientists aplenty converged on Rothamsted to examine the work in progress. In addition to Boussingault and Caldwell, William H. Brewer, professor of agriculture at Yale's Sheffield Scientific School, visited and came away impressed. Thomas Graham, first president of the London Chemical Society, known for his work with gases, came at the start of the experiment. Eventually, even Ville himself arrived. Pugh's confidence in Ville was such that he would not trust Ville's unaccompanied presence among his plants.[58]

In the late winter of 1859, the results were conclusive and the methodology left no room for doubt. Both Boussingault, whose results were confirmed, and Ville, whose results were disproved, accepted Pugh's findings without argument or qualification.

In the case of graminaceous plants (grasses), Boussingault was completely vindicated, as in no case was any evidence of an assimilation of free nitrogen found. In the case of leguminous plants (peas and beans), however, results were indeterminate, but the results were stated in such a way as to allow for possible revision in the future.[59] And revisions were made, a quarter-century later, by methods of bacteriology virtually unknown in Pugh's time. It was found that the roots of legumes (such as peas and beans) have small tubercles containing bacteria that have the power of taking up free nitrogen of the air and converting it to a form of combined nitrogen utilized by the plant.[60]

The one inadvertent flaw in Pugh's research was his careful sterilization of all soils and apparatus, which destroyed any micro-organic life. Thirty years after the fact, Lawes and Gilbert themselves revised the record: "If, therefore, it should be established that fixation does take place under [the microorganisms'] influence, and that such influence is essential for the development of the action, the conclusions, both of Boussingault and ourselves, from the results in question, are so far vitiated."[61]

In 1861 Pugh and his colleagues Lawes and Gilbert published the results of their investigation in a 146-page report, *On the Sources of the Nitrogen of Vegetation; With Special Reference to the Question Whether Plants Assimilate Free or Uncombined Nitrogen*. As the junior member of this trio, Pugh was listed as the third author, but by all accounts he was the principal researcher.[62] The direct outgrowth of Pugh's work was the modern nitrogen fertilizer industry (ammonia and nitrates), which in turn became "the most important famine reducing factor in the world today."[63]

Pugh's investigation of nitrogen fixation won him widespread recognition by scientists in England and on the Continent, even before the results were in. "I have had a jolly time attending all the meetings of the Chem. Soc. and some of the Royal Soc. To meet such men as Faraday, Lyell, Graham, Hoffman, &c., &c., is not 'small potatoes by any means,'" he wrote to Johnson.[64] Pugh, who remained lifelong friends of Lawes and Gilbert, became something of a minor sensation at parties at Lawes's manor. Although Pugh was stoic, disciplined, and of the strictest morals, he also was tall, well built, handsome, distinguished, and unmarried, and thus he attracted the attention of the opposite sex. "An occasional soiree has afforded opportunities for doing the social in the society of the ladies and I have done much more of this kind of social in England than anywhere else in Europe."[65]

In the spring of 1859 Pugh presented his results via lecture to a room packed with scientists and men of affairs at the nearby Harpenden Lecture

FIGURE 8 *Pugh's research exhibit.*

Institution and Reading Club, founded a year earlier in 1858. Pugh displayed a four- by eight-foot diagram of his experiment. He spoke about the importance of agriculture, reminding his audience that the fate of nations turned on the quality of their agriculture. Pugh pointed out that Napoleon, after having conquered Italy, Austria, and Prussia, was defeated in Russia not by the enemy but by the hunger of his troops resulting from the infertility of the soil. Pugh then elaborated on all of his experiments, describing the composition of soil and explaining his proof about the absence of free assimilation of nitrogen in graminaceous plants. The Harpenden audience was captivated by Pugh's presentation, and the evening ended with high praise for the young American scientist.[66]

Through his work at Rothamsted, Pugh's reputation was cemented in the international scientific community. As noted nearly a quarter-century after the experiment in Johnson and Cameron's *Elements of Agricultural Chemistry and Geology* (1883): "The most elaborate and, in our judgment, the most conclusive contribution to the elucidation of this question are the experimental results of Messrs. Lawes, Gilbert, and Pugh, published in the transactions of the Royal

Society, part II, 1860. In this elaborate memoir the experiments of all previous investigators are examined, criticized, and in many instances repeated. The original experiments devised by Messrs. Laws, Gilbert, and Pugh, were carried out with the most minute attention to details, and with every precaution against error. The results confirm those of Boussingault, and disprove Ville's conclusions."[67]

At Rothamsted Pugh also conducted research in vegetable physiology and nitric acid, the latter resulting in an article published by the Chemical Society of London. This same society conferred upon him the status of Fellow, his most cherished honor, which was later inscribed on his tombstone.[68]

In the wake of the completed nitrogen experiment, Lawes beseeched Pugh to stay on at Rothamsted, offering him a handsome salary and superb facilities to continue his research. Pugh, by this time one of the foremost young scientists in Europe, was surely tempted to remain and explore new frontiers of knowledge at arguably the world's finest agricultural research facility. But he was determined to complete the plan he had laid out for himself before departing America—to return and create a college dedicated to scientific agricultural education—the model institution for America. It was, as Pugh put it, an endeavor in which "the harvest is great and the laborers few."[69]

CHAPTER 3

A New School, a New President, a New Movement

DURING HIS YEARS IN Europe in pursuit of a scientific education, Evan Pugh kept a larger object in mind: creating the model agricultural college for America. Years before the 1862 Morrill Land-Grant College Act was signed into law by President Abraham Lincoln, Pugh had a clear vision of what an American agricultural college should be and should do. And he wanted to be the one to build it, preferably in his home state of Pennsylvania. As early as 1855, he informed a trustee of the newly chartered Farmers' High School of Pennsylvania that he had left Pennsylvania to study in Germany in order to "fit" himself as a scientist qualified to develop and lead a scientifically based agricultural college such as the one they envisioned.[1]

Pugh's time in Europe paralleled the founding and early development of the institution he eventually would come to lead. Although an ocean away, Pugh periodically signaled his interest in an appointment at the school either as professor or president. As the decade of the 1850s entered its final year, the trajectories of Pugh's education abroad and the school's "completion" coincided propitiously. The Farmers' High School opened for instruction in February 1859, just as Pugh was finishing his work at Rothamsted and communicating with the president of the school's governing board about accepting the presidency.

The origins of the school, however, stretched back to the opening of the decade, when Pugh was principal and teacher of the Jordan Bank Academy in Chester County. The Farmers' High School grew out of the Pennsylvania State Agricultural Society, formed in 1851. The society sponsored a convention in 1853 to discuss a course of action in regard to the proposed school. The committee appointed to study the matter recommended that it not be near a large town or city, but still have convenient access to agricultural markets. The curriculum should include classical subjects as well as agricultural courses, and students should be required to perform manual labor. To differentiate the institution from the collegiate mainstream of classical or literary colleges—and to address the suspicions of farmers about such institutions and their pernicious influence on young men—the committee came up with the title of "The Farmers' High School." Nonetheless, the academic work was to be of collegiate grade, with baccalaureate degrees conferred.[2]

The Pennsylvania legislature authorized a charter for the school in April 1854—specifying sixty-five trustees, one from each county agricultural society. Because this unwieldy number made it difficult to gather a quorum for an inaugural meeting, the state agricultural society asked the legislature to pass a new charter stipulating only thirteen trustees. This new act of incorporation, from which the Pennsylvania State University dates its birth, was signed by Governor James Pollock on February 22, 1855. Pugh, meanwhile, was transitioning from Leipzig to Göttingen.

The founder of the Pennsylvania State Agricultural Society was Frederick O. Watts, a Cumberland County attorney and judge and a business developer for county railroad lines and gas and water companies. A graduate of Dickinson College, class of 1824, he also was a gentleman farmer and agricultural reformer, experimenting on his 116-acre farm outside Carlisle. He used his new leadership position in the agricultural society to push the state legislature to establish an agricultural college.

Writing to Pennsylvania governor William Bigler in January 1854, Watts outlined the contours of the desired agricultural college, noting that how students were to be educated was "not so well understood." He stated that existing colleges were not adapted to education "for the business of agriculture" due to expense, the nature of the education they offered, and the habits of mind they inculcated—habits of idleness that militated against those required for farming. In Watts's view, the institution need not be as scientifically oriented as Pugh later would insist it be: "It is not proposed . . . to educate young men . . . for the professional pursuit of scientific subjects; but to teach them that

which is valuable for a farmer to know." He recommended courses in the English language, mathematics, geography, chemistry, botany, astronomy, and related subjects as well as the "art of farming."

Start-up costs, he estimated, would be $38,000—for a 300-acre farm, additional buildings, and equipment. This would be funded by a $20,000 appropriation from the state, a $10,000 grant from the state agricultural society, and a mortgage of $8,000. Operational costs would total $16,000 per year—$10,000 for the support of professors and pupils, $2,000 for the principal's salary, with an additional $4,000 to support three additional professors. These costs would be funded via an annual state appropriation of $5,000; through tuition revenue totaling $15,000, based on $75 per year from 200 students, and $2,000 from the sale of farm produce. The revenue plan would produce $22,000—$6,000 more than planned; the surplus would be used to expand the institution over time.[3]

Chartering the Farmers' High School was one thing; putting it into actual operation was quite another. Indeed, it would take a full four years until the school was in position to accept its first students in February 1859 and to secure Pugh as president shortly thereafter.

Of the thirteen trustees authorized by the new charter of February 22, 1855, four were to be ex officio: the governor of the Commonwealth, the secretary of the Commonwealth, the president of the Pennsylvania State Agriculture Society, and the principal of the school. Nine additional trustees were named in the charter: the aforesaid Frederick Watts of Cumberland County, who would be elected president of the Board of Trustees; Alfred Elwyn of Philadelphia, a member of the Philadelphia Society for Promoting Agriculture; Algernon Roberts, also of Philadelphia, a former ironmaster and now a gentleman farmer, and also a member of Philadelphia Society for Promoting Agriculture; Hugh N. McAllister, of Centre County, a prominent attorney; Robert Walker of Allegheny County, another former businessman now turned to farming, and the founding secretary of the state agricultural society in 1851; James Miles of Erie County, a judge with interests in land development; John Strohm of Lancaster County, a teacher, surveyor, Pennsylvania legislator, and U.S. representative in Congress; A. O. Hiester of Dauphin County, a lawyer and judge, with interests in banking and manufacturing, including iron forges; and William Jessup of Susquehanna County, a Yale graduate and prominent attorney with interests in coal mining and railroads.

As the board's makeup attests, these men represented broad statewide support for the Farmers' High School, as opposed to local or parochial interests. Politically, these board members tended to be Whigs—in favor of internal tariffs to protect domestic industry, internal infrastructure projects such as canals and later railroads, and conservative fiscal policies. Their interests extended not only to agriculture but also to industry and other ventures designed to move the state and nation forward. Nationally, the tensions over slavery eventually split the Whig Party apart, and most of the Pennsylvania Whigs, including these governing board members, moved to the Republican Party in support of Lincoln, himself a former Whig.[4]

The Board of Trustees having been established, the next item of business was to select a location for the new school. Offers, including land, farms, and money, came from men in Allegheny, Blair, Dauphin, Erie, Franklin, and Union counties. The successful offer came from Centre County, which, as its name denotes, was centrally located, but also, as a later Penn State president would describe it, "equally inaccessible from all parts of the state."

The Centre County offer included 200 acres of land from ironmaster James Irvin as well as $10,000 to be gathered by subscription from the people of Centre County and adjacent Huntingdon County. Despite the various offers and the politics inherent to each, the Board of Trustees selected the Centre County location with little dissension. In his so-called Barn Speech of 1857, Watts defended the committee's decision to select Centre County, stating that objective considerations concerning "soil, surface, exposure, healthful-ness, and centrality" rather than local preferences held sway.[5]

The next problem to be solved was the physical plant. Accepting Trustee Hugh N. McAllister's building plan, the board contracted with a Carlisle company, Turner and Natcher, to erect the main college building for $55,000. Work began in the summer of 1856, when Pugh was in Heidelberg. Although three stories of one of three main sections were completed by 1857, progress slowed considerably, caused in large part by the Panic of 1857 and the finan-cial problems it posed to the construction firm. Work was abandoned by the summer of 1858, when Pugh was at Rothamsted.

Despite the economic malaise, the legislature in May 1857 appropriated $25,000 to the institution with the promise of an equal amount if $25,000 were to be raised through private subscription. In the summer of 1858 the trustees authorized the purchase of an additional 200 acres of land from Irvin, renewed the campaign for subscriptions, and set entrance require-ments for students: They must have attained the age of sixteen and were to be of good moral character, and qualified by the public elementary schools of the state. Tuition, room and board, and incidental expenses were set at $100 per session, the academic year beginning in February and ending in December, thus following the agricultural calendar. One hundred students were to be admitted on the recommendation of the various county agricul-tural societies, apportioned among the counties according to the size of their tax base.

In December 1858, though the college building was still two-thirds unfinished, the trustees authorized putting the school into operation by the following February. The subjects advertised for instruction covered a wide range, from mathematics to marketing to agricultural genetics. The first col-lege catalog in 1859 described the institution's mission in a fashion far more scientific than what Watts had outlined in 1854: "to afford a system of instruc-tion as extensive and thorough as the usual course of our best colleges, to emphasize scientific instruction, and to develop to the fullest extent possible those departments of all science which have a practical or theoretical bearing upon agriculture and agricultural interest."[6] This stronger scientific focus very likely was due to Pugh's influence on key trustees from abroad.

"A new light is about to break upon the agricultural community," Watts proclaimed in his annual report.[7] And on February 16, 1859, with sixty-nine students present, four faculty members but no president, a building one-third complete in an improbable location, but with well-defined purpose and lofty ambition, the Farmers' High School of Pennsylvania opened its doors and went to work. It would take eight more months, however, until Pugh could arrive.

Anticipated as his coming was, Pugh was not the first candidate to be offered the presidency. The initial offer went to Charles B. Trego in 1855, the year of the institution's incorporation. At a meeting of the trustees on September 12 to accept the offer of land from Irvin to place the school in Centre County, a search committee for a "principal" recommended Trego and was then instructed by the board to approach him about the position. Trego had strong credentials, not least of which was his service in the Pennsylvania legislature, which was considered to be an advantage. Born and raised on a Bucks County farm in southeastern Pennsylvania and, like Pugh, largely self-educated, Trego had served as assistant state geologist from 1837 to 1841. In that capacity, he conducted the first geological survey of the Commonwealth, publishing a 400-page *Geography of Pennsylvania*. At the time the offer was made, Trego was professor of geology at the University of Pennsylvania, in the newly established (1852) School of Mines, Arts, and Manufactures.

But Trego turned down the offer from the Farmers' High School, upset because of the crossed signals he had received. One trustee told him he had been chosen while another said that board had only favorably received the nomination but not definitely accepted it. "I believe it is usual for a person who is actually appointed to any station of trust and responsibility to have some authentic or official notice of the fact," Trego wrote to Watts. Trego was dismayed as well by what he saw as the limited capacity of the state agricultural society to fund the school as well as its remote location in Centre County.[8] Meanwhile, the School of Mines, Arts, and Manufactures never found its footing; Trego remained its only faculty member from 1855 until the Civil War, when operations were suspended. After the Trego debacle, the principalship went unfilled for years. As the institution prepared to open to students in February 1859, William G. Waring, who had been serving as superintendent of gardens and nurseries, was appointed professor of horticulture and acting principal. As such, Waring was the chief academic and executive officer pending the appointment of a new president, striving to get the new school off the ground.[9]

In 1855, as the Trego affair was still in play, the trustees were looking not only for a president but also for prospective faculty members, particularly

a professor of chemistry. Accordingly, Farmers' High School trustee Alfred
L. Elwyn wrote to Samuel W. Johnson, the Yale-educated chemist who a
year earlier had returned to the United States after studying with Pugh at
Leipzig. Elwyn was a Chester Countian and a colleague and friend of William
Darlington, with similar agricultural and scientific interests. He had grad-
uated from Harvard in 1823 and earned his M.D. from the University of
Pennsylvania in 1831, but never practiced medicine. He was one of the found-
ers of the Pennsylvania State Agricultural Society, and an early member of the
American Association for the Advancement of Science and the Academy of
Natural Sciences. Although a founding trustee of the Farmers' High School,
Elwyn would step down from that post in 1858. With others, however, he
became instrumental in the drawn-out process that resulted in the eventual
selection of Pugh not only as professor of chemistry but as president.[10]

In his response to Elwyn, Johnson strongly recommended Pugh. Elwyn
did not offer the professorship outright to Pugh, who at the time was a student
at Göttingen, but was certainly assessing his interest. Pugh took advantage of
the opportunity and responded to Elwyn at length. He lamented that farmers
were poorly served in terms of education, which could change only if scientific
agriculture were to be put in place to appeal to their interests. But scientific
agriculture was virtually nonexistent in America, despite the nation's "many
agricultural journals" and books on the subject, though none of them were
truly scientific. "When agricultural science is properly developed its subjects
will be such as can only be understood by *Study*."[11]

Pugh insisted that that development and introduction of agricultural science to farmers would have to be done carefully, as their skepticism was already
high. "Quacking has already done our cause no little harm and hundreds of
farmers are disgusted at what they (with too much reason) term scientific
humbug." An "earnest effort in proper hands" could get things moving in the
right direction. Pugh wanted Pennsylvania to take the lead in this mater by
"founding an Agricultural College with its necessary appendages." He noted
that the "character" of the first such college would be paramount, as new institutions emulating the model would begin to sprout up across the country. Pugh
volunteered his services for the professorship, but not immediately. He wanted
more information about the plans for the Farmers' High School so that, during
his last year of study, he could purchase books and apparatus accordingly.[12]

Then he went a bit further, offering recommendations for the new school:
that it should focus on the "wants of Farmers' sons"; that it should be financially self-sustaining, over and above the value of students' manual labor and

the profits of its agricultural products; that it be free to investigate and experiment "without any regard to pecuniary loss or gain by the individual results"; that the faculty be of strong scientific reputation among the country's and world's best scientists and be "an original scientific agricultural investigator"; that the school continually gather various "soils, minerals, manures, plants, etc." for investigation; and that the school should establish a newspaper, publishing the results of its research for the benefit of the farmer. Here, Pugh was envisioning what would become known as "cooperative extension"— outreach by land-grant college experts to put new knowledge into the hands of American farmers—sixty years before such a system became institutionalized and supported at the federal level via the Smith-Lever Act of 1915. Pugh refrained from discussing the details of curricula and admissions, but noted that a chemical laboratory, a botanical garden, and rooms for mineralogical and geological specimens would be essential.[13]

For Pugh, eager to help shape such an institution, it would be four more years of study and research before he would feel ready to return to America. But writing to Elwyn in 1855, at age twenty-seven, he knew what agricultural colleges needed to be and to do to win the confidence of both scientists, the generators of knowledge, and farmers, the end users of that knowledge. Properly organized and run, Pugh maintained, agricultural colleges could be the lead agents in transforming American agriculture into the scientific enterprise that would generate vast improvements in productivity, profitability, and national prosperity.

In subsequent communications, Pugh emphasized another essential point: that the presidents of agricultural colleges must be scientists first and foremost, "because the expenditures for *material*, as *auxiliaries to study* in a Scientific College must always be great, and they are such as can only be properly *regulated, encouraged* and *controlled* by a scientific man. No scientific Institution ever has been, or ever can be successful as such, the control of which, either *directly* or indirectly, is not vested in a scientific man."[14] Scientific control, scientific method, scientific integrity, with the resultant scientific benefits: These were to be the four implicit cornerstones of Pugh's model agricultural college.

During his years in Europe, Pugh continued to express his interest in returning to Pennsylvania as professor of chemistry and even as president of its new agricultural college. Following up on his letter to Elwyn, Pugh wrote Johnson to inform him that he "would be willing to accept the position of Principal in the School" and that he would "take it *gladly* at the end of two years," when he supposed he would be finished with Europe. He then asked if

Johnson would "be good enough" to inform Elwyn "of my intention."[15] Pugh
believed that should he gain a position, whether as professor or president, he
could profoundly influence the direction of the school. Even if the arrangements were not "the best in the world" for agricultural science, Pugh had no
doubts that he "might bend matters gradually into a proper course. One must
first gain the confidence of interested persons, and then *influence* over them
follows."[16]

In addition to his letters to Elwyn and Johnson, Pugh wrote Darlington
nearly two years later to reiterate his intensifying interest in a position and to
express his concern that he might have got off on a bad footing responding to
Elwyn. Pugh's ostensible purpose in writing was to introduce George Caldwell,
who had been a fellow student with him at Göttingen, to Darlington. Caldwell
was interested in learning more about a faculty vacancy in natural science at
the University at Lewisburg, Pennsylvania (now Bucknell University). Pugh
vouched strongly for Caldwell (whom he later would bring to the Agricultural
College of Pennsylvania as professor of chemistry). Pugh also took the opportunity to let Darlington know of his continuing interest in the Farmers' High
School. But to that point, Pugh was concerned that, in his earlier letter to
Elwyn, he might have made the wrong impression.

> Dr. Elwyn wrote to me through Prof. Johnston of Yale College over a
> year ago to know if I would accept the professorship of chemistry in the
> college. I replied at some length, stating what I thought should be kept in
> mind as of fundamental importance in starting his college. In Dr. Elwyn's
> reply he did not disguise the fact that he thought I was too theoretical and
> that to "run a straight furrow" was of more importance than he thought
> I supposed. I had dwelt upon the importance of our lack of *Agricultural
> principles* rather than Ag. practice which the student could learn at home
> and I am happy to say that I have no one who has had anything to do
> with agricultural teaching who does not agree with me upon the point at
> issue. And I have talked upon this subject with all the great teachers of
> Ag. Chemistry in Germany, France & England and I cannot think that
> Dr. Elwyn would be of different opinion could we talk the matter over.[17]

Evincing a devotion to his home state that was typical of the era, Pugh
offered that he was certain that such a school in Pennsylvania could, with
proper management, be made "second to none of the kind in the world."
Feeling somewhat in the dark about how the Farmers' High School was

progressing, he asked Darlington if he would "promote my interest with regard to the professorship in question."[18] A few days later, Pugh's colleague Caldwell followed up with Darlington, asking for insight about the vacancy at Lewisburg. Caldwell ended his missive with a ringing endorsement of Pugh, who was "now engaged in the settlement of the most interesting questions in Agricultural Chemistry . . . no man could be better fitted for such a place than he is."[19]

Pugh's reputation, already strong with his earned Ph.D. from Göttingen, grew even more so by virtue of his association with Rothamsted, the most prestigious research facility of its kind. As 1858 drew to a close, the trustees were resolved to bring him back to Pennsylvania to lead the fledgling Farmers' High School. In early February 1859 Watts, continuing as president of the Board of Trustees, extended to Pugh the offer to serve not only as professor but also as president of the institution, which finally was about to open its doors to students. In his response to Watts of March 3, 1859, Pugh accepted the offer, though he negotiated for a delay in his arrival so as to complete his work at Rothamsted. Nonetheless, Pugh was thrilled to accept "a position . . . to which I had hoped to devote the labors of my life." Pugh added that he hoped to make the institution "the central point from which the knowledge of the theory and practice of agriculture should go forth to the country" as well as "a central point to which the farmers of the whole country could look with confidence for advice" on all things agricultural. Pugh stressed the importance of collections of geological minerals and botanical and zoological specimens for the purpose of illustrating lectures. He offered to bring with him his own "tolerable good collections" for use at the institution. He further suggested that, if the trustees would see fit to invest $500 to $1,000 for the purchase of scientific equipment, he would be pleased to travel to Berlin or Paris to purchase the best such apparatus available—certainly more advanced than what might be available in America.[20]

Watts was delighted with Pugh's acceptance. He approved his request to be allowed to complete his experimental work at Rothamsted and agreed to refer to the trustees Pugh's offer to buy apparatus. "Ours is among the first indeed . . . the very first that has gone into operation; for whilst there is an Agr. School in Michigan it differs from ours in what we deem essential features," Watts said, congratulating Pugh for the opportunity now before him "of so moulding the Farmers' High School . . . as to make it do a perfect work."[21] Soon after, the trustees did send Pugh $1,000, and the president-elect traveled to universities and laboratories throughout Germany—including many of his old haunts—to pick up the best equipment money could buy. (Some of this same equipment—as well as Pugh's aforementioned botanical collection—is still preserved and in the possession of the Pennsylvania State University.)

In Philadelphia, a few days before leaving for the Farmers' High School to assume the presidency, Pugh wrote to his colleague Johnson with an important question: "Do you know any good book on *Ag. Science* for a text book, a book more thorough, more advanced and with about 1,000 fewer mistakes in it than *J.L. Campbell's A.M.*?"[22] Here Pugh was referring to *A Manual of Scientific and Practical Agriculture for the School and the Farm*, published in 1859 by J. L. Campbell, professor of physical science at Washington College in Virginia. Other America textbooks on the subject had been produced since 1824, most notably *Elements of Scientific Agriculture* by Yale's John Pritkin Norton in 1850, but most were outdated and rife with error, none of them being up to Pugh's European standard.[23] Pugh suggested to Johnson that they put their heads together and write some textbooks that could be adopted by teachers of agricultural science across the country. Pugh's recommendations for new texts covered the universe, extending to elementary and general chemistry; agricultural chemistry; geology as applied to agriculture along with physical geography and meteorology; agricultural botany; agricultural practice as related to implements and machines; veterinary surgery; agricultural zoology, physiology, and anatomy; agricultural mathematics including surveying, crystallography, mechanics, and the theory of machines; and political, national, and social economy.[24]

Here was Pugh's dilemma and challenge: He was returning to America as one of the best-educated young scientists in the Western World, with a clear purpose in mind: To invent a new kind of educational institution designed, through science and its applications, to improve the state of American agriculture. Yet at the time in America there existed very little agricultural science per se, no curriculum for teaching the subject, and virtually no institutions of higher learning devoted to the task. All of this and more would Pugh take on as the central challenge of his life.

The Movement for Agricultural Reform and Agricultural Colleges

The aborning institution of which Pugh was now president was one of only two state-sponsored agricultural colleges to be established in the United States that would actually graduate baccalaureate students by the beginning of the Civil War. These were the Michigan Agricultural College, which ultimately became Michigan State University (1965), and the Farmers' High School, which ultimately became the Pennsylvania State University (1953). Both would be designated as land-grant colleges by their respective states shortly after the Morrill Act became law in July 1862.

But agricultural colleges were a long time in coming. The movement to establish such colleges grew out of the plight of the American farmer—particularly in the Northeast. In that populous region, soil exhaustion had become a fact of life after generations of poor agricultural practices born of ignorance or, more accurately, the absence of science. With no agricultural science, no agricultural education, there was an abundance of superstitious practices among farmers in the colonial and early national periods. They planned their work according to phases of the moon and signs of the Zodiac. Planting, slaughtering, and building were timed to coincide with sundry astronomical influences, the waxing and waning of the moon, and its position relative to the constellations. According to the Pennsylvania historian Wayland F. Dunaway, "It was commonly believed that cattle would be healthy if the stable were covered in cobwebs, that newly purchased pigs should be backed into the sty, that thunder in March foretold a rich harvest, and so on."[25]

In the United States, the science of agriculture did not coalesce and emerge as a coherent body of knowledge until the last thirty years of the nineteenth century, by which time Pugh was long gone. Science historian Margaret Rossiter observed that agricultural science actually did not come into being until after the federal Hatch Act of 1887 had brought a national system of agricultural experiment stations to life—most of them attached to land-grant colleges.[26] Europe, as has been noted, was far ahead of the United States. In Great Britain, two influential agricultural research stations got their start in the early 1840s, Rothamsted being the more consequential. In the German states, the first state-supported agricultural research station was established in 1852, and more than seventy such stations were in operation by the mid-1870s. Not until the late 1890s would American agricultural science begin to approximate that of the Europeans.[27]

That is not to say that interest in agricultural science and experimentation was entirely absent in America. The aforementioned American Philosophical Society, founded by Benjamin Franklin in 1744, published in its *Transactions* many articles and tried to stimulate interest in scientific farming. The Philadelphia Society for Promoting Agriculture, founded in 1785, encouraged improved methods of farming as well. Two early presidents, George Washington and Thomas Jefferson, were noted agricultural experimenters in their own right. In a 1796 address Washington called for a federally funded board of agriculture to serve as a center for encouraging experimentation, but it never came into being during his life.[28]

Meanwhile, settlement and farming pressed ever westward. In the early National era, the Northwest Territory (the upper Midwest beyond the Appalachians, bounded by the Ohio and Mississippi rivers and the Great Lakes) as well as the larger Mississippi Valley became open to settlement and cultivation. Pioneers attracted to its rich virgin soil eventually became a competitive threat to their brethren in the Northeast. The latter were faced with the dilemma of moving west or adopting new farming practices and remedies that would improve productivity and profits. These considerations made them increasingly receptive to innovation in their question for new crops and new procedures—and increasingly susceptible to quackery and miracle cures.

Farmers began to complain about their plight. The details about their economic distress, as well as their perceived sense of social inferiority and political impotence, began to work their way into letters, into the agricultural press, and into speeches by champions of "the common man." The catalyst for their dissension was the Panic of 1837 and the crop failures of 1837 and 1838, prompting agricultural productivity to become a pressing issue not only for farmers but also for the nation as a whole, as plentiful food supplies were essential for workers in the nascent industrial economy.[29] To be sure, some progress was being made to help the American farmer. The newly developing systems of canals and railroads expedited the transport of farm products to new markets. New inventions such as the steel plowshare for breaking up tough soil, the reaper for harvesting grain, and the combine to cut, thresh, and clean grain boosted agricultural productivity as well.

At about the same time, around 1840, the urban industrial movement reached the takeoff stage in America. In the cities, mechanics, tradesmen, and laborers formed associations to advance their interests. A similar class-consciousness began to burn among the nation's farmers, fanned by a new breed of agricultural reformer: the editors of agricultural newspapers and journals. Politicians, too, began to appeal to the farmers' discontent, amplifying the distress, disparities, and discrimination that had been thrust upon the nation's largest political constituency. At mid-century, the national agricultural community was vast, indeed. By 1850 fully 84 percent of the American public still lived in rural areas, the large majority engaged in farming.[30]

The state agricultural society movement, dominated by gentlemen-farmers and men of affairs, also reached the takeoff stage in the 1840s and 1850s.

In fact, the movement culminated in 1852 with the creation of a national organization, the United States Agricultural Society. Among other things, the national society would advocate for a federal Department of Agriculture, finally established in 1862, the same year that saw passage of the Morrill Act and the Homestead Act.

The American agricultural reform movement of the 1830s, '40s, '50s, and beyond, has come under greater scholarly attention in recent years. As historian Ariel Ron has argued, this was nothing less than a major social movement, centered in the Greater Northeast—"an incipient restructuring of the American state along the lines of administrative bureaucracy and interest-group politics." In fact, beyond the better-known oppositional and reform movements of the nineteenth century such as abolitionism, temperance, and women's rights, it created an entirely new kind of social movement: the "state-allied or state-constructive movements." In other words, the agricultural reform movement originated in the grassroots but ultimately succeeded only by demanding greater involvement by the federal government to solve large-scale societal problems, thus ushering in the advent of the modern bureaucratic state.[31]

The agricultural reform movement was, without question, a true mass movement. The rapid growth of farm journals, newspapers, and other periodicals began in the 1830s and exploded over the next two decades. By 1852 there were some thirty active farm journals with a total circulation as high as 500,000 nationally.[32] One of the most prominent was the *Pennsylvania Farm Journal*, published in Chester County under the editorship of J. Lacey Darlington and of which Pugh was an avid reader. Another was *The Farmer and Gardener*, published in Philadelphia under the editorship of A. M. Spangler and William Saunders. Both of these journals editorialized for state-sponsored agricultural colleges and supported the Farmers' High School. *The Farmer and Gardener*, for example, editorialized in 1861 for the passage of a $50,000 state appropriation to complete the college building, calling on its readers to write to their representatives in Harrisburg "urging them not only to vote for this bill, but to work with their fellow members to secure its passage."[33] In this fashion, through its publications, the agricultural reform movement built a national communications network of unprecedented proportions and influence.

Coupled with the agricultural press were state agricultural fairs, executed on a grand scale by the standards of the day. Pennsylvania's 1854 agricultural fair, for example, attracted 100,000 visitors. These annual gatherings were events at once social and educational, and they carried political implications.

They featured a multiplicity of exhibits and new tools and machines and, of course, facilitated conversations and subsequent political action as circumstances warranted.[34]

This movement, uniting America's largest vocational constituency, intensified as problems increased. Besides soil depletion in the Northeast, which spurred interest in fertilization and the rotation of crops, there was a "dramatically worsening pest environment." In addition, the opening of lands in the Midwest and beyond sounded the death knell for the grain culture of the Northeast and fueled the outmigration of farm families from the region. The byword of the day became "scientific agriculture," increasingly viewed by reformers as the ultimate solution to problems of American agriculture.[35] From an early age, Pugh was one of its most vociferous advocates.

The agricultural college movement took its first tentative steps in conjunction with these dynamics. The first notable articulation of the idea for agricultural colleges in America came in 1819, from Simeon De Witt, surveyor-general of the state of New York, in his pamphlet *Consideration of the Necessity of Establishing an Agricultural College, and Having More of the Children of Wealthy Citizens Educated for the Profession of Farming*. The Troy Polytechnic Institute, founded in 1824 and later to become Rensselaer Polytechnic Institute, was a viable precursor of an agricultural college, though engineering (the mechanic arts) soon superseded agriculture in the school's curriculum. Other "farm schools" came into being on a less ambitious scale. In 1823 the Gardiner Lyceum, along Maine's Kennebec River, became the first institution to offer "scientific" agriculture, so called. The Boston Asylum and Farm School was founded in 1832 for poor children. The Cream Hill Agricultural School in rural Connecticut was founded in 1845 and continued successfully until 1869.[36]

Perhaps the most interesting institution before the Civil War was the Farmers' College, founded by Freeman Cary in 1846 near Cincinnati, Ohio. In many ways, it presaged the land-grant college in striving to offer practical education to regional farmers and mechanics, in addition to the traditional classical curriculum. The Farmers' College peaked in the mid-1850s with an enrollment of 330 students, but was plagued by chronic financial difficulties, receiving its support largely through the sale of subscriptions. By the end of the Civil War, it was in serious decline. In fact, in 1863 a Farmers' College faculty member wrote Pugh asking for his guidance on teaching agricultural science: "From my amateur Stand point the only embarrassing feature is to know where to enter, upon the vast field of instruction which has remained all untouched thus far." Although the Farmers' College made a bid to become Ohio's land-grant institution, the designation went elsewhere. The school continued to struggle and in 1884 was reorganized and renamed.[37]

Other agricultural colleges had been promoted, but not established. In 1825 a four-year Massachusetts Agricultural College was proposed. In 1837 a committee of the Pennsylvania state legislature reported that agriculture "must in some way be interwoven with our system of education" and broached the idea of establishing an agricultural school and an experiment farm. Of all the false starts, however, one of the best known was the People's College in the upstate New York town of Havana. Planning for the school began in 1848 but the cornerstone was not laid until a decade later. Founded by a group of progressive thinkers, the college embarked on a broad, ambitious, and egalitarian mission. Agriculture and the industrial arts were to be interwoven with the curriculum, manual labor was required of all students, which were to include women as well as men. The People's College finally opened in 1860, but was foreclosed by the start of the Civil War. From 1848 onward, however, the plans for the People's College attracted considerable attention and inspired kindred thinking elsewhere.[38]

Of course, the very idea of an "agricultural college" was a radical concept, oxymoronic in certain quarters, a wide departure from the mainstream of American colleges in the mid-nineteenth century. And the agricultural college movement, however halting, took place in the midst of a great expansion of collegiate institutions. The number of American colleges doubled between 1840 and 1860, from 107 to 209. But the average enrollments of those institutions grew much more slowly, from an average of 78 students in 1840 to 73 in 1850 to 79 by 1860.[39] Not until after the Civil War did institutional enrollments begin to expand, and then in only a handful of schools. Cornell, "the first visible, spectacular fruit of the Morrill Act," opened in 1868 with a freshman class of 400—a number unheard of at the time.[40] Those who planned the Farmers' High School in 1855 set comparatively high enrollment goals, at least by the standards of the day. At a time when the average college enrollment was about 75 students, the Farmers' High School predicated its original business plan on 200 matriculants, each paying $75 in annual tuition.[41] The college building was designed to accommodate more than 300 students, and Pugh wanted to see the institution enrolling between 400 and 800 students.

The two attempts to establish agricultural colleges that were durably successful occurred almost simultaneously in Michigan and Pennsylvania, with the acts of incorporation for each being signed in February 1855. In Michigan

FIGURE 10   *Students clearing campus land.*

the state agricultural society, founded in 1849, began to lobby for the establishment of a state agricultural college. A committee of the society visited the
University of Michigan in 1854 to determine whether the agricultural college
should be appended to it. Committee members talked with President Henry
P. Tappan and listened to three scientific lectures, but found the university's
offerings insufficient for the making of a practical farmer. "An agricultural college should be separate from any other institution," the committee declared,
and it successfully lobbied for a new institution. The governor of Michigan
signed the act of incorporation on February 12, 1855, placing the new agricultural college on a farm near Lansing and under the jurisdiction of the
state board of education. The college was dedicated in May 1857, entrance
examinations were held, and an entering class of seventy-three students was
admitted.[42]

In a few other states, efforts also were made to establish agricultural
colleges. The Maryland Agricultural College, chartered in 1856, opened for
instruction in 1859 but was woefully deficient in providing any kind of agricultural education. In 1858 the state of Iowa appropriated $10,000 and created

a board of trustees for the Iowa State Agricultural College and Farm, but the institution was not able to begin operation until 1869, long after the Morrill Act was passed.

Thus, as the 1860s began, there were three self-described agricultural institutions in some manner of operation at the collegiate level. These were the fledgling schools that in time would become Michigan State University, the Pennsylvania State University, and the University of Maryland. But as will be discussed later, neither Michigan nor Maryland, in their early years of struggle, would be as assiduously scientific as the Pennsylvania institution under Pugh's leadership.

A final differentiating factor for the Farmers' High School, and for the Michigan and Maryland agricultural colleges as well, was their public or state-sponsored status. This was a unique status that Pugh, the trustees, and other advocates would emphasize with increasing force to the Pennsylvania legislature as the 1860s ground on. The overwhelming proportion of colleges during the mid-nineteenth century was private, in the modern meaning of the word. Of the 180 or so colleges founded between 1820 and 1860, only 10 were state controlled; almost all the rest were affiliated with a religious denomination.[43] Thus the agricultural college movement, soon to morph into land-grant colleges with sponsorship from the federal as well as state governments, was opening the gates to a new era in American higher education.

CHAPTER 4

Beginning the Presidency

PUGH'S ARRIVAL ON THE grounds of the Farmers' High School on October 26, 1859, marked the culmination of six years of intensive scientific preparation in Europe. His education in Germany and France and research at Rothamsted were now ordered to a different purpose, his long-held dream. Even before leaving the United States in 1853, after serving as principal of his own Jordan Bank Academy, Pugh had envisioned building the model agricultural college for Pennsylvania and the nation. Now his time had come.

Pugh was hired sight unseen, without interviews, selection committees, or the other trappings of the modern presidential search process. Though the hiring was consummated with Pugh's acceptance of trustee president Watts's offer in March 1859, Watts had never met Pugh. Their first meeting did not occur until late September 1859, in Philadelphia, where Watts "received favorable impressions of him," as he wrote to William Waring, the acting principal of the Farmers' High School.[1]

Oddly, in the minutes of the Board of Trustees, there is no reference to any formal offer being made to Pugh, or of his acceptance, or of the board's voting on the appointment. The first mention of Pugh appears in the board's minutes of its December 5, 1859, meeting, at which Pugh's salary was set at $1,500 per year.[2] Due to the penurious condition of the school, the amount was actually $500 less than what Watts had listed for the president's salary in his 1854 letter to Governor Bigler. Pugh was appointed not only as president but also as professor of scientific agriculture, chemistry, mineralogy, and geology.

Just as Pugh had formed a solid working relationship with Watts, he forged an equally beneficial relationship with Hugh N. McAllister, the trustee from Bellefonte who met Pugh at the train station and drove him to campus. It was well that he should. Watts and McAllister, far more than any other trustees, shouldered the major work of moving the institution forward in its early years. Watts was located in Carlisle, Cumberland County, about eighty-five miles southeast of the Farmers' High School, but McAllister was close at hand, his farm outside Bellefonte being only about twelve miles from campus.

Twenty years older than Pugh, McAllister was an 1833 graduate of Jefferson College in southwestern Pennsylvania. He read law in Bellefonte and eventually attended the Dickinson School of Law in Carlisle. He practiced law for thirty-eight years; in 1859 he went into partnership with James A. Beaver, who later became president of the college's Board of Trustees and governor of Pennsylvania. Centre County's most distinguished attorney, McAllister turned down several judicial posts offered by Pennsylvania governors in the 1850s and, although well beyond military age, served for a brief time in the Union army.

Through all of this, his interest in the school never abated. For nearly twenty years, from 1854 until his death in 1873, as historian Erwin Runkle noted, "there was scarcely a day which did not have some task for the college which demanded his thought or counsel."[3]

McAllister, like Watts, had been a strong champion for establishing an agricultural college in Pennsylvania. He was one of the three trustees charged with planning the school's physical facilities, especially the college building. He and Watts also planned all of the school's outbuildings, and it was McAllister who was asked to oversee the construction of everything. When the Panic of 1857 halted construction, McAllister donated $500 to help meet expenses and raised an additional $5,700 through a local fundraising campaign, though it was not enough to resume the work.[4] It would not be the last time McAllister would help with the financial needs of the institution, however.

The Pugh Papers overflow with letters between Pugh and McAllister detailing the minutia of building, and advocating for, the institution. Pugh would ask McAllister to come to campus to evaluate the poor window placement in the college building. The president would explain new hiring and firings, the ordering of supplies and equipment, as well as situations involving students being called to war, suffering from illnesses, and breaking campus rules. Pugh could complain candidly to McAllister, which he did early and often, especially with regard to the continual interruptions to the construction of the college building. For his part, McAllister never wavered in his support of Pugh and the school.

Upon his arrival at the school, Pugh also needed to familiarize himself with Centre County, located in the geographic center of the state. There was no town surrounding the Farmers' High School, and hence no immediate distractions for its students. A topographical map of Centre County from 1861 denoted the location merely as the "Farmers' High School of Pa." As Pugh traversed the countryside, Centre County would have appeared bucolic and sparsely populated, sprinkled with small farms and a few scattered villages. The 1860 U.S. Census counted Centre County's population at exactly 27,000, about 1 percent of the state's population of 2,823,024.[5]

The first land-claim was made in 1763, at the end of the French and Indian War. Population grew slowly, gradually attracting Scots-Irish and Germans, or "Pennsylvania Dutch." English and Welsh settlers—the latter tending to be Quaker, like Pugh—came later.[6] By 1800 the area had grown to slightly more than 4,000 residents, enough to warrant its formal establishment by carving it out of four adjoining counties. Two closely located towns—Milesburg and

Bellefonte—were incorporated as boroughs, with Bellefonte, the larger town, being named the county seat.[7]

Surprisingly, perhaps, the county's pastoral appearance masked a vibrant industrial base. By mid-century, central Pennsylvania—particularly the counties of Centre, Huntingdon, Blair, Clinton, and Mifflin—had grown into the greatest iron-producing region in the United States, with forty-six furnaces and forty-two forges.[8] The demand for high-grade "Juniata Iron," named for the nearby Juniata River valley, was insatiable, with the "pig iron" being shipped to markets in Philadelphia and Pittsburgh. The iron industry developed because of the combination of natural resources in the region: pockets of iron ore near the surface, rather than in deep veins, where it could be quarried rather than mined; abundant hardwood forests, which provided the fuel as trees were felled and slow-burned into charcoal to fire the furnaces; seams of limestone, also required for the manufacturing process; and abundant streams to provide waterpower.[9]

In Centre County, iron-making got under way in the 1790s. The first operation to be established was Centre Furnace, the vestigial remains of which are located on the eastern border of the present-day Penn State University Park campus. Centre Furnace eventually was purchased by James Irvin, who became known as "the great ironmaster of central Pennsylvania, with 13 iron plants in five counties under his control."[10] The most productive operation in Irvin's iron empire was Centre Furnace. This considerable source of wealth enabled Irvin to make the offer of 200 acres of adjoining land to the site selection committee of the state agricultural society. Thus, Centre Furnace literally fired the founding of the Farmers' High School. The iron industry also influenced local agriculture. Iron-making necessitated a large, specialized workforce, a manorial community of sorts, which, of course, demanded copious amounts of food, thus accelerating the expansion of agriculture in the rich soils of Centre County.

In 1815 such iron-making opportunities induced the Valentine and Thomas families, Welsh Quakers from Chester County, to move to Centre County. They developed two large iron-making operations in and near Bellefonte.[11] The arrival of these same families would, decades later, influence Pugh's life. Very early in his presidency, he visited ironmaster Abram Valentine in Bellefonte to discuss the mineral assets of the region. There, he met and fell in love with the ironmaster's daughter.

With his background in scientific and practical agriculture, chemistry, mineralogy, metallurgy, botany, and geology, Pugh had landed in a locale well suited to those interests. Now he could turn his attention to getting the Farmers' High School on a solid footing by addressing student conduct, reorganizing the curriculum, shoring up its finances, completing the college building, and promoting the "great experiment."

Addressing Student Conduct

Pugh had arrived at the institution very late in its first academic year, which had opened on February 15, 1859, and was slated to end on December 15. In the meantime, the students had enjoyed their experience without his guiding presence and things had gotten a bit out of hand. Discipline was a constant problem at the Farmers' High School, as it was in American colleges generally. Far removed from the enticements of city life, and facing a regimented life of classes, manual labor, and other requirements such as chapel, Farmers' High School students fell to entertaining themselves for amusement. They indulged themselves through pranks, hi-jinks, and even drunkenness when they could find a tavern owner in one of the nearby villages eager to ply them with alcohol. Aside from admitting students nominated by county agricultural societies, the school also became something of a dumping ground for young men who had been expelled from other colleges for academic failure or breaches of discipline.[12]

Pugh's first order of business was to draw up a printed set of rules and regulations for student behavior. "Three years' experience with 25 to 35 scholars from 15 to 30 years of age taught me that the principle of 'no rules' was bad," he told McAllister. Pugh's philosophy was to use the carrot as well as the stick. He proposed a medal to reward truly excellent students who coupled high academic performance to exemplary behavior, constituting an honorary class of no more than twenty who should be treated as "gentlemen," an example to the others.[13] In his first year, Pugh sought mightily to appeal to the better angels of the students' nature. When that failed, however, he had no second thoughts about expelling the miscreants, if such extremes were deemed necessary. Beyond the orderly conduct of the educational process, student discipline was important to Pugh for a larger reason. Pugh was determined that the Farmers' High School succeed. It was an experiment being watched by its sponsoring state and the national agricultural community, and he wanted his students to be as committed to its success as he was.

Pugh made an immediate impression upon his students, physically as well as intellectually. At six feet two inches in height, and of strong, muscular build, he was commanding in stature if not intimidating. But his countenance and comportment were even more impressive. Students knew he meant business. Tellico Johnson, one of the first students, later recalled that although one of the other faculty members suffered a blow during a dining hall food fight, "No one dared throw butter at Dr. Pugh. . . . He did his duty and expected everyone else to do theirs, and woe unto you if you failed."[14] An early incident, also in the dining hall, set the tone. Young Walter Pierce had skipped an algebra class. Pierce made it through the rest of the day, his teacher apparently ignoring the transgression. As evening approached, he might have felt that he had gotten away with it.

The students filed into the dining hall and food was served. Before the grace, Pugh rose from his table and addressed the room sternly: "Mr. Pierce was absent from his class in algebra. He will leave the table." In stunned silence, the students looked to Pierce for his response. Pierce in turn looked down at his bowl, picked up his spoon, and began slurping his soup. Pugh sprang from his chair, caught Pierce by the collar, and swept him out the door. The students learned that night that Pugh would brook no violation of the rules.[15]

At the beginning of the school's second academic year in February 1860, after three months in office, Pugh laid out his philosophy and expectations for the study body in his inaugural address, "On the Mutual Relations of the Teacher and the Taught." Published soon after as a twenty-six-page pamphlet, it might have been the longest talk his young charges had ever heard.

Pugh began with an excoriation of the "code of honor" commonplace among college students that induced them not to tattle on their fellows who broke the rules. This code produced an ethos of antagonism between students and teachers that undermined the very purpose of higher education. Pugh declared the code "false in theory and pernicious in practice."[16] Pugh wanted a dynamic of mutual respect and cooperation that would underlie the educational objectives for the Farmers' High School and distinguish it from all the rest. He observed that an "incredibly large" number of American college students had made their way "without even learning how to study, much less laying up well systemized stores of knowledge." He didn't want his students to pass through college life "in this disreputable manner" (5). Pugh cited example after example of the "immorality" of undermining pedagogical authority and consequently subverting the educational enterprise. "Every hour that the teacher must waste in suppressing insubordination in colleges, is more than an hour lost . . . which he might devote to preparing the material for his classes in the lecture, or recitation room" (12).

Discussing the various moral grades of men, Pugh characterized his students as mainly good but warned of the harm that could be wrought by only a few bad apples. His own experience showed him that less than 10 percent of any given student body exerted a negative influence. "But 5 or 6 evil-disposed students in a hundred, may exert a most pernicious influence, if the 100 are without much experience." Thus it was the leaders of insubordination who deserved to be punished, not the entire student body, even though all of them seemingly might have been involved (16, 17).

After admonishing any potential troublemakers, Pugh appealed to the better natures of those students who were attending the institution in hopes of succeeding. "We are here with the eyes of the friends of agricultural education, in every civilized country in the world . . . for the avowed purpose of trying an experiment which has never been successfully performed in any country in the world . . . to demonstrate the practicability of combining agriculture practice with the study of agricultural principles in an educational institution." The task of inventing an agricultural college and a subsequent national system of agricultural education and research was enormous, he maintained, requiring generations of work before it would be completed. But at the Farmers' High School, the hard work was at least beginning. Pugh stressed that he had visited many agricultural schools and colleges in Europe, and "in none of them is the fundamental idea of thorough study and manual labor, together with the idea of the dignity of labor, maintained as it is maintained at the present moment in the Agricultural College of Pennsylvania" (21–23).

As he built toward the climax, Pugh waxed teleological, citing the institution's ultimate purpose and the constituencies that would benefit:

We owe it to the friends of this Institution, and to the people of our great Keystone State . . . that we resolve not to let this great experiment fail. We owe it to the cause of agricultural science, now struggling in its infancy, without proper means for its promulgation, that we carry on our enterprise with a resolute and persevering energy. We owe it to the cause of agricultural practice now groping its way in the labyrinthine uncertainties of empiricism, quackery and ignorance, that the light of science be set upon to guide it in the onward march of modern improvement. We owe it to the agriculturalist himself who treads upon a soil rich in subjects of thought, and who feeds and cultivates his crops that reward his labors by processes he know nothing about, that we develop a system of instruction which shall unlock the beauties and the mysteries of nature around him.

. . . And lastly, my young friends, we owe it to ourselves, that we should now so shape our course and mould our actions, that when life's early vigour shall have passed, and we look back from a ripe-old age upon our duties in connexion with the Farm School, we shall have the pleasure of feeling that we have done all that lay in our power to acquit ourselves in a manner worthy of the responsibilities that evolved upon us. (23, 24)

Urging his students to help him in the unfinished task of completing the school's main building and grounds, Pugh dangled the eventual verdict of history in front of them. Future generations, he said, "will either censure our mistakes . . . or they will point with pride to our efforts . . . which made it possible to show, upon the soil of Pennsylvania for the first time in the world, that the idea of study and labor, as proposed at this institution, is practicable" (25).

However eloquent, Pugh's rhetoric could not transform student nature. As the school year began in mid-February 1860, a number of students got themselves in trouble by drinking excessively at a village tavern a few miles distant. Pugh went after the tavern owner with a vengeance, taking him to court and demanding two alternatives: either the offending party leave the area and sell or rent his establishment to a more responsible person or face a lawsuit in Centre County court. "Mercy to this rum-selling clique is giving *injustice* to the Institution and every parent that patronizes it," Pugh told McAllister.[17] Though Pugh saw justice served in this case, the problem of student drinking would not dissolve itself during his presidency.

Reorganizing the Curriculum

The institution's charter, as approved by the Pennsylvania legislature in 1855, included two major educational goals: to provide students with a knowledge of English language, grammar, geography, history, mathematics, chemistry, and such other branches of natural and exact sciences as necessary for "the proper education of a farmer" and to require that students perform all the labor "necessary in the cultivation of the farm."[18]

Pugh would quickly expand the institution's mission and scope and revise the curriculum accordingly. By 1862, according to the annual report, the over-arching goal was "to associate a high degree of intelligence with the practice of Agriculture and the industrial arts, and to seek to make use of this intelli-gence in developing the agricultural and industrial resources of the country, and protecting its interests." The institution would accomplish this mission through four objectives: teaching all the natural sciences, focusing on those that have practical applications; requiring manual labor as a condition of matriculation; conducting research so as to contribute to the development of the agricultural sciences; and supporting the industrial interests of the state by educating its farmers.[19] Pugh's goals, save for manual labor, seem prescient for the time, auguring the teaching, research, and service mission of the as-yet-unborn land-grant college and, indeed, the modern public research university.

Pugh's larger purpose in coming to the Farmers' High School was to advance the interests of the state and nation, through the introduction of scientific education and research with their resultant applications for agriculture and industry. He and other leaders knew that industrialization and urbanization could not occur without concomitant progress from the agricultural sector. That was particularly apparent in the nation's two greatest industrial powers and most populous states, New York and Pennsylvania, of which Pugh was a deeply loyal son. In 1860 New York had nearly 3.9 million inhabitants, Pennsylvania 2.9 million. At the same time, both were huge agricultural states. New York ranked first in improved farmland, with 14.4 million acres with a cash value of $803 million, while Pennsylvania ranked third (after Ohio) in the same measures: 10.5 million acres of improved farmland valued at $662 million.[20]

Having set standards and expectations for student behavior, Pugh next turned his attention to a panoply of major tasks: reorganizing the curriculum; ensuring that work (by the students) was progressing on the college farm and its related operations; acquainting himself with the school's precarious finances; and making the case for the future of the institution—in addition to dozens of sundry duties and details attendant to getting an experimental institution off the ground. All of this work was laid out in the institution's first *Catalogue of the Officers and Students for the Second Annual Session, Together with a Financial Report of the Affairs of the Institution.* Written by Pugh toward the end of the second academic year, the report was submitted to the Board of Trustees. President Watts, in turn, submitted it to the president of the Pennsylvania State Agricultural Society, James Haldeman, on December 7, 1860. The catalog provided a detailed picture of the college in all aspects.

The faculty stood at five; collectively, they were heavily oriented toward science. Pugh was now professor of chemistry, scientific and practical agriculture, mineralogy, and analytical mechanics. David Wilson, the vice president, served as professor of the English language and literature and moral and intellectual philosophy, as well as superintendent of the agricultural department.

William G. Waring, who had served as principal before Pugh's arrival, was professor of horticulture and general superintendent of the gardens and nursery department. J. S. Whitman was professor of botany, physiology, zoology, veterinary science, and geology. R. C. Allison was professor of mathematics, astronomy, and natural philosophy.

Total enrollment for the college stood at 110 students for the 1860 academic year—30 in the second class; 53 in the third class, and 27 in the fourth class. This was down slightly from the 119 ultimately enrolled during the inaugural 1859 academic year. The students came from thirty-eight of the extant sixty-six counties of Pennsylvania. Pugh noted that applications and letters of inquiry had come from students and sponsors beyond Pennsylvania's borders. But in keeping with the expressed intentions of the trustees and the state agricultural society to educate Pennsylvania students first and foremost, and because of the limited capacity of the college building only one-third finished, the out-of-state interest was kept at bay.

The four-year curriculum, strongly oriented to science and mathematics, was ordered as follows:

> First Year—Arithmetic, Elementary Algebra, Botany, Elementary Anatomy and Physiology, Geography and Elementary Astronomy, English Grammar and Composition, Elocution, History, Practical Agriculture and the details of management on the College Farm
>
> Second Year—Advanced Algebra and Geometry, General Chemistry, Vegetable Anatomy and Physiology, Zoology and Veterinary, Geology, Paleontology, Physical Geography, Practical Agriculture and Horticulture, Logic and Rhetoric
>
> Third Year—Surveying, Leveling, Drafting, the use of instruments, Analytical Geometry, Elementary Calculus, Natural Philosophy, Qualitative Chemical Analysis, Veterinary Surgery, Entomology, Agricultural Botany, Practical Agriculture and Pomology, Political and Social Economy
>
> Fourth Year—Analytical Geometry, Differential and Integral Calculus, Engineering, Drafting, Mechanical Drawing, Quantitative Chemical Analysis, Veterinary Pharmacy, Gardening, Agricultural Accounts and Farm Management, Moral and Intellectual Philosophy[21]

The Farmers' High School offered a prescribed curriculum, a lockstep progression for students leading to the bachelor of scientific agriculture degree, the first degree so titled and so structured in America. To gain some perspective, it is instructive to compare the Farmers' High School curriculum to that of Yale's School of Applied Chemistry, the leading scientific institution of the day, established some thirteen years earlier in 1847, as well as that of Union College, the first institution to introduce a science curriculum, nearly twenty years earlier than Yale.

Yale's School of Applied Chemistry later transitioned into the Yale Scientific School and, ultimately, the endowed Sheffield Scientific School. Yale's curriculum was laboratory-intensive and much less prescriptive than that of the Farmers' High School, although the latter also required substantial laboratory work within the course matrix.

At Yale, the school's original faculty were John Pritkin Norton, professor of agricultural chemistry, and Benjamin Silliman Jr., professor of chemistry and kindred sciences as applied to the arts. Both had earned considerable scientific reputations. According to the Sheffield School's early historian, Russell H. Crittendon, each of the handful of original students "was more or less a law unto himself and his one object was work. . . . The instruction they received was radically different from the usual type of college classroom work." Learning came mainly through personal interaction in the laboratory, where students "worked out for themselves chemical reactions, studied the behavior of acids, bases, and salts, applied analytical methods . . . and in various ways gained first hand knowledge of the facts and principles upon which chemical laws are based."[22]

In addition to the laboratory work, there were two formal courses of lectures—one by Norton on the agricultural chemistry during the second term and one by Silliman Jr. on applied chemistry and mineralogy, given during the third term. By 1852 the degree Bachelor of Philosophy was established, for which students qualified by passing examinations in at least three branches of study—in the physical and mathematical sciences and either German or French. By 1852 six of the eight students who had completed this program were granted the B.Phil. and thus became the first graduates of the Scientific School. Three of the six later became professors in the school, including Samuel W. Johnson.[23]

Before Yale, Union College in Schenectady, New York, became the first American institution to introduce a comprehensive science curriculum, at least comprehensive by the standards of the day. Eliphalet Nott, one of the most progressive educational leaders of the nineteenth century, served as Union's president for an astounding sixty-two years, from 1804 until 1866. Like Pugh, Nott began his presidency at age thirty-one, but he lived much longer and was able to bring Union into early national leadership in science education. Union introduced the B.A. degree in science in 1828, offering its students a choice in any combination of the traditional classical and the new scientific course, creating what was very likely the first elective system in American higher education. Union's scientific course offered professional preparation in such fields as engineering, education, medicine, law, and mining, and it attracted students in droves, particularly transfer students. In 1830, just two years after the scientific course was introduced, Union graduated ninety-six students, Yale seventy-one, Harvard forty-eight, and Princeton twenty.[24] However progressive it was, Union's early emphasis on science did not address agriculture.

Pugh and the trustees were looking to construct a very different kind of scientific school, oriented entirely toward the science of agriculture, with ambitions toward a larger student constituency than either Yale's Sheffield School or the earlier Union College. Although it is useful to compare and contrast the scientific approach and curricula of these two schools to that of the later Farmers' High School, the three institutions differed substantially in mission, scope, and orientation.

Even as he introduced the prescribed "thorough course" leading to the Bachelor of Scientific Agriculture degree, Pugh was looking forward to the day when he could broaden the Farmers' High School's curricular offerings, an eventuality he said could happen when the college building was completed. Pugh envisioned a need to differentiate the curriculum for various ability levels and educational goals. He advocated for an elementary/secondary department, affording preparation specifically designed for admittance to an agricultural or scientific college; a special partial course for students who could not take the whole four-year course; a purely practical course, affording some connection to science for students who sought more knowledge in production farming; and at the top the "thorough course" for those with high academic talent, immersing them in the scientific principles of agricultural practice—the only curriculum in place when Pugh wrote the catalog in 1860. Pugh foresaw the need to generate a critical mass of students—in varying states of ability and desire—in order to finance the entire enterprise, thus ensuring that agricultural science at the highest level could be offered to the truly talented.[25]

Addressing Institutional Finances

Beyond student conduct and curricular reform, Pugh was necessarily preoccupied with institutional finances. He set up three major funds and reported receipts and expenditures for both 1859 and 1860. The Students' Fund included all debtor and creditor accounts pertaining to the institution since the opening of the school; essentially, this was the school's operating account. The Nursery Fund was dedicated to the income and costs associated with that operation. The Permanent Fund, or Building Fund, included monies coming from the state, from private subscriptions (fundraising), and from the expenditures for capital improvements. Pugh noted, however, that the Students' Fund—"as the most accessible source of money"—also had been used to support improvements across the institution. For example, $2,912.39 had been drawn from the Students' Fund in 1859 and 1860 to support expenses for the nursery. In all, expenditures for operating the institution in its entirety—including faculty salaries, food, and physical plant—were listed at $12,590.21 for 1859 and a like amount, $12,938.85 for 1860. Income derived from students provided 86 percent of the total: $11,275 for 1859 and $10,800 for 1860. Then, as now, the institution relied heavily on tuition and fees to cover operating costs (17–21).

Pugh's greatest concern was that student enrollment was far too small for the efficient operation of the school. He knew that enrollment could not increase appreciably from the trustees' initial target of 200 until the college building was completed and more dormitory rooms made available. "It requires nearly as much expenditure in Professors' Salaries, and in Farm and Garden Superintendence, with 110 Students as it would with three times this number. . . . It requires nearly as much time and effort to conduct a single Student, through all the details of an experimental science . . . as it would to lead 50 Students in a class to the same point" (22).

The report of the Permanent Fund—monies derived for capital expenditures—painted a fuller picture of public support for the Farmers' High School from 1857 through 1860. Funds from subscription campaigns in fifteen Pennsylvania counties amounted to $20,116.56—from a high of $8,199.64 from Centre County to a low of $10.00 from Clearfield County. Added to that were $10,000 from the State Agricultural Society; a $10,000 pledge from two prominent Centre Countians, trustees Hugh McAllister and Andrew Curtin, to cover the guarantee for the subscription campaign for Centre and Huntingdon counties; $25,000 from the state treasury for the initial appropriation in 1857 for the college building; $21,411.05 from the state treasurer on certificate and governor's warrant; $4,467 from the estate of Elliott Cresson, the school's first benefaction of the kind; and other sundry sources. The grand total was $103,320.39 in revenue for the Permanent Fund. Expenditures had exceeded income, however, by $3,535 (25–27).

FIGURE 12   *Students cultivating land by College Building.*

Institutional property was inventoried as well. The Farm consisted of 400 acres, made serviceable by virtue of student labor: "All of it . . . has been broken up, and the principal part of the stones picked off it; the stumps have been grubbed up, fences built, and hedges and orchards planted, so as to bring it into good condition for future cropping, and thus very materially enhance its value," Pugh reported. Farm buildings included a double-decked barn, hog pen, blacksmith shop, carpenter shop and tool house, wash-house for the students' clothes, and two frame houses.

The college building was another story altogether. No progress had been made since 1858, when construction was halted due to lack of funds and the contractor's financial problems; in fact, subcontractors had filed various liens against the contractor for nonpayment. An adjacent temporary building, used as a kitchen and dining hall, had been erected. Piles of construction material lay nearby—limestone, bricks, lumber, cast-iron window and door sills, and so forth—awaiting the day when construction of the college building might resume.

In his concluding remarks, Pugh noted that the work required for the operation of an agricultural college and farm involved more responsibility than was required for an "ordinary institution of learning." Nonetheless, the school's progress during his first year demonstrated "that even in our present unorganized state, it is *practicable*, and if properly organized would be *entirely successful.*" Pugh then sounded a cautionary note, asserting that the institution must soon be scaled in size appropriately to succeed. And scaling the institution properly could not be accomplished without the necessary funds to complete its facilities. Without those funds, the experiment would fail. He noted that certain critics of the school had faulted the trustees for starting a school upon too large a scale. "It is said that they should have constructed a building that would have been complete for 100 students, rather than have commenced with one for 400 students. . . . *A school like this can succeed only as a large school.* It can only be *completely organized* as a large school, and without complete organization it *cannot prosper.* A small Agricultural school, complete in itself, *would go down as a result of its inefficiency*" (30).

If the institution failed to complete the college building, Pugh observed, "Our experiment would fail *because the conditions upon which its friends had predicated its success had never been supplied.*" The failure would have repercussions far beyond the borders of Pennsylvania, he added. It would represent "a loss of confidence in the principle" behind agricultural colleges and would discourage similar attempts elsewhere. "*It cannot live long as it has been living,*" Pugh warned. "The friend of Agricultural education everywhere in the State should know that about $120,000 have already been expended here, and that $50,000 are wanted to make the material for which this sum has been spent. . . . It cannot be too distinctly understood, that without an additional expenditure of $50,000, the $120,000 already spent must become almost a total loss. Our buildings must be completed speedily, or our school must cease to exist" (29–31).

Meeting on December 5, 1860, the Board of Trustees heard Pugh's report and ordered that it be printed for wider circulation. Heeding Pugh's words about the urgency of completing the college building, they resolved to make that happen by applying for $50,000 from the state legislature for that purpose at its next session in January 1861.[26]

Taking the Case to the Public

Early in his presidency, Evan Pugh saw the need to take the case for support of the Farmers' High School and scientific agriculture to wider audiences in Pennsylvania and beyond. He was a fierce promoter of the school and would remain as such for the duration of his presidency. Within his first two months, he sent copies of the school's catalog to every member of the Pennsylvania legislature, to newspaper editors across the state, and to "life members" of the Pennsylvania State Agricultural Society.[27] He also considered public speaking engagements but conceded that such efforts would be hard to accomplish. "Between government and teaching not much time is left from coming in contact with the great public exterior to ourselves," he told McAllister.[28] Nevertheless, he sallied forth. In October 1860 he spoke to the fall meeting of the Cumberland County Agricultural Society. Pugh's appearance was arranged by Society president Watts, who wanted to introduce the new Farmers' High School president to constituents in his home county. In any event, Pugh's address—*What Science Has Done and May Do for Agriculture*—was published as a thirty-nine-page booklet by the society and sent to influential persons across the state as well as selected organizations across the nation.

Pugh's address did not center on local interests in Cumberland County. Rather, it was a manifesto for a system of agricultural science and education in the United States that should, he postulated, surpass similar systems extant in Europe and the British Isles. From his work, travels, and observations in Europe, Pugh had gained wide knowledge of what other nations had done and were doing on these fronts. America, he declared, had yet to even get started; accordingly, he laid out a master plan of what was needed to move ahead of Europe. He wanted nothing less than a national system of agricultural science and education, the apex of which would be the American agricultural college, based, he hoped, on the model he was building at the Farmers' High School.

Pugh did not intend to flatter his audience but rather to impress upon them "*how much they have yet to learn*, and how much they should do that *has not been done*." He criticized American agriculture as merely "jogging along, unaided by science, at the old rate of our forefathers of half a crop, one-fourth of a crop, or no crop at all to the acre. We have been retrograding rather than progressing in that which constitutes the fundamental basis of all agricultural theory and practice. I mean the *rotation of crops*, and the *maintenance of constant fertility* in the soil."[29]

Pugh raised the specter of soil exhaustion and the consequence of starvation in certain parts of the country. "Before that time comes, let us hope that science will be appreciated and her teachings headed, and that the farmer will learn to restore the exhausted materials that he annually takes from his land in grain and meat." Pugh cited the recent national excitement over the introduction of guano—a natural manure composed of the excrement of seabirds—a fad he condemned for being "so mixed up with quackery, fraud and ignorance." He cited further instances of fraud with artificial manures and called for a national system of research and regulation to ensure quality in "manufactured manure" and protect the farmer (8–10).

Pugh compared agricultural practices and crop yields between the United States and the more scientifically oriented cultures of Great Britain (England, Scotland, Wales, Ireland). In England, he noted, the population had doubled, and with it a doubling of consumption of agricultural products, yet the price of agricultural produce had declined significantly. Even in Ireland, previously devastated by the potato famine, the traditional method of cropping that exhausted the soil had been abandoned in favor of scientifically based methods, placing the nation "beyond the power of any disaster . . . as that of 1846" (16, 18).

What brought British and European nations into advanced agricultural practice and productivity, Pugh pointed out, was their comparatively sophisticated system of research and education. The Scots, at first, took the lead in agricultural improvement, he said, with the Highland Agricultural Society of Scotland, founded in 1783, out of which came the first Agricultural Chemistry Association. Faith in the benefits of science was such that sixty Scottish farmers banded together to hire an analytical chemist for a five-year period (19). Describing progress along similar lines in England, Pugh cited examples of how consulting chemists had aided the Royal Agricultural Society of England (1828), particularly in regard to exposing not only the manufacture and sale of fraudulent manures but animal nutrients as well. "It has detected poisons and adulterations in cattle foods and has exposed the charlatanry of those who would sell 'patent cattle foods' with extraordinary fattening qualities" (23).

As important as research and investigation were, the linchpin to agricultural progress on a broad scale was agricultural education, Pugh emphasized, "for the obvious reason that science cannot be *understood* or *applied* without scientific education." And science cannot be taught through "popular lectures," he added. Pugh provided an overview of agricultural education in the British Isles and Europe. Recounting his visit to the Royal Agricultural College at Cirencester, England, Pugh noted that the institution was flourishing with eighty students, eight professors, and with ample resources extending to buildings, botanical gardens, and the college farm of 450 acres. The professor of chemistry at the Royal College had three laboratory assistants making analyses of manures, salts, cattle food, and so forth, in the process protecting the agricultural community from fraud. When Pugh told the faculty he was returning to America to build a similar institution, "they told me not to get discouraged, to not expect an agricultural community to wake up at once to the importance of an agricultural education . . . that such an effort only could succeed by dint of hard labor and continual perseverance" (24–26).

Cirencester's was exactly the kind of institutional dynamic Pugh wanted to bring to life at the Farmers' High School. But the larger, well-articulated system of agricultural education Pugh hoped would take root in the United States was to be found in "Germany, the land of learning . . . with her half a hundred Universities. Germany has been first and foremost on the subject of Agricultural Education." Pugh described the various levels of agricultural education extant in the German states—the elementary agricultural schools, the higher agricultural schools, the agricultural chairs at its leading universities, and specialized agricultural institutions connected to certain universities. Undergirding the German system were the agricultural investigation stations, providing the knowledge platform upon which agriculture education could take place on such a grand scale (27–30).

Pugh castigated the United States for its lack of progress. "Where are her Agricultural Schools? Where are her Agricultural Colleges? Where are her Agricultural Investigations? . . . Where are our Agricultural Chemists? . . . Where are our Agricultural Bureaus to collect agricultural statistics, and enable us to know just what the country is doing and what it is not?" Pugh had surveyed the American landscape of agricultural higher education and found it a disaster in the making. He noted that Michigan's Agricultural College had failed, that Maryland's was not working, that the aborning New York Agricultural College at Ovid was impoverished, and that Pennsylvania's "had come to a stand-still, for want of funds." Equally discouraging, the United States lacked even a single agricultural experiment station, "at which the innumerable questions suggested by agricultural practice, are being solved" (34).

Pugh was a cosmopolitan, first and foremost, but he also was a loyal son of Pennsylvania. As such, he wanted the Keystone State to exert leadership in getting the agricultural college movement off the ground. He was mortified that a fellow Pennsylvanian, U.S. president James Buchanan, had vetoed Congressman Justin Morrill's 1857 land-grant college legislation, an action he viewed "with shame and sorrow" (35).

Having laid out the history of international agricultural science and education, Pugh climaxed his address with his vision for the United States. He wanted agricultural colleges of a high order established across the nation, teaching agricultural principles in connection with practice. "They must stand in the same relation to Agriculture that our highest Military Academies stand to the art and science of war," he said. Its faculty members must be researchers as well as teachers, Pugh emphasized, constituting "a higher class of men in relation to what they have to teach, than those need be who teach the older and more fully developed sciences."

His concluding remarks emphasized the potential for leadership offered by the Farmers' High School of Pennsylvania: "If this Institution is sustained as it should be; if its buildings are completed upon the original plan, and it receives a reasonable support I have not the slightest doubt that it could be made the best Agricultural Institution in the world." And the model institution Pugh would create would produce additional institutions of similar quality across the nation, superseding those of Europe. That would happen because of the unique character of American institutions, the national consensus regarding the dignity of labor, the relative lack of social classes or castes, and the sheer size of the American agricultural community—"All will enable us to build up the best Agricultural Schools in the world, and we must do it! *We must do it in Pennsylvania,* and I think, gentlemen that we *will do it*" (36, 37).

But Pugh wasn't finished. He also called for state chemists, state-funded agricultural professorships, agricultural scientific investigation stations connected to agricultural colleges, state chemists also connected to agricultural colleges, an organized system for collecting agricultural statistics on a national scale, and a "National Agricultural Bureau, that should represent the agricultural interest in the National Legislature, and serve as a kind of union between all the isolated agricultural interests of the country" (38).

Pugh's vision, expressed that crisp October day in the rolling Cumberland Valley of south-central Pennsylvania, would come to pass eventually, though it would take decades of effort and struggle and he would not live to see the final results. The Morrill Land-Grant College Act would make it through Congress in 1862 and be signed into law; this enabling legislation would set in motion a national system of colleges, supported by the federal and state governments, in which the "leading object" would be "to teach such branches of learning as are related to agriculture and the mechanic arts." Pugh would also see Lincoln's establishment, in May 1862, of the U.S. Department of Agriculture, with a commissioner but without cabinet status, though that would come later, in 1889. In 1887, some twenty-three years after Pugh's death, would come the federal Hatch Act, providing for the establishment of agricultural experiment stations with annual federal funding, most all of the stations being attached to land-grant colleges. In 1890 would come the second Morrill Act, a general institutional aid bill for land-grant colleges, providing annual funding for a wide variety of programs and assuring the colleges' sustenance. In 1906 came the Adams Act—which provided for additional federal funding for agricultural experiment stations. As a result of these developments and many more in the twentieth century, the United States would emerge as the most agriculturally productive nation in the history of the world—while feeding much of it in the process. Pugh foresaw many of these needed advancements, and he devoted his life to working toward their realization as best he could.

By the fall of 1860, a year into his presidency, Pugh had won the confidence of the school's Board of Trustees. In a letter to McAllister, Watts cited a report Pugh had drafted for him. "Dr. Pugh writes frankly and generously and I must say that the more I know of him the better I like him." Noting that the onus of building the faculty should fall directly on Pugh rather than the trustees, Watts added, "I have said to him . . . that the organization of faculty must be a work of time and that the duty of doing it well must devolve upon him ultimately—he has more interest and will have more zeal in doing the work well than even you or I. He is young . . . energetic and writes as if he had devoted himself to the object of building the institution up into fame."[30]

CHAPTER 5

The Institution Hits Its Stride

LITTLE MORE THAN FOURTEEN months after his arrival at the Farmers' High School, Evan Pugh turned the calendar from 1860 and prepared for the beginning of the 1861 academic session, his second full year in the presidency. It was to be an extraordinary year. The United States would split apart, with the southern states seceding and commencing the bloodiest war in American history. Notwithstanding the larger crisis, the Farmers' High School, ensconced in its peaceful valley ninety-five miles north of the Mason-Dixon Line, would make signal accomplishments on three fronts. Pugh and the trustees would convince the Pennsylvania legislature to provide funding for the completion of the college building; construction would begin in the summer, providing for the eventual completion of the facility that would allow the institution to grow in student enrollment and benefit from economies of scale. Most significantly, the first entering class from 1859 would yield the institution's first graduates in December 1861, with eleven of them earning the Bachelor of Scientific Agriculture degree—the first such degree of its kind in America. In addition, Pugh would expand and diversify the curriculum, adding two new courses of study that would attract more students but would not require the mathematical rigor of the "full course." And, not least, he would inaugurate graduate study—a program leading to the first master of scientific agriculture degree to be granted in America.

The first priority of the new school year was to procure the money needed to complete the still-only-one-third-finished college building, as the trustees had resolved to do at their last meeting in the waning weeks of 1860. This time, the efforts of Pugh, Watts, McAllister, and their allies in the Pennsylvania legislature and statewide agricultural community paid dividends, due in no small part to the perceptions of progress at the Farmers' High School since Pugh had come on board.

On April 18, a week after Fort Sumter had been fired upon, the Pennsylvania legislature appropriated $49,900 for the building's completion—the second appropriation in the institution's brief history. But this victory did not come without a struggle. There was legislative opposition stemming from a variety of concerns: the restricted purposes of the school (it was established for "special classes"); the perception that the school would generate no benefits whatso-ever; the penurious condition of the state treasury; and the specter of unpaid bills of creditors of the former contractor. One representative said he could vote affirmatively only "if buildings and ground are owned by the State."[1]

But the support in the House was overwhelming, and the appropriations bill passed by a nearly 2-to-1 ratio, 57–31. The bill had been introduced in early 1861 by William C. Duncan of Centre County, who "championed it ably."[2] It was referred to the Ways and Means Committee, before which Pugh and several trustees appeared and made the case for its passage. In addition, to show how much work remained to be done, Pugh took a photograph of the incomplete main building to the hearing.[3] Several county agricultural societies expressed their support via letters and resolutions, and "friends of agriculture" across the state made visits to legislators and wrote letters as well. The agricul-tural press also advocated for the bill.

Despite the victory in the House, the battle left Pugh with a bitter taste in his mouth. As he wrote Samuel Johnson on March 13, a month before the bill's eventual success, "I am a little blue about it." Pugh was distressed because his vacation time was "wasted with those legislative blockheads" and because "honesty has not availed us in a righteous course." Above everything else loomed the real possibility that the school "must cease to go on if we don't get money." Pugh conceded that the school wasn't executing its mission because it was "too poor to do what will be creditable to us." Finally, should the bill be defeated, Pugh would exact a toll, as he was determined "that a knowledge of the evil that some devil dodging politicians have done shall live after them."[4]

In the Senate, the bill passed by a ratio of 3 to 2 (18–12). Here, strong champions emerged. Senator Winthrop Ketcham pointed out that legisla-tion had been passed to benefit interests in the mining, manufacturing, and commercial sectors, but not so for agriculture. Senator Alexander McClure

FIGURE 13 *Pugh's photograph of incomplete College Building, 1861.*

also championed the bill, vowing to vote against all other appropriation bills until the Farmers' High School bill passed.[5] But it was Colonel Andrew Gregg, senator from the school's home district in Centre County, who led the fight and secured the needed votes.[6] Also, it did not hurt that Andrew Curtin of Centre County, a former elected member of the institution's Board of Trustees, had been elected governor of Pennsylvania in 1860. He also supported the measure and signed it into law.

The importance of this legislative victory cannot be emphasized enough. It saved the school from failure, plain and simple. As Pugh recounted it, Pennsylvania, a great agricultural state, "was saved the disgrace of allowing an Agricultural College it had attempted to found, to break up in the act of being founded." The money already invested in the institution, $150,000 in Pugh's estimation, "was saved from being sacrificed." But more to the point, "our old Commonwealth has succeeded in bringing the first Agricultural School in the United States into successful operation."[7]

Watts was elated. He had never felt "more overjoyed than I do now at your success in Harrisburg," he told Pugh. The money would not only allow the institution to pursue its plans but also enable it to "build upon the confidence" that the legislature had expressed in the institution's management.[8]

FIGURE 14 *Construction progress on College Building, 1862.*

The trustees lost no time in following up. Meeting two weeks later in special session, they appointed a special committee of Pugh, Watts, and McAllister to make any needed modifications in the original plan and to employ a contractor to complete the work and get the building "under roof" by November 1, 1862—eighteen months' time.[9] The trustees hired George W. Tate of Bellefonte for $41,500 to complete the building under the original plan. At their next meeting nearly six months later, the trustees realized that the construction contract did not provide for the entire completion of the building, as it made no provisions for heating and furnishing the structure. The trustees authorized extending the contract with Tate (or another contractor, if needed) to include these essential features at a cost not to exceed $20,000, for which another mortgage would need to be secured.[10]

In the Farmers' High School Catalogue for 1861, published half a year later in early 1862, Pugh noted optimistically that construction had resumed over the summer and that "the whole is now under roof, and will be completed during the present winter and fore part of next summer."[11] But the work soon slowed down, in large part because of the shortage of labor and materials consumed by the war; the building would not be finished until December 1863, more than a year after the original trustees' deadline.[12]

At completion, the building was large by the standards of the day, designed to accommodate just about everything and everybody. Towering five stories above the basement, 234 feet wide and 130 feet deep (at its deepest part), the building encompassed a central core on a north–south axis, perpendicular to two long wings running east to west. The completed structure provided 165 dormitory rooms, each 10 by 18 feet and 9 to 11 feet high, sufficient to accommodate 330 students on the second through fifth floors. Other facilities included the library, the geographical and mineralogical museum, an anatomical museum, and a museum of agricultural productions, a chemical laboratory "for beginners" in the basement, laboratories for more advanced students, recitation rooms, rooms with apparatus for "special scientific investigations," lecture rooms, a chapel, kitchen and dining room, halls for the two literary societies, and a room for the proposed elementary or preparatory department, not to mention living facilities for the president and faculty. An indoor privy was provided on every floor, a five-story protrusion from the rear of the central core and affectionately referred to as the "shot tower." In all, the college building housed a veritable city, or at least an academical village, to borrow Thomas Jefferson's term. Although many other buildings would be erected after Pugh's day, "Old Main," as it later came to be called, would serve as the only major building for the duration of Pugh's presidency and would stand until 1929 when, because of structural deficiencies, it would be torn down. A new "Old Main" of roughly the same dimensions but of neo-classical architecture, would be erected on the same spot in 1930 with the same limestone blocks recycled from the original.

Enrollment for the institution stood at 88 for the 1861 academic year, a decline of twenty-two students from the total enrollment of 110 in 1860. This 1861 enrollment included twenty-one in the fourth class (freshmen), twenty-one in the third class (sophomores), twenty-nine in the second class (juniors), and seventeen in the senior or graduating class. The graduating class had been whittled down considerably from the fifty-five who entered as such in 1859, declining to thirty in 1860, and dropping to seventeen in 1861, of whom only eleven qualified for a B.S.A. degree. War and sickness were taking a toll as well. Of the seventeen members of the graduating class, two left to join the Union army in October 1861 and four more were "called away by sickness early in the session."[13]

Nonetheless, the Farmers' High School produced its first graduates. In December 1861 the eleven students qualified to graduate were awarded the first bachelor of scientific agriculture degrees in America. In the 1861 catalog, their grades were listed in seven subject areas—mathematics, chemistry, botany and horticulture, English literature, geology and mineralogy, zoology and veterinary, and practical agriculture—and then averaged. Each graduate was rank ordered, with James Miles Jr. of Erie County placing first with a 9.83 average on a 10.00 scale and the eleventh-ranked graduate, C. E. Troutman of Philadelphia, earning a 7.01 average.

In addition to finishing their course work and passing their examinations, graduates were required to complete a dissertation. For the most part, the eleven students teamed up in twos to coauthor such a work. The aforementioned James Miles and classmate A. C. Church of Luzerne County joined forces for a dissertation "On Indian Corn (Zea Maize)." Their investigation dealt with ascertaining the proper depth for planting maize, with some comparative examinations for oats and beans. It also explored the relative amounts of nitrogen and ash in the components of fully developed corn plants—the corn, cob, husk, tassel, silk, stem, and leaf. J. D. Isett of Huntingdon County and John N. Banks of Juniata County wrote their dissertation, titled "On the Iron Ores of Nittany Valley." They analyzed the principal iron ores of their locality together with the ferruginous and sandy limestones found with the ores. They also discussed the origin of the ores and the modes of preparing it for the iron furnace, as well as the process for reducing it. Samuel Holliday of Erie County and E. P. McCormick of Clinton County analyzed six artificial fertilizers—both superphosphates and phosphates, including the superphosphate manufactured by Lawes at Rothamsted. They evaluated the relative quality and unique characteristics of each. Their findings were slated to be sent to agricultural journals.[14]

Pugh insisted on the highest academic standards, and those eleven young men who graduated in December 1861 had survived a demanding scientific gauntlet. They had completed their baccalaureate degree work in three years, having entered the school in 1859 with advanced standing in the "third class" (sophomores). "This was also the first class that graduated at an Agricultural College in the United States," Pugh said, "and they graduated upon a higher scientific educational standard than is required at any other Agricultural College in the world."[15] According to historian Wayland Dunaway, each of them became "useful citizens of the Commonwealth." Eight of them lived to celebrate the fiftieth anniversary of the class in 1911, two became trustees of the college, and one, C. Alfred Smith, became a professor of chemistry at the college for a period.[16]

The "full course" these students pursued offered a rigorous array of theoretical and practical instruction, in addition to three hours of manual labor

FIGURE 15 *First graduating class, 1861.*

daily. As Pugh explained it, the students first encountered the sciences from a theoretical perspective, and then studied their practical applications to agriculture and industry. They would study chemistry in the classroom and laboratory until deemed ready to analyze various substances such as "as ores, rocks and minerals for the miner; slags, fuel, metals and alloys for the furnace operator; residual products for the manufacturing chemist; poisonous substances and abnormal secretions for the physician; adulterated articles for the consumer; and soils, marls, limestones, phosphates, guanoes, ashes, and all other articles used or consumed in agriculture, for the farmer." Pugh had his students devoting considerable effort to the analysis of the various manufactured manures found in the marketplace. His goal was to have their results published in the agricultural press, so as to steer farmers away from faulty products and toward useful ones. On the college farm, Pugh had his students carrying out a course of large-scale experiments to analyze different kinds of manures on various plants; then he had them repeat the experiments on a small scale so they could become familiar with the experimental process and, with the use of "a few simple manures," ascertain what would work to best effect with the various soils in question—"a desideratum once sought by soil analysts, but never attained by them."[17]

FIGURE 16
C. Alfred Smith, B.S.A.,
1861, M.S.A., 1863.

While his main objective was to train the inaugural generation of scientific agriculturalists, Pugh realized that the institution could boost enrollment and still accomplish its mission by accommodating students either uninterested in, or unqualified for, the mathematically based "full course." Thus he introduced the "Partial Scientific and Practical Course," designed for talented but mathematically challenged students who might instead find success in the natural sciences. Students in the Partial Scientific and Practical Course would pursue the subjects as offered by the "full course" with the exception of analytical geometry, differential and integral calculus, and "the higher mathematics."

For those students wishing to gain only a basic introduction to the agricultural arts and sciences without the demands of more formal study, Pugh introduced the "Practical Course." This was designed for students who could not devote years of their life to a baccalaureate degree program, but who wanted, over a briefer residency, to simply observe "the various arts and operations of the Farm, Garden, and Nursery; and at the same time attend some of the classes of the College, and thus get a general idea of the subjects taught, without studying them with sufficient thoroughness to graduate."[18]

At this same early time, Pugh moved in the opposite direction as well, establishing the Master of Scientific and Practical Agriculture degree (M.S.A.), advertised for the first time in the 1861 catalog. Eligibility went to baccalaureate-degree holders who had been out in the world for at least three years, during which time they were to demonstrate "a continued interest in agriculture or the industrial arts . . . or devoted the time to any intellectual pursuit"—not quite an honorary degree but conferred via the president's judgment according to the rather vague criteria. Also eligible were graduates who would "remain one more year at the institution and devote the time to scientific investigation."[19]

Two students were enrolled as the original M.S.A. candidates. C. Alfred Smith, of the Class of 1861, was the first to receive the degree, on January 3, 1863, when the school was on winter hiatus. Smith had stayed on after graduation to conduct experiments and generally assist the president. Smith, Pugh wrote, "possesses a very good general knowledge of practical, analytical, and pharmaceutical chemistry and will be able to work successfully at any ordinary chemical work." After signing the certificate, Pugh added, "In view of Mr. Smith's year spent as a resident graduate, he receives the degree of Master of Scientific and Practical Agriculture."[20] The conferral of that degree marks the beginning of graduate work at the institution, though advanced study would not be formalized and expanded until the establishment of the Graduate School in 1922.

The other M.S.A. student was Augustus King, the son of Columbia College (later Columbia University) president Charles King. The younger King was not a graduate of the Farmers' High School, but President King had somehow learned about the institution and contacted Pugh about sending his son there. In early February 1862 Pugh visited President King in New York City to discuss the matter, gaining King's confidence and the resultant matriculation of his son.[21] In August 1862, before finishing his degree requirements, Augustus went home to visit his father in New York and there contracted typhoid fever and died. Columbia students kept coming, and in 1863–64 three of them were enrolled for graduate work at the institution. With Pugh's death, however, the Columbia pipeline dried up.[22]

Finally, Pugh began to cast a wider net for students of more diverse backgrounds and interests. He noted that the Farmers' High School was designed "to occupy a place not before occupied, rather than to come into competition with any other institution" of higher learning. He reached out "to persons in cities who may wish their sons to become acquainted with the details of practical agriculture and science." And he especially emphasized the school's proficiency in chemistry that could lead to careers in pharmacy, manufacturing, mining, and engineering. Interested students would find "rare opportunities at a comparatively insignificant cost at the Farm School."[23]

Notwithstanding the national trauma of the Civil War, and the early Union defeat at Bull Run, the year 1861 had produced brightening prospects for the Farmers' High School—funds to complete the college building, its first graduates, and expanded curricula and outreach for more students.

The Turning Point

Building on the advances of 1861, the following year—the fourth year of operation—would see the Farmers' High School reach the turning point of its early history. With the state appropriation secured, construction of the college building resumed, though progress would soon slow down, requiring an additional year to finish the task. To more accurately reflect its collegiate stature and better position it to receive the benefits of the Morrill Land-Grant College Act, the Farmers' High School would change its name to the Agricultural College of Pennsylvania. Two months after the name change, the Morrill Act was signed by Lincoln on July 2. Pugh and his key allies in Pennsylvania's agricultural community had played an important role in pushing for the passage of the legislation. As Pugh matter-of-factly described the shape of things in his 1862 catalog, published in September of that year: "The present session was opened on the 19th of February, 1862, and is now more than half completed; the college is full, notwithstanding the disturbed state of the country, and all its affairs are working more satisfactorily than they have ever done before."[24]

Looking backward, the institution's progress in the face of "the disturbed state of the country" is impressive—particularly compared with the handful of aborning agricultural colleges that halted or suspended plans and operations in the face of the national crisis. And crisis it was. In 1862 the Civil War intensified, spread, and raged to a degree unimagined in 1861, as the carnage at Shiloh, the Seven Days, Second Manassas, Antietam, and Fredericksburg attested. As the year closed, the Union was clouded with pessimism; prospects for victory seemed to be fading fast, given the military successes of the surging Confederacy.

Nevertheless, Pugh was fixated on building the school quickly, and he strove to accentuate the institution's accomplishments. Despite the unfinished college building and the constant struggle for revenue, the school had received "a degree of patronage unprecedented in the history of Agricultural Colleges." Enrollments had built up to the institution's physical capacity, save for the dip in 1861. The school also was attracting "many . . . from other states, who could not be admitted." With such progress, Pugh expressed confidence in the "ultimate success" of the experiment. This was particularly true "now that its college buildings are completed"—which was wishful thinking, not the reality—"and the Agricultural College Bill [Morrill Act] has passed Congress."[25]

Pugh's confidence in the comparative success of his institution was well placed. Intensely interested in other attempts at launching agricultural colleges, Pugh early on in his tenure wrote presidents and professors at these institutions for information about their status, made a visit to the Maryland Agricultural College, and mailed his institution's catalogs to numerous colleges, both fledgling and established. The Civil War, he soon found, had crushed the plans of various northern states to get agricultural colleges organized and into operation. Nonetheless, these states and institutions also were watching, with keen interest, his experiment in Pennsylvania.

In response to Pugh's query, Samuel Foster, president pro tem at Iowa State Farmers' College, said, "We have no school of the kind yet in this state," though they had a tract of 628 acres with a working farm. The Iowa legislature had passed enabling legislation for the school in March 1858, providing a $10,000 appropriation, and the local county pledged an equal amount, but there progress ended as the war began. "I doubt if the School is needed until peace and prosperity is restored," Foster said. To Pugh's surprise, Foster added that he had visited the Farmers' College of Pennsylvania in September 1859, a month before Pugh took office. "I esteem it the model school of America. Am pleased to hear of the progress of the building and prosperity of the institution."[26]

The New York State Agricultural College at Ovid had received its enabling legislation in March 1856, but problems with the building contractor delayed the start of instruction until December 1860, with twenty-seven students present. Then things started to unravel. J. P. Kimball, the school's professor of chemistry and economic geology, had, like Pugh, received his Ph.D. at Göttingen. He began corresponding with Pugh as soon as the latter had arrived at the Farmers' High School. "I have advised two, and may more, of my students to go to you when we break up," Kimball stated.[27] By the fall of 1861 Kimball painted a more dire picture. The legislature had failed to pass a $50,000 appropriation for the school, and the school's enrollment had dropped from ninety to about thirty. "The war has spoiled all our pretty plans for us," Kimball said. "Money and students have gone to war. . . . It would give me full pleasure to fall in with you again."[28]

Two months into his presidency, Pugh came to the attention of the Massachusetts Society for the Promotion of Agriculture and Agricultural Education, interested in the "plan, progress, and prospects of your institution."[29] By 1861 a gubernatorial commission had been appointed to plan for an agricultural school, and Pugh was asked for copies of his reports. The commission member noted that he was "impressed with the idea that your school comes more nearly within the circle of your society than any other."[30]

In response to Pugh's queries, Charles Calvert, president of the Maryland Agricultural College, invited him for a site visit.[31] In late January and early February 1860, Pugh made the trip, swinging east to visit the Millersville State Normal School in Lancaster County, then down to Baltimore and Washington, and then to nearby College Park, home of the Maryland Agricultural College. Pugh visited Calvert for several hours. He reported that "there is not much to learn from their operations." He found a very large main building, five stories tall, expensively carpeted, and "furnished as an aristocratic school."[32]

Assessing the State of American Agricultural Colleges

In his 1862 catalog, Pugh encapsulated his findings of the efforts to establish American agricultural colleges. He noted that students were admitted to Michigan's agricultural college in May 1857 and declared, "To Michigan belongs the honor of having put the first State Agricultural College in the United States in operation, but for some cause this College has been obliged to suspend operation." That cause, he later determined, was the withdrawal of students to fight for the Union. The Maryland Agricultural College, Pugh observed, was incorporated in 1856 and opened for students in 1859, and had been in operation since that time. "It differs from the Agricultural College of Pennsylvania, in its course of instruction, being more nearly allied to that of ordinary literary colleges, and consequently having a less scientific course, and in its not requiring manual labor of each student upon the farm." The Iowa State Agricultural College and Farm, he noted, was incorporated in March 1858 and some provisions were made for the erection of buildings, but no students were enrolled and further operations were suspended because of the war. As for New York, Pugh described the long struggle to establish the New York State Agricultural College, incorporated in 1853, but not opening its doors until December 1860, and soon after failing financially and going out of business. New York's People's College, partly but not entirely devoted to agriculture, also was incorporated in 1853 but was yet to open for business. In Massachusetts a school of agriculture was incorporated in 1856 but not yet founded. In Minnesota the agricultural college was incorporated in 1858 but had yet to erect any buildings. In Ohio, Pugh noted, the subject of an agricultural college had been before the legislature several times, but "nothing tangible, so far as we know, has resulted from its actions." Pugh did reference the Farmers' College, a private enterprise near Cincinnati, but observed that "the course of instruction does not differ essentially from that of an ordinary literary college." And in Illinois, Pugh reported, nothing had happened at the state level, despite repeated efforts to found an agricultural college; a private counterpart near Chicago was in the embryonic state but was languishing for lack of support.[33]

Pugh's reportage on the nascent agricultural college movement was substantially accurate. But further analysis provides additional insight to these early efforts, particularly in regard to Pugh's claim that his was the model institution of its kind. The Agricultural College of the State of Michigan found its enabling legislation in the Michigan State Constitution of 1850, which mandated that "the Legislature shall encourage the promotion of intellectual, scientific and agricultural improvements; and shall, as soon as practicable, provide for the establishment of an agricultural school."[34] Presciently, perhaps, the Michigan legislature that same year petitioned Congress to donate 350,000 acres of federal land to the state to allow it to found agricultural schools, but the request fell on deaf ears (23).

The state constitution did not address the question of where the agricultural school was to be situated—at the extant University of Michigan or elsewhere. Accordingly, a long fight ensued. There was some talk of establishing it at the state normal school at Ypsilanti. At the University of Michigan, Henry Tappan, who assumed the presidency in 1852, also expressed some qualified interest in securing the school. Although Tappan was willing to establish an agricultural "department," he refused to entertain the requirement for a model farm, and so split sharply from the agricultural interests of the state, who deemed a new school, in East Lansing, near the state capital, to be the better choice.

Joseph R. Williams, editor of the *Toledo Blade* and decidedly not a scientist, was named president in May 1857. That same month, seventy-three students showed up to enroll, of whom fifty-nine were judged to be adequately prepared for admission. Nevertheless, with students on board and classes under way, the Michigan Agricultural College began describing itself as the national model leading a national movement, eliciting praise from agricultural interests across the country. As President Williams reported to the State Board of Education in December 1858: "The institution continued to attract the interest in other states. It should be a subject of honorable pride in Michigan, that her example in taking the lead in a great movement, indicative of educational progress, is so generally applauded, and in fact, imitated." Minnesota and Iowa had "almost literally copied" the college's enabling legislation, he said, adding that other states had expressed interest in establishing similar institutions (31).

What was odd about the Michigan Agricultural College was its curriculum—seemingly as oriented to the liberal arts as to agricultural science. The college did not require Greek or Latin, but it offered both "an English and a Scientific course." Apparently, the first students "demanded that they received a liberal education that encompassed more than learning about agriculture." These early students had a "deep interest in literature and history" (29–35). It seems strange that students attending a self-described agricultural college would agitate for a curriculum that was the norm in traditional classical colleges.

Then things began to wobble. President Williams resigned in March 1859, less than two years after he began. His problem was spending too much money and advocating a broad curriculum incorporating both an English course and practical agriculture. John Gregory, superintendent of public instruction for the state, took the reins, parsimoniously underspending the budget to the extent that the legislature reclaimed the unused portion. More significantly, Gregory changed the curriculum drastically, moving it from a four-year course to a two-year program designed to teach farm management and little else (39–40). Faculty member Lewis Fisk, who was serving concurrently as president pro tem of the school, championed a return to the four-year curriculum. He had the strong support of both the faculty and student body. Fisk proclaimed, "There is probably not one young man that has come here for the sole purpose of studying the science of agriculture." The students evidently met and voted for a restoration of the former curriculum, offering "the old academic studies for those who wished—the purely agricultural for all who wished. All voted for the academic" (41). With the concurrence of the legislature, the dual curriculum was reinstated in 1861, offering both a liberal arts and an agricultural course, the former far more popular than the latter.

In his report, Pugh noted that the Michigan Agricultural College had been forced to suspend operations. The Michigan Agricultural College historian Keith R. Widder observed, however, that although the Civil War caused disruptions in the development of the college, "it did not prevent it from moving forward" (48).

Michigan Agricultural College did graduate its first students—seven in all—in November 1861, a month before the Farmers' High School graduated its first eleven students. But to a man, Michigan's students graduated in absentia with the Bachelor of Science degree; they were excused to serve in the Union army and allowed to leave school before they formally were graduated. In 1862 Michigan Agricultural College installed a new president, its third in five years: Theophilus C. Abbot, who would stay in office for twenty-three years and stabilize the institution. Abbot had been serving as a professor of English literature at the school since 1858.

Though both the Michigan Agricultural College and the Farmers' High School would claim the mantle of being the first *successful* state-sponsored agricultural college in America, it is somewhat problematic to ferret out the truth of those assertions. In the case of Pennsylvania's example, however, it is worth pointing out that the Farmers' High School was headed by a scientist-of-renown who insisted that the presidents of such institutions be scientists first and foremost. Pugh took special care in designing a truly scientific curriculum oriented heavily toward producing graduates in the nascent agricultural sciences—indeed, it was for that scientific education and nothing else that they came to the institution. The Michigan curriculum favored the liberal arts as much as it did practical agriculture, and most of its students favored the former. Also of interest: Pugh's first class—those first eleven graduates—were awarded the degree Bachelor of Scientific Agriculture (B.S.A.), the first degree of its kind in America, as opposed to the more general bachelor of science. Pugh's Pennsylvania institution also would award the first graduate degree in agriculture—the Master of Scientific Agriculture—in 1863.

And despite the war's drain on manpower, the Farmers' High School/ Agricultural College of Pennsylvania would surpass the Michigan Agricultural College in enrollments during those four disrupted years. The Agricultural College of Pennsylvania enrolled 88 students in 1861, 110 in 1862, 142 in 1863, and 146 in 1864. The Michigan Agricultural College enrolled 65 students in 1861, 74 in 1862, 60 in 1863, and 62 in 1864 (48). During the Civil War, then, the Agricultural College of Pennsylvania was twice as large as the Michigan Agricultural College and more thoroughly oriented to a curriculum of scientific agriculture.

Maryland's experiment with an agricultural college is also consistent with Pugh's observation that the institution was more literary than scientific. In his 2005 volume, the historian of the University of Maryland, George H. Callcott, concurred: "The Maryland Agricultural College at College Park was just emerging as a rather traditional residential college, mainly for farmers' sons."[35] Maryland, a slave state, had seen its agricultural economy slide into serious decline during the first half of the nineteenth century. Its chief export crop—tobacco—was no longer favored by Europeans, whose tastes had turned to more exotic varieties.

The prime mover of Maryland's agricultural college was the aristocratic planter Charles Calvert, a direct descendant of the colony's founder some seven generations earlier. Calvert enlisted the support of his peers, all of whom were stockholders in the new institution. Thus, the movement for the college "came not from small farmers, but from large planters—both generous and self-serving—who wanted to educate their own sons and the sons of their well-off neighbors." In 1856 the Maryland General Assembly voted to establish the college, provided that the trustees raise $50,000. With that act, the state of Maryland had chartered the third state-sponsored agricultural college in America. Opening ceremonies were held in October 1859. The founding president floundered quickly, so Calvert assumed the office and hired another faculty member to teach English history, philosophy, and Christianity. He also found a prominent Washington scientist to teach entomology and botany. After a year, Calvert hired the principal of a local academy to serve as president. The end result was exactly as Pugh had described it. As Callcott concluded, "The planters of Maryland had created for themselves a mostly traditional college—traditional in its small size, its elitist enrollment, its curriculum, its routine. Their dream of a new kind of a practical education, of scientific agriculture, of elevating the farmers of the state, had hardly materialized."[36]

In Massachusetts, a bastion of private colleges, nothing would happen until well after the passage of the Morrill Act. As Pugh reported, the legislature in 1856 issued a charter for a Massachusetts School of Agriculture to a group of eastern Massachusetts interests. Some years earlier, the legislature had appointed a commission charged with making a systematic study of agricultural education in Europe. The plan emerging from that study, written by Edward Hitchcock of Amherst, fell on deaf ears in the legislature, but it did prompt the formation of the State Board of Agriculture in 1852, which created new momentum for the institution. The charter for the school was shifted from Boston to Springfield in 1860. The Morrill Act of 1862 prompted interest by Harvard, the newly forming Massachusetts Institute of Technology, Amherst, and Williams colleges. The state accepted the provisions of the

Morrill Act on April 18, 1863, and shortly thereafter passed legislation to split the land grant, the mechanic arts eventually going to MIT. Managing to survive years of intense political wrangling, the Massachusetts Agricultural College in Amherst would finally open for instruction on October 2, 1867.[37]

In Iowa, as Pugh reported correctly, the Iowa State Agricultural College and Farm was incorporated in March 1858 and some provisions were made for the erection of buildings, but further operations were suspended because of the war. Iowa's early claim to fame, however, was that it became the first state to accept the provisions of the Morrill Act, which it did on September 11, 1862, about five months before Michigan and Pennsylvania did so. The first president of the State Agricultural College and Model Farm, however, was not appointed until 1868 and its first class of students was enrolled beginning in 1869. Not until 1872 would it graduate its first class—twenty-five men and two women.[38]

To Iowa's north, the University of Minnesota nearly died aborning. Chartered by the territorial legislature in 1851, the institution hired its first chancellor, a minister, in 1858, the year Minnesota was granted statehood status. The institution was pretty much done in by the Panic of 1857, and despite an attempt at reorganization, the school essentially collapsed as the Civil War began. As the University of Minnesota historian put it: "The end of the university seemed really to have come."[39] As for Ohio and Illinois, also of interest to Pugh, their agricultural colleges would not become operational until after the Civil War. The Illinois Industrial University, later the University of Illinois, would be founded in 1867 and opened for instruction in 1868. The Ohio Agricultural and Mechanical College, later the Ohio State University, would be chartered in 1870 and opened for instruction in 1873.

Thus three state-sponsored agricultural colleges—so called—were in actual operation, with students and faculty, before 1860, although one of them, Maryland, was more traditional and "literary" than agricultural. Michigan's was as much literary, if not more so, than it was agricultural. Nonetheless, the agricultural colleges of Michigan and Pennsylvania, both chartered in 1855, emerged as the land-grant college equivalent of ancient Rome's mythological founding twins, Romulus and Remus. Michigan and Pennsylvania became the founding twins of the pre–Civil War state-sponsored agricultural college movement that would soon morph into the American land-grant college system. In 1955, the two institutions—by that time Michigan State College and the Pennsylvania State University—were commemorated for their centennials with a U.S. Post Office special-issue commemorative stamp, additional testimony to their shared historical stature.

Changing the Institution's Name

The gains Pugh had engineered for the Farmers' High School in 1861 and 1862 provided the platform for him to change the institution's name. The change—to the Agricultural College of Pennsylvania, as it finally turned out—had been very much on Pugh's mind. Since beginning his presidency, he frequently referred to the institution as the Agricultural College, not the Farmers' High School. At its chartering, in 1854 and 1855, the institution was designed to be of collegiate grade. The sense of the founders, however, was that the word "college" would, among the farming community, evoke a gentlemen's institution promoting idle habits and haughty condescension toward the laboring classes. But with the funds for the college building having been secured a year earlier, and having graduated its first students, the trustees concurred with Pugh that the time was right to adopt a name more reflective of the institution's purpose and stature. Equally important, they wanted to position the institution so as to qualify it explicitly to receive the benefits of the Morrill "agricultural college" bill that was moving through Congress at the same time.

The change didn't come about without some internal discussion, however. Pugh had intended to take the matter to the Pennsylvania legislature for approval. He also wanted to include the word "State" somewhere in the new name, hoping to ensure a continuing financial obligation from the Commonwealth. Though approving "entirely of your proposition to change our corporate name," Watts pointed out that it wasn't necessary to ask the legislature for approval; an act passed in 1843 empowered the several Courts of Quarter Sessions in the Commonwealth, upon the petition of the parties in intent, to change the "name, style, and title of any corporation" within their respective counties. "From both education and experience I prefer a resort to a Court rather than the Legislature," Watts said. "As to the name: There is a 'Penna. Col.' at Gettysburg and I do not like the use of the word State—perhaps it is because I like brevity and I think with that omission in your proposition it will do and call it 'Penna. Agl. College."[40]

Trustee McAllister presented the petition for change to the Court of Quarter Sessions for Centre County; after its approval there, the matter went to the Board of Trustees, which ratified the name change during its meeting of May 6, 1862.[41] Pugh had even designed a new seal for the college, which was approved by the trustees at the same May meeting.[42] Thus, the Farmers' High School of Pennsylvania became the Agricultural College of Pennsylvania, a

FIGURE 17 *The President's House, of Pugh's design, ca. 1872.*

name it would retain for twelve years, until it became the Pennsylvania State College in 1874.

Besides the college building, there was another construction project on Pugh's mind. Dissatisfied with his cramped quarters in the college building, and looking to the day when he would take a wife, Pugh struck an agreement with the trustees to build a house on the campus for the college president. He proposed to donate one-third of the cost, $1,000, if the trustees would provide the remainder, $2,000. The site for the house was about 150 yards southwest of the college building. Pugh designed the two-story limestone edifice in the style of a typical Pennsylvania farmhouse of the era and oversaw its construction, even furnishing his own labor at times. He would not live to see the completion of the house, but his successors would occupy the home from 1864 through 1970. The house still stands, its exterior much altered from the original, and still functions as part of the newer Hintz Family Alumni Center, dedicated in 2001.

At the same May 1862 meeting, the trustees appointed a committee of three—Pugh, Watts, and McAllister—to prepare a magnum opus to be used for public relations purposes, to attract students, political support, and patronage. This became a sixty-three-page document, written entirely by Pugh and titled *The Agricultural College of Pennsylvania . . . September 1862.* The work presented a detailed history of agricultural science in Europe and America, with an equally detailed history of the origins of the Agricultural College in question. Also presented were "the aims, object, progress, and present conditions and prospects of the institution."

The "objects" of the institution—its mission, in modern parlance—bear some examination. The four major objects were to function simultaneously as an educational institution, a practical institution, an experimental institution, and a servant of the state, in particular, protecting its agricultural interests. Pugh's vision presaged, once again, the mission of the land-grant college and the modern public research university.

As an educational institution, the Agricultural College professed to include the entire range of the natural sciences, particularly those that had a practical bearing. "Since agriculture more than any other of the industrial arts, is important to man, and since . . . more scientific knowledge is required than for all other industrial arts combined, it . . . should receive by far the highest degree of attention."[43] Pugh intended not to educate everyone in the industrial classes, but only a relative few, so that they "may infuse new life and intelligence into the several communities they enter." Pugh again wanted to create the example and set the standards for other institutions to follow.

As a practical institution, the college needed to ensure that an essential part of the students' education be devoted to practical application, "in the field and laboratory" . . . with manual labor deemed essential "for the preservation of health, and the maintenance of habits of industry" (46).

As an experimental institution, Pugh said, the college had great opportunities before it—"an unbounded field of labor"—but a long way to go. The principles of agricultural science were only beginning to be developed; the labor, expense, and time involved in making agricultural experiments were enormous, with the result "that as yet little has been done in that direction." Pugh looked to the recently passed Morrill Act for salvation in that regard. Even with that, he cautioned, the results would not be immediate. "They will, however, ultimately pay a thousand fold" (47).

Finally, the college had a significant role to play in public service, or "protecting the industrial interests of the state, and most especially the agricultural interest," as Pugh put it. He particularly wanted to protect farmers from the rampant quackery and profit-mongering that plagued the rural community. Farmers had the ability to test agricultural tools and implements, as well as seeds and plants, but their methods of testing manures, chemical salts, guanoes, phosphates, poudrettes, and other fertilizers were not well developed. "And hence we find that the market is filled with worthless or very high priced manures, such as the farmer never would purchase, if he knew their composition and real value" (47–48).

The 1862 catalog is notable in that Pugh was able to present, in some detail, the scientific collections reposing in the college as important resources for instruction and experimentation—collections remarkable in their extent and diversity for so recently founded and geographically remote an institution. For the most part, these collections had been gathered by Pugh during his travels in Europe and England for the college he would someday build.

For mathematics, these "auxiliaries to study" included a transit instrument, ordinary surveying apparatus, with compass, and mathematical figures and forms for illustrating geometric and crystallographic principles. For natural philosophy, the school offered a large electrical machine, air pumps, a magnetic machine, galvanic batteries, and other apparatus related to optics, statics, dynamics, mechanics, pneumatics, and so forth.

For chemistry, the institution presented a bonanza of state-of-the-science equipment. Before returning to the United States, Pugh had requested and received from the trustees $1,000 to purchase the best equipment that Europe had to offer. The main building featured a large chemical laboratory for beginning students, two smaller labs for advanced students, and a few private labs for "special agricultural scientific investigations." In addition, there were collections of marls, artificial manures, limestones, ores, and minerals from different locales in America and Europe.

But Pugh was hardly satisfied with the college's facilities and equipment for chemistry, and so he committed one-third of his salary, $500 per year, to purchasing the best chemical apparatus available. To Pugh chemistry was both the queen and the *sine qua non* of the agricultural sciences; he knew precisely what equipment was needed and where to get it. For geology and paleontology, the college featured 6,000 specimens—rocks, limestones, fossils, ores from across Pennsylvania, complemented by a large collection from Europe that Pugh had gathered in his studies and travels. Pugh also provided a collection of ordinary and rare minerals for mineralogy and crystallography. Perhaps most extraordinary, however, was the botanical collection Pugh had assembled for scientific use by the agricultural college he someday hoped to lead. As described earlier, this was a veritable herbarium, with more than 3,000 specimens, that Pugh had gathered and purchased near Heidelberg, Germany, in 1856 (53–54).

For practical agriculture and horticulture, the college offered a 400-acre farm, along with a vineyard, orchards, and a small nursery. "Experiments with all the chemical elements of manures are carried out every session, for the purpose of illustrating the effect of each element alone and in combination, as also experiments as to the time of planting and sowing seeds and applying manures," Pugh wrote. "Each Student will have an opportunity of learning all the varied operations of ordinary farm, garden and nursery work, in connexion [*sic*] with the management of farm stock."

In addition, the main building offered a library with "an extensive collection" of literary and scientific works, with maps, diagrams, and charts, as well as a separate reading room. Two rooms were set apart for the two student societies, the Cresson Literary Society and the Washington Agricultural Society. Each student was required to belong to one of them, as they afforded social as well as intellectual opportunities such as debating and presenting papers on various topics.

The college also was able to attract, as donations, some state-of-the-art farm machinery, in particular, two reapers and mowers. The first was McCormick's Combined Self-raking Reaper and Mower, manufactured in Chicago and costing $175. The second machine was Pennock's Iron Harvester, another combined reaper and mower manufactured in Chester County, Pennsylvania, and costing $135. Both drew favorable reviews. Pugh concluded that the McCormick reaper would be "unequalled for any other in the world for large farms and the less expensive Pennock harvester would be more than suitable for smaller farms" (60, 61).

Pugh concluded the 1862 catalog with a statement of intent about new lines of research. This work would focus on "the raising of improved stock . . . the value of different food under different circumstances for fattening purposes . . . [and] the preservation and use of liquid manures." He conceded that such research had been "neglected to attend to the more strictly educational department of the institution" (63).

By September 1862, with the war raging no more than 120 miles away at South Mountain and Antietam, the Agricultural College of Pennsylvania was deemed a hard-won success by Pugh and the trustees—the first successful agricultural college in America, as he characterized it. The funds for the main building had been secured the year previous and construction had resumed with the end in sight, if not in fact. In actuality, Pugh's description of the college building and other facilities was prospective rather than retrospective, not as the college actually was at the date of publication but as it was to be the following year; in fact, the section introducing the buildings was titled "The College As It Will Be In Operation Next Year, 1863." Nonetheless, the institution had improved the farm, orchard, and outbuildings. Despite the war's continual drain of college-age boys and men, enrollment continued to grow, equipment and amenities had been added, and the institution had adopted a new name to better reflect its purpose and stature. Perhaps most significant, the college graduated fifteen students in December 1862—an increase of 36 percent over the eleven graduates in 1861. This would represent a high watermark of sorts—the college's largest graduating class until 1890.[44] Thus, in its four years of operation, the institution had finally turned the corner. But Pugh's greatest challenge—qualifying the institution for the benefits of the Morrill Act and protecting that status from jealous competitors—would lie ahead.

CHAPTER 6

Pugh's Standing in the American Scientific Community

DESPITE HIS PHYSICAL ISOLATION in rural central Pennsylvania, Evan Pugh enjoyed high standing not only as the visionary president of an experimental agricultural college but also as a scientist of international distinction and a science administrator who could exert leadership at the federal level. Pugh's expertise, vision, and organizational acumen came into play as the nation began to craft the legislation and policies, and build up the infrastructure, for improving American agriculture.

Pugh's early success with the Agricultural College of Pennsylvania was due in no small part to his scientific training. Indeed, of the several attempts before the Civil War to found agricultural colleges, only one of them—and the only one with a true scientific curriculum—would be led by a scientist. And Pugh argued two essential points at every opportunity: that agricultural colleges, as scientific institutions, must be independent and free of any attachment to a classical or "literary college," so that their mission and finances not be compromised; and that scientific institutions must be led by a scientist, who, unlike his classically educated counterparts, would best understand how to build, finance, and structure such an institution for success. In these respects, Pugh was on the leading edge of his era. Higher education reformers such as William Barton Rogers, who founded Massachusetts Institute of Technology in 1861 and began instruction in 1865, and Charles W. Eliot, a faculty member at

MIT who went on to become president of Harvard University, both believed that independent institutions offered the best model for scientific studies. Yale and Harvard had moved in this direction in the late 1840s, establishing plans for separate schools of science and practical studies yet still attached, at least to some degree, to their parent institutions. But lack of adequate facilities, opportunities for student laboratory experiences, and sufficient financial underpinnings hindered their development.[1]

Yale's scientists held a high opinion of Pugh. Benjamin Silliman Jr. (1816–85), one of the two founding faculty members of Yale's School of Applied Chemistry, and the son of Benjamin Silliman (1779–1864), professor of chemistry and natural history at Yale for more than fifty years, was especially impressed with Pugh. Silliman Jr. likely learned about Pugh from fellow Yale professor Samuel Johnson, but in any event was well aware of Pugh's work at Rothamsted and his several publications.

The Sillimans, father and son, were major forces in the development of American science. Both were among the fifty original members elected to the National Academy of Sciences in 1863. Assuming his professorship in 1802, Silliman Sr. was the prime mover in building the sciences at Yale, establishing the department that ultimately evolved into the School of Applied Chemistry and later the Sheffield Scientific School. Silliman Jr., a chemist and geologist, wrote an 1855 report that was a major factor in the birth of the American oil industry. In 1838 he took over the editorship, along with Charles Dwight Dana, of the *American Journal of Science and the Arts*. The publication, generally referred to as "Silliman's Journal," had been founded by his father in 1818.[2]

Silliman Jr. played at least a minor role in supporting Pugh for the presidency of the Farmers' High School. Writing in December 1859 to express his pleasure in Pugh's new position, Silliman demurred from taking credit. "My limited agency in your nomination would have been of no avail had not your prior devotion to your service won you a reputation which rendered it a small matter of whose agency your name was brought to the notice of the Trustees." Silliman also asked Pugh to send him a few of his published papers from his work in Europe for the *Journal*.[3] In Silliman Jr.'s view, Pugh as an accomplished scientist was the ideal leader to establish the nation's first scientifically based agricultural college. As Pugh's former student C. Alfred Smith recalled, it was Silliman Jr. "who insisted that he knew 'of but one man in the world who could bring the Agricultural College to the desired standard'—that man was Evan Pugh."[4]

After concluding his research at Rothamsted and presenting his lecture at Harpenden, Pugh was elected a fellow of the Chemical Society of London. The society had been founded in 1841, granted a royal charter in 1847, and amalgamated with other scientific organizations into the Royal Society of Chemistry in 1980.[5] The fellowship was Pugh's proudest scientific recognition, bestowed by England's greatest chemists. His tombstone in Bellefonte's Union Cemetery reads: "First President of the Pennsylvania Agricultural College and Fellow of the London Chemical Society."

In the summer of 1860, nine months into his presidency, Pugh presented his Rothamsted experiment to the fourteenth annual meeting of the American Association for the Advancement of Science in Newport, Rhode Island. He also presented the results of an experiment analyzing rainwater collected at sea while he was making the return voyage to America the year previous. At Newport, Pugh was able to meet Benjamin Silliman Jr., William Barton Rogers, and Joseph Henry, the first secretary of the Smithsonian Institution, as well as others, including some "old friends" from his student days in Europe. Writing to McAllister to illustrate the large amounts of money required for new scientific facilities, Pugh reported that Louis Agassiz detailed plans for a new zoological collection at Harvard, courtesy of a $50,000 gift and other contributions totaling $225,000. A new chemistry laboratory at Harvard was being built with a $40,000 gift and another at Yale for $50,000. "This shows the way the wind blows in these quarters," he observed.[6]

In the fall of 1862, Pugh was elected to the American Philosophical Society, the organization founded in 1743 by Benjamin Franklin for the promotion of useful knowledge. The news came as a surprise. Pugh was nominated in April 1862 by his early supporter and former Farmers' High School trustee, Dr. Alfred L. Elwyn, in conjunction with J. Peter Lesley, the secretary of the society, on the basis of his presidency of the Farmers' High School and his "distinguished scientific attainments."[7] In his response to Lesley, Pugh said he was "not aware who has been so kind as to present my name" but was nevertheless "highly flattered by the honor."[8] Pugh provided a copy of his Rothamsted investigation to the Society.

As for his affiliation with American Association for the Advancement of Science (AAAS), Pugh later was recognized as one of the 337 leading scientists of AAAS, the organization formed in 1848 from the expansion of the Association of American Geologists and Naturalists. In her *Formation of the American Scientific Community* (1975), historian Sally G. Kohlstedt found that nearly every American scientist was affiliated with the AAAS during its formative years. She developed a biographical directory of all members of the AAAS between 1848 and 1860 and categorized them as "ordinary members"— which included more than 1,700 scientists—and the "leadership," consisting of 337 scientists who participated in AAAS by publishing one or more papers or by serving on one of more committees. Kohlstedt further divided the "leadership" into "primary" and "secondary" classifications – primary if the scientist published two or more articles in different years, held two or more offices, was a member of a standing committee, or had a combination of publications and offices. Evan Pugh, whose first year of AAAS membership was 1860, was listed in the highest echelon of American scientists of his era as a "primary leader."[9]

By this time, Pugh had four principal publications to his credit: "Hämatinsalpetersäure identisch mit Pikraminsäure," *Journal für Praktische Chemie* 15 (1855): 362–69; "Miscellaneous Chemical Analysis" (inaugural diss., University of Göttingen, 1856); "On a New Method for the Quantitative Estimation of Nitric Acid," *Quarterly Journal of the Chemical Society* 12 (1860): 35–42; and "On the Sources of the Nitrogen of Vegetation, with Special Reference to the Question Whether Plants Assimilate Free or Uncombined Nitrogen," *Philosophical Transactions* 151 (1861): 431–577 (with Lawes and Gilbert).[10]

Pugh's 1862 publication *The Agricultural College of Pennsylvania* was widely circulated across the northern states, particularly to the agricultural press, and in Europe as well. The publication not only detailed the recent progress, current condition, and future prospects of the institution proper but also put it into larger context with Pugh's "succinct history of agricultural education in Europe and America." Pugh construed the new Agricultural College of Pennsylvania to be both the logical expression of a movement that had begun in Europe in the eighteenth century and the educational capstone of the American experience within that international movement. Thus, the publication represented a "coming out" party of sorts for the college, which just four months earlier had discarded the restrictive Farmers' High School name in favor of the new identity more accurately describing its stature and purpose.[11]

Even with the incessant demands of building and leading the college, Pugh was in constant communication on the wider topics of agricultural science and education. His counsel was sought by others in the movement, particularly officials in the federal government. He was eager to share his advice, and he did not shy away from lending it proactively, not necessarily waiting to be asked. In 1860, for example, in an initiative suggestive of the federal research grant system of the twentieth century, he wrote to Samuel W. Johnson suggesting "a plan for making a series of experiments on ag. practice with manures and a project for getting 10 or 15000 dollars from Congress to do it with."[12]

With agricultural science being in the early formative stage, high-quality textbooks on state-of-the-art agricultural chemistry were yet to be written. Pugh kept pressing Johnson to complete the textbook his former Leipzig colleague was working on at Yale. Pugh hadn't yet adopted a textbook on the subject and the press of duties had prevented him from arranging his materials for the course he was to teach. As a stopgap, Pugh had selected two books, which he deemed substandard. "I want a better book on Ag. than any I know of. . . . I like what I have seen of your work and want to know if it will all be out soon. I must have something at once as we have a class that must graduate this fall."[13] Johnson's text would not materialize in time for Pugh's purposes. But the wait would be worth it, at least for the rising generation of academic chemists. Johnson would become well known for his translations of the famous manuals of Fresenius, which became the standard work for introducing a generation of American chemists to qualitative and quantitative analysis, in his 1864 *Manual of Qualitative Analysis* and his 1870 *System of Instruction in Quantitative Chemical Analysis.*[14]

In October 1861 Pugh told Johnson that he had been asked to write a short article for the U.S. Patent Office on agricultural colleges (at the time, the U.S. Bureau of Agriculture was a division of the U.S. Patent Office). Pugh was intending to provide statistics he already had gathered in regard to the European agricultural colleges. He also was intending to include information about emerging efforts to establish such institutions in America. "Could you just tell me the aims, objects, expectations and desires of your Yale effort—and whether your past experience encourages you to go on with it. Also whether you are getting up any other agl. colleges in New England." Pugh added that he had recently heard from a committee established for that purpose by the governor of Massachusetts but feared "the war will stop their effort."[15]

Pugh followed up with Johnson a month later, thanking him for supplying the requested data and elaborating on Johnson's own doubts as to the limits Yale faced in furthering agricultural education. Pugh observed that Yale was too far north for a good agricultural school, its climate and soil insufficiently representative of the country at large. In addition, Yale was "too much within the circle of excitements common to citylife," referencing one of the strongest arguments for locating agricultural colleges in rural locales.

And, more damning, Yale's scientific school, even though separate, was still attached to Yale.

> It [an agricultural college] is just about 5 times as difficult to keep in orderly operation as an ordinary college and hence it ought to have 5 times the facilities for maintaining order and controlling all sources of disorder than an ordinary college has. And lastly and most important . . . I do not think that an agl. college can flourish under the wing of a literary college to which it is subordinate. The literary college will sap its vitality, rob it of its enthusiasm, take away its best students and finally appropriate its means of subsistence. . . . We here with imperfect organization over head and ears in debt with buildings half finished and only 100 students have *consumed* annually about $400 worth of apparatus and reagents—no purely literary man could see the use of all that expenditure and hence it could not be made through him.[16]

Perhaps the most telling attestation of Pugh's reputation is that he was twice offered the post of chief chemist for the U.S. Bureau of Agriculture and later U.S. Department of Agriculture. A Penn State scientist, speaking at the 1928 centenary of Pugh's birth, declared that U.S. government officials first offered him the post while he was still in England. It was a "splendid opportunity for the 31-year-old scientist, but his ambition to teach others the intricacies of agricultural chemistry and to bring about better conditions for farm people, finally led him to refuse this offer and accept the post at the little Farmers' High School."[17] That statement, however, was apocryphal, as there is no evidence in the Pugh papers of his turning down the post at this early juncture to accept the Farmers' High School presidency.

But the offer was to come soon enough. In 1862, during the school's winter break, Pugh made an extensive trip—to New Haven, Connecticut, to visit Samuel Johnson and Benjamin Silliman Jr. and inspect Yale's laboratories and museums; to New York City, where he visited President Charles King of Columbia College; to Harrisburg; to Philadelphia; and to Chester County to take a few new students back to campus. But his first and most important stop was in Washington, D.C. In the nation's capital, he talked with agricultural leaders in the throes of preparing to transition from the Bureau of Agriculture in the U.S. Patent Office to the new U.S. Department of Agriculture, which would be established on May 15, 1862, when Lincoln signed the enabling legislation.

Pugh met first with Isaac Newton, a prominent Pennsylvania dairy farmer who was serving as superintendent of the Bureau of Agriculture; when the U.S. Department of Agriculture was established about three months after Pugh's visit, Newton would be appointed by Lincoln as the new department's first commissioner. Pugh was distressed by what he learned. In the Bureau of Agriculture, all of the clerks and subordinates were political appointees lacking any knowledge of scientific agriculture. The constant turmoil and political maneuvering among the bureau's staff was one of the reasons behind the establishment of a new, more professional cabinet-level department, Pugh observed.

Pugh then met with Owen Lovejoy, a Republican congressman from Illinois, a noted abolitionist and close friend of Lincoln, and the chair of the House committee on agriculture. Pugh found that "several ill-digested plans for a Bureau have been proposed and two or three of them presented to com-mittee." Pugh urged that Lovejoy establish "a more efficient scientific Dept. than any of the friends of the bill seemed to have any idea of." Lovejoy listened attentively and requested that Pugh draw up a "summary of arguments in its favor" and send it to him as soon as possible. In New Haven, Pugh urged the Yale scientists and Silliman Jr. to write to Lovejoy as well. Pugh was confident that "a little work might secure a useful Bureau, but without it only a miserable political humbug will be established. The men in Washington now in charge of the measure are as ignorant of what should be done as South Sea Islanders."[18]

In person, Pugh made an impression on both Newton and Lovejoy. Newton, in fact, sounded him out about his interest in accepting one of most important scientific posts in the new Department of Agriculture, that of chief chemist, leading the entire chemistry section. Pugh's name had been bandied about, and he had the previous fall done a brief survey for Newton on the status of the agricultural college movement. Responding via letter a month later, Pugh outlined how the chemistry section should be organized, but then declined any interest in leading it. Although flattered by the nomination, he "could not . . . leave this place for any other, however great the inducements." Pugh offered to consult with whoever might be appointed and volunteered to make the college farm available for any experiments the bureau might want to conduct. He dangled the possibility that at some future date he might consider such an offer, but not until the college were established and operating smoothly. Pugh would not leave if there were any possibility "that its scientific character would degenerate into a mere ordinary college course." If, however, he felt fully confident in the college's success, he "would like a position in such a scientific chair as I believe I could do more good investigating scientific Agl. questions than teaching, but at present duty demands my presence here."[19]

Pugh provided counsel on nearly every aspect of how the new federal agency should be organized and staffed. In terms of its section head, the "chief chemist," Pugh made the case for a scientist of international standing: "It is *indispensable*" that the chief be conversant in German and French and familiar with the scientific agriculture literature of both countries. Ideally, the successful candidate also should have seen the European scientists at work and even have been involved personally with their research. Pugh recommended his Yale colleague Samuel Johnson, the only American who, in his estimation, could bring such a background to the post. Though Pugh said the chief chemist should be free to hire his own assistants, Pugh recommended two Europeans—"Dr. Julius Sachs of Bonn . . . or Dr. Knope of Leipzig. Both of them told me three years ago that they would come to this country if a good opportunity is offered for investigation." The salary he recommended was $3,000 per year for Johnson (and another $3,000 to be split among the assistants). That was twice the salary Pugh was making in his presidency. As for the head of the botany section, Pugh noted that a botanist "who is not also a very good Agricultural Chemist will not be able to do much for agriculture." Pugh recommended Professor William H. Brewer, formerly of the failing New York State Agricultural College in Ovid, New York, who at the time was serving as botanist for the California Geological Survey. Like Johnson, Pugh said, Brewer had the advantage of a European education.

Pugh also laid out the costs for the new Department of Agriculture: For the salaries of the seven or so scientists and assistant scientists, a total of $14,400. To that he pegged the cost of a new "first rate laboratory worthy of our country" at $50,000. Failing that, an old building could be "fitted up," but he estimated the cost of doing that and providing the necessary facilities at $19,600. He did argue for, eventually, a building "like that of the Smithsonian Institution . . . but a year's experience in an old building would enable those interested in it to see more fully just what is needed." To this first-year expense totaling $34,000, he added $17,900 annually for keeping it maintained.

As for the department's research agenda, Pugh made special mention of the importance of analyzing the leading manures on the market. Protecting farmers against "the shameful imposition of manure dealers alone would save the agricultural interest of the country more than 5 times the amount annually." He recommended seven lines of research: the prevention of potato disease; special manures for special crops; the preparation and preservation of manures and the byproducts of factories that could be utilized as plant nutrients; the uses and abuses of lime in agriculture; the effectiveness of artificial manures in the marketplace; the nutritional value of livestock feed; and the unique composition of various soils and methods of rehabilitation.[20]

A few days later, Pugh followed up on his advice to Newton and Lovejoy with a paper on what he deemed to be an essential complementary institution —"A National Agricultural Investigation Station." Pugh noted that, dating back to 1852, agricultural investigation stations had been established across continental Europe. Their components consisted of a laboratory for "chemical, physiological, and microscopical investigations"; a large farm for experiments in real conditions; and facilities for "testing the fattening qualities of different kinds of food for cattle."

He elaborated on the practical results obtained from such stations, deeming them revolutionary for the agriculture industry. He cited the example of his colleague John Lawes of Rothamsted and the super-phosphate of lime he discovered. Lawes's manufacturing enterprise, now shipping the product worldwide, had "originated in the beaker glass of his experimental chemical laboratory." Noting his own experimental work at Rothamsted, Pugh said he had visited similar stations "at Berlin, Dresden, Leipsic, Stuttgart, Bonn and Paris and have worked in some of them" and was "personally acquainted with professors in all of them." The experiment stations were accepted across Europe as being necessary to the advancement of agriculture and were receiving increased "patronage from the State and from public spirited private individuals." The research emphases of these European scientists, Pugh pointed out, were in chemistry, botany, and zoology as related to agriculture and requiring expertise in agricultural chemistry, vegetable physiology, and animal chemistry. He concluded by itemizing the expenses attendant to setting up a national experiment station, as he had in his previous letter.[21]

Despite his two extensive responses to Newton and Lovejoy, Pugh was not sanguine about the immediate prospects for success. "I laid out a plan for them that will take $100,000 to start upon," he told Johnson. "I don't expect they will get more done than talk this winter. The bill as reported is a humbug but it may be made something of yet."[22]

The second offer for the position of chief chemist, U.S. Department of Agriculture, came in 1863, when Pugh was in Oxford, Pennsylvania, recovering from his broken arm. The letter to Pugh arrived at the Agricultural College and was opened by College Vice President David Wilson. Wilson sent it on to Pugh, along with a letter from Paschall Morris, editor and proprietor of *The*

Practical Farmer and Rural Advertiser, urging him to accept the post.[23] Again, Pugh turned the offer down, telling Wilson:

> I refused to accept the head of that department [chemistry] when it was offered me two years ago—because I wanted to devote myself to agricultural education, in the State Agricultural College called or to be called into existence by the Congressional Appropriation. The best way to do this I conceive is to make our own college a model which other Agricultural Colleges will adopt . . . to do this I am resolved to stay with our College, while God gives me strength to perform my duties there, whatever may be the pecuniary inducements or prospects of honor elsewhere. It is my duty and my destiny to do so, and I shall seek honors in the path of duty and destiny rather than at Washington.[24]

Writing to Pugh in September 1863, his chemistry assistant and protégé C. Alfred Smith voiced relief: "I am very glad you will not accept the Washington offer."[25]

Agricultural Research and Experiment Stations

His advocacy notwithstanding, Pugh would not live to see the beginnings of the agricultural experiment station movement in America—though his best friend Samuel Johnson would play the seminal role.

The movement to establish agricultural experiment stations is generally credited to Johnson, although Harvard (through the Bussey Institution) established the first privately endowed station in 1871. Nonetheless, in 1875, through Johnson's influence, the Connecticut legislature made a small appropriation to aid the cost of a two-year program of agricultural experimentation, to be conducted by William O. Atwater (who received his Yale Ph.D. under Johnson) at Wesleyan University in Middletown, Connecticut. Two years later, the legislature approved the establishment of the Connecticut Agricultural Experiment Station, under Johnson's direction. The station was moved from Middletown to Yale and later New Haven.[26]

Federal aid for state experiment stations began with the Hatch Act of 1887, which authorized direct annual appropriations of federal funds to each state to establish an agricultural experiment station generally under the direction of its land-grant college. Penn State's seventh president, George W. Atherton, played a substantial role in drafting the bill that Congressman William

H. Hatch of Missouri introduced. The federal Office of Experiment Stations came into being under the U.S. Department of Agriculture in 1888, the year after the Hatch Act, with the aforesaid Atwater as its first director.[27]

The 1880s also gave rise to new scientific organizations of the sort Pugh would have endorsed. The Association of Official Agricultural Chemists was established in 1880, its original agenda being to standardize tests and measurements across state lines. In similar fashion, at the 1880 meeting of the American Association for the Advancement of Science, a group of horticulturalists organized the Society for the Promotion of Agricultural Science—to "help raise the level of agricultural science in the country."[28]

But the greatest development was that of the U.S. Department of Agriculture, which was elevated to cabinet-level status with a secretary in 1889. Under the direction of Secretary "Tama Jim" Wilson, appointed in 1897, the USDA would undergo a vast expansion, emerging as the world's leading scientific research organization, with a staff of 11,000 and a budget of $21.2 million by 1912.[29] The USDA came to establish several large experiment stations of its own, including the Henry A. Wallace Beltsville (Maryland) Agricultural Research Center, which in turn includes the National Agricultural Library and the U.S. National Arboretum in Washington, D.C.

Evan Pugh foresaw the need for all of these developments, and he advocated vigorously to bring them into being. Although the press of duties at the Agricultural College constricted his ability to carry out his own original research, until the end of his days he remained a staunch champion for a national coordinating agency and research infrastructure for the advancement of agricultural science. How he might have influenced the course of events had he lived beyond 1864 is open to speculation, but there is no question that his expertise and insight would have played a major role.

CHAPTER 7

Campaigning for the Morrill
Land-Grant College Act

EVAN PUGH HAD A deep, abiding interest in the Morrill Land-Grant College Act of 1862. He was a strong advocate of state financial support for agricultural schools and colleges, as he had seen what had been accomplished through such means for German institutions during his years abroad. The passage of the Morrill Act ultimately would generate the funds needed to build his agricultural college out to effective scale, which to Pugh's way of thinking meant at least 400 students, nearly 30 faculty members, and an annual income approaching $50,000—big numbers by the standards of the day.[1] But his larger goal was focused on the benefits the act would bring to the whole of American agriculture and national progress. As the only scientist–college president with an active interest in the legislation, Pugh held a uniquely informed perspective of what the act could accomplish. At least one scholar credits Pugh with being the bellwether scientist in the effort to bring the measure to fruition: "Except for Evan Pugh, a Göttingen Ph.D. in chemistry and head of a state-supported agricultural college in Pennsylvania, scientists had done little to promote the bill."[2] Pugh worked very closely with James Tracy Hale, the congressional representative from the college's district and also an Agricultural College trustee, who in turn worked closely with fellow representative Justin S. Morrill and others in Congress to ensure the bill's passage.

Forces Behind the Legislation

Though it passed Congress with little fanfare, the Morrill Act has been deemed a watershed piece of federal legislation with important implications for the nation's development—economically, socially, scientifically, and technologically. It was one of several farsighted pieces of legislation passed the same year by the Thirty-Seventh Congress that distributed federal land to accelerate the nation's advancement in several key ways—courtesy, in no small measure, of southern secession and the absence of conservative representatives and senators. Salient among this legislation was the Homestead Act, which eventually distributed 234 million acres of land by allowing any qualified person (who had never taken up arms against the U.S. government, was twenty-one years or older, or the head of a family) to file a claim for up to 160 acres of federally owned land in exchange for five years of residence and the cultivation and improvement of the property. Other vital legislation was the Pacific Railway Act, which begat a series of measures to promote construction of the transcontinental railroad through the issuance of government bonds and federal lands to railroad companies. The third broad-scale distribution of federal lands came through the Morrill Act, which distributed more than 17.4 million acres to the states for specific higher education purposes.[3] Despite the immediate concerns posed by the Civil War, the farsighted Thirty-Seventh Congress was looking ahead to its successful conclusion and the rapid resumption of manifest destiny.

As historian Ariel Ron has postulated, the federal government's ownership of the vast public land domain constituted an unprecedented fiscal resource, a "reserve of wealth" that the government "spent" to support a wide range of policy goals, including immigration and settlement, transportation infrastructure, social welfare, debt financing, war and conquest, and public education, among other uses. Rather than resorting to increased taxation of the citizenry to support policy objectives, or borrowing money from foreign governments, the government used the treasure trove of public land for the broad purposes of national economic development.[4] In terms of primary and secondary education, for example, the Northwest Ordinance of 1787 established the federal policy of surveying western lands according to a system of square townships, each township encompassing one square mile divided into thirty-six "sections." The sixteenth section—later expanded to two sections— of every township was to be used to endow a local school fund.

The Morrill Act represented the federal government's first policy involvement with higher education. The legislation offered to each state that accepted its terms 30,000 acres of federal land for each of its congressional representatives and U.S. senators. The land was to be sold and the proceeds used to establish an endowment to support "at least one college where the leading object shall be, without excluding other scientific and classical studies, and including military tactics, to teach such branches of learning as are related to agriculture and the mechanic arts, in such manner as the legislatures of the States may respectively prescribe, in order to promote the liberal and practical education of the industrial classes in the several pursuits and professions of life."[5]

The act promised a bonanza for the more populous eastern states. New York, the largest state, received title to 980,000 acres. Pennsylvania, the second-most populous, acquired 780,000 acres. By contrast, Rhode Island, eastern but small, was awarded 120,000 acres.[6] Ultimately, the Agricultural College of Pennsylvania realized $439,000, about 56 cents per acre, from the sale of its federal land entitlement. The funds did not begin to materialize, however, until well after Pugh had passed from the scene.

In sheer numbers alone, the act's influence was felt quickly in the decade following the Civil War. By the late 1870s, some thirty-seven land-grant colleges were in operation. As additional states and possessions were added to the national fabric, the act eventually designated fifty-eight land-grant campuses, systems, and/or allied institutions. The 1890 Morrill Act brought an additional seventeen historically black colleges and universities, mostly in the South, into the land-grant college system. Thirty-one Native American tribal colleges were accorded land-grant status in 1994 as well, through representation via a single system, creating 106 land-grant institutions nationally.

As the 1960s approached, the impending centennial of the Morrill Act was marked with a number of scholarly outpourings celebrating what was deemed to be the unqualified success of the legislation. The scholarly consensus held that, with the Morrill Act, the government had responded to popular demand in offering a modern alternative to traditional, classically oriented colleges, thus "democratizing" American higher education. As he prepared his Godkin lectures at Harvard in 1963, Clark Kerr, then the president of the University of California, wrote: "Two great impacts, beyond all other forces, have molded the modern American university system and made it distinctive." Both impacts, Kerr said, came primarily from the federal government in response to national needs. "The first was the land grant movement," which "set the tone for the development of American universities, both public and private, for most of the ensuing hundred years." Calling it "one of the most seminal pieces of legislation ever enacted," Kerr said the movement represented the response to the "rapid industrial and agricultural development" of America in the mid-nineteenth century. Pointing to the significant impact of the German research university model on the development of land-grant colleges, Kerr said the "second great impact" on the modern American university began "with federal support of scientific research during World War II."[7]

In the half-century since the centennial, higher education historians have revised the traditional historiographical consensus of the land-grant college movement. It is now seen as a less democratically triumphant and more complex and nuanced phenomenon, balancing a multiplicity of interests and causes, divergent as well as convergent. In their study, "The Welding of Opposite Views: Land-Grant Historiography at 150 years," Nathan Sorber and Roger Geiger examine the corpus of revisionist writing that has moved beyond the romantic democratization thesis of expanding access through the addition of practical subject matter. The movement's other forces, at once complementary and competing, have to do with the rise of science, international competition, industrialization, agricultural modernization, academic professionalism, an emerging middle class, nation-building and bureaucratization, and more. It is the *tension* of these interplaying forces and opposite views, rather than the simple democratizing process, that "has proved decisive in the development of the land-grant colleges." Accordingly, Sorber and Geiger urged scholars to continue moving the historiography of the land-grant movement "from celebratory to empirical ground."[8]

None of this newer scholarship professes to mute the influence of the Morrill Act. Rather, it is concerned with interpreting it accurately, objectively, and fully. Writing in his 2015 *History of American Higher Education*, for example, Geiger observed that the Morrill Act "conveyed far-reaching aims to institutionalize practical fields of study, meld them with liberal education, open them to a new class of students, and charge the states with finding the means to accomplish all of it. The act immediately affected the expansion and structure of higher education and, eventually, the productivity of the American economy."[9]

The Morrill Act itself was the product of decades of agrarian agitation and legislative interest. The major source was the advocacy emanating from the hundreds of state and local agricultural societies and the agricultural press, as noted previously. Indeed, Justin Morrill himself was a leading influence in his Orange County Agricultural Society in eastern Vermont.[10] In the mid-Atlantic states, New England, and the upper Midwest, these societies and their journalistic allies pushed hard for the establishment of agricultural colleges, which they deemed essential for increasing agricultural productivity and solving the national "Farm Problem" related chiefly to soil exhaustion.

In early 1853, for example, the *Pennsylvania Farm Journal,* published in West Chester, in Pugh's home county, and edited by J. Lacey Darlington, editorialized for an agricultural college and model farm for Pennsylvania. The editorial appeared eight months before Pugh set sail for Germany and certainly caught his attention, as he kept the edition among his personal papers. The *Journal* cited efforts to establish an agricultural department in connection with nearby Delaware College as well as efforts by the State Agricultural Society of Maryland to endow a professorship of agricultural chemistry in connection with St. John's College in Annapolis. "Is Pennsylvania going to be behindhand?" the editorial challenged. "Are our farmers so far ahead of those north and south of them, that no instruction is needed? Is the theory and practice of agriculture in Pennsylvania already perfect, and are the great fundamental principles . . . better understood here than in our sister states?" The editorial went on to call for a "model and experimental farm," an "Agricultural Professorship," and advocacy for those goals "by our State Society at its approaching meeting," with subsequent action to be taken by the Pennsylvania legislature.[11]

The nation's sectional tensions were playing out ferociously in Congress during the 1850s, and legislation typically was viewed from a sectional perspective, not a national one. Indeed, the United States at this time has been described as "three countries living under the same flag, the Northeast, the South, and the West."[12] These sectional tensions came into play when Vermont representative Justin S. Morrill introduced his first land-grant college bill, in December 1857—a year that also ushered in an economic depression. In contrast to the equality of land grants favored by western interests, Morrill proposed a flat grant of 60,000 acres to each state followed by a proportional grant of 20,000 more acres for each congressional representative, favoring the more populous East. Morrill's bill left it to the states to realize what they could through selling their land grants. And while Morrill advocated for practical education, he did not omit classical studies from his plan.

The alliance of the South and West mounted opposition to the bill. Chief among the objections was the "unconstitutionality" of the proposed federal incursion into state prerogative, a trampling of states' rights, as southern legislators argued. Nonetheless, the bill passed the House and Senate by slim margins. In February 1859 President James Buchanan vetoed the bill. He too found it to be unconstitutional. He also deemed the bill to be a dangerous financial drain on the national treasury; a burden to the newer states in the West because of the land speculation that would work against their interests; an exercise in futility because the federal government could not compel the states to carry out the mandate of the act; and a threat to existing colleges.[13] While working at Rothamsted, Pugh got wind of Buchanan's veto and expressed his disgust.[14]

After the secession of the southern states and the outbreak of hostilities, Morrill introduced a revised bill on December 16, 1861, with some major differences from its predecessor: the western territories and the states in rebellion were omitted as beneficiaries; the land grant for each member of Congress was increased from 20,000 to 30,000 acres; and military tactics were included in the curriculum, a desideratum made evident by the poor performance of Union armies in the war's opening year.

Western states still viewed the bill as inimical to their interests. They believed it would preclude the intent of the Homestead Act, as eastern land speculators would buy up the Morrill bill's land grants and hold onto it until prices would rise, retarding the growth of farms and communities. Nonetheless, with the absence of southern opposition, the bill sailed through both houses. It first passed the Senate by a vote of 32 to 7 on June 11, 1862. The House concurred on June 19, by a vote of 90 to 25. President Lincoln, who had no particularly strong feelings about the bill, yet whose support "was never in doubt," as Morrill later put it, signed the measure unceremoniously on July 2.[15]

Morrill's motives in introducing the bill covered a complex web of concerns. According to Roger Geiger, they addressed, first and foremost, educational opportunity for the industrial classes, which at the time encompassed four out of five American adults. Second was the desire to provide practical education in the various avocations, agriculture and engineering foremost among them but by no means the entire universe of practical subject matter. Third, Morrill sought to elevate the practical arts alongside scientific and classical studies and to thus advance those subjects in connection with higher education. The fourth goal was to promote the nation's economic development through research and experimentation—scientifically rooted, of course—as well as education.[16]

The nation was beginning to industrialize rapidly, although the Civil War—a "locomotive of history," as Karl Marx called such major conflicts—would accelerate the process dramatically. Leaders knew the nation could not urbanize and industrialize without the foundation provided by an increasingly productive agricultural sector. Other factors were involved as well. The perceived reluctance of existing colleges to tend to new subjects and new kinds of students was a major concern. The perceived inability of the newer, less affluent, and less populous states (twenty new states were admitted to the Union between 1820 and 1860) to provide modern colleges of practical orientation without federal help was also under consideration. The rapid dissipation of public lands to private interests as well as increasing concern over soil deterioration, spreading ever westward as settlers broke new ground, entered the picture. Looming in the background was the fear that the United States should not fall further behind Europe, with its burgeoning agricultural and industrial movements. And not least was the political urgency of bringing the industrial movement, especially the agrarian interests, into the fold of the new Republican Party.[17]

The 1862 Morrill Act—officially "An Act donating Public Lands to the several States and Territories which may provide Colleges for the benefit of Agriculture and the Mechanic Arts"—introduced a new dimension to American higher education. It was to establish colleges for the underserved industrial classes, to be sure, but in a way that was broad and liberal, offering arts and humanities, but emphasizing science, applied science, engineering and technology, and military science. In so doing, it pushed the whole of American higher education in a more utilitarian, practical direction. Nonetheless, the act was never intended to produce narrow vocationalists. As Morrill was quoted by his colleague George W. Atherton, president of the Pennsylvania State College, in a 1900 speech: "It is perhaps needless to say that these colleges were not established or endowed for the sole purpose of teaching agriculture" nor was it intended "to force the boys of farmers . . . so to study that they should all come out farmers . . . not manual but intellectual instruction was the paramount object. . . . Classical studies . . . must be included." The act proposed "a system of broad education by colleges, not limited to a superficial and dwarfed training such as might be had at an industrial school, nor a mere manual training such as might be supplied by a foreman."[18]

Pugh's Role in the Passage of the Morrill Bill

Ascertaining Pugh's precise role in influencing the passage of the Morrill Bill during the winter and spring of 1862 is difficult, but there is no question that he was involved both indirectly and directly. He is credited with wielding influence on the final result by an assortment of scholars, though the specifics of his actions are described in vague, general terms. Penn State historian Margaret T. Riley says that Pugh went "to Washington in the line of duty, however, as did Penn State's trustees and leaders from other states, notably Illinois, Massachusetts, New York, Michigan, and Connecticut . . . to exert influence on the formulation and passage of the Morrill Act."[19] As noted previously, Robert Bruce, in *The Launching of Modern American Science, 1846–1876*, credits Pugh as being the only scientist actively engaged in the effort.[20] Earle D. Ross, the seminal land-grant college historian, said that Pugh was one of four college presidents who worked vigorously for the passage of the 1862 Morrill Act. In fact, Ross observed, "Pugh led the Pennsylvania group with characteristic zeal and with effective if not determining influence on the final result."[21] Penn State historian Asa E. Martin, in a 1942 article in *Pennsylvania History*, was the least specific. He said that "certainly the agricultural interests of Pennsylvania were extremely active in support of both the Morrill Act of 1859 . . . and that of 1862 . . . and the Farmers' High School of Pennsylvania was expected to be the recipient of the financial benefits conferred by the act."[22] Certainly Pugh was in Washington in late January and early February 1862, but the chief object of his visit was to confer with the director of the U.S. Bureau of Agriculture and a congressional sponsor to advise on how the anticipated U.S. Department of Agriculture might be structured and effectively focused. Pugh made no mention of any meeting during this time to discuss the Morrill bill.[23]

Given what was at stake, Pugh and the trustees were in constant conversation and activity with regard to the Morrill bill, particularly with their congressional representative and fellow Agricultural College trustee, James T. Hale from Centre County, as well as others in the state's agricultural community. In his *Organizational Plan for Agricultural Colleges*, published in January 1864, Pugh stated categorically, "The friends of the Agricultural College of Pennsylvania secured the passage of the Land Grant bill by Congress. A member of their Board of Trustees (then as now a prominent member of Congress) devoted almost an entire session in Congress to its passage, and other friends of the college visited Washington several times for the same purpose. Without their aid, the bill would not have passed."[24] A Pennsylvania state senator, Heister Clymer of Berks County, also cited Hale's work in Washington, conferring on the congressman "great credit" for his work in achieving the act's passage. "Possibly there was no one of the floor of Congress more interested in that proposition or who lent more efficient aid in the passage of the law."[25]

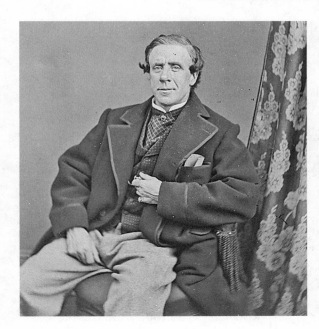

FIGURE 18
*James T. Hale, college
trustee and member, U.S.
House of Representatives,
1859–65.*

Without question, Hale was the indispensable legislator who engineered major successes for the Agricultural College of Pennsylvania on both
the national and state levels in the early 1860s, representing Centre County
from the Thirty-Sixth through the Thirty-Eighth Congress (1859–65). Born
in 1810 in Towanda, Pennsylvania, to a family of farmers, Hale studied law
under his uncle in Lewistown, Pennsylvania, and moved to Bellefonte in 1832.
Continuing to practice law, he was appointed president judge of the twen-
ty-fifth judicial district for a few months in 1851, returning to the practice of
law until 1856. He then became part owner and president of a large timber and
coal company, holding that post until 1860. He joined the new Republican
Party and was elected to Congress, representing Pennsylvania's Eighteenth
District (Centre, Clinton, Lycoming, Mifflin, Potter, and Tioga counties),
re-elected in 1860, and again in 1862, remaining in Congress through March
1865. At the end of March 1865, while engaged in legal work in Bellefonte,
Hale became ill and died quickly thereafter on April 6, at age fifty-four.[26]

General James A. Beaver, a later president of the college's Board of
Trustees, a governor of Pennsylvania, and finally the interim president of
the college itself, memorialized Hale as "not only a man of great ability but a
diplomat as well." He was "the devoted champion of the land grant act" who
"efficiently aided Mr. Morrill . . . in securing its passage." Hale also would

extend his influence to the Pennsylvania legislature when "called to Harrisburg to assist in the passage of measures affecting the welfare of the College."[27]

The Morrill Act and Its Acceptance in Pennsylvania

Working with the U.S. Congress for the passage of the Morrill bill was one thing; getting the terms of the act accepted by the Pennsylvania legislature was quite another. It was to the latter imperative that Pugh and the trustees turned their attention shortly after Lincoln had signed the act on July 2, 1862.

The Morrill Act provided some strong provisions about the use of the funds, placing significant obligations on the states willing to comply with the act. Section 4 of the act mandated that the funds derived by each state from the sale of apportioned federal land or land scrip be invested in stocks yielding not less than 5 percent per year in interest. The monies realized from the sales were to be held in perpetuity, as the principal of the endowment, and never diminished. The annual interest "shall be inviolably appropriated by each State . . . to the endowment, support and maintenance of at least one college where the leading object shall be . . . to teach such branches of learning as are related to agriculture and the mechanic arts, in such manner as the legislatures of the states may respectively prescribe."[28]

The sale of the public land entitlement was tricky business, however. Each state (sec. 2) was entitled to first claim public land (listed at $1.25 per acre) within its own borders; in those states, particularly in the Northeast, where there was no remaining public land, or very limited amounts thereof, they were to be issued land "scrip," a paper entitlement to the allocated amount of federal lands, to make up the difference. With land scrip, the states were prohibited from actually locating the land they wanted to sell within the borders of any other state; instead, they were free to sell the scrip to private agents and land speculators, who in turn could locate it in whatever state they chose. To prevent a land grab in any particular state, however, the act set a limit of 1 million acres per state that could be claimed by land agents and speculators.[29] As things stood, only ten states were in position to claim existing federal land within their own borders; twenty-seven states had to look outside their borders. Those twenty-seven states encompassed the eastern seaboard states that had been the original thirteen colonies, including Pennsylvania, all of which had no remaining public land to distribute.

Section 7 required states interested in claiming the benefits of the act to accept its terms via legislative action within three years dating from July 23,

1866. Going further, the act (sec. 5) required each state accepting its provisions to establish within five years at least one college dedicated to the purposes of act; the penalty for not doing so would be a cancellation of the grant to the state and the requirement that it reimburse the federal government for the entire amount of land sales generated by that state. Additionally, to provide accountability, the act also required an annual report by the college, to be sent to all other colleges designated by the act and to the U.S. secretary of the interior.

Significantly, the Morrill Act prohibited any portion of the endowment, or interest generated, from being applied, "directly or indirectly, under any pretence whatever, to the purchase, erection, preservation, or repair of any building or buildings." Thus, the responsibility for the campus physical plant would rest with the states and the institutions proper, not the federal government.[30] In this respect, the Morrill Act's imminent passage prompted a shift in the college's financial strategy by Pugh and the trustees. Their original plan was to ask the Pennsylvania legislature for an endowment to support the construction of the college's buildings. As confidence grew in the prospects for the Morrill bill and the institutional endowment it would create, they "promised the Legislature, when asking for money to complete the College buildings, not to ask the State for an endowment."[31]

And so in Pennsylvania and other states, the race was on. The trustees of the Agricultural College of Pennsylvania lost no time in preparing for the legislative campaign. At their September 2, 1862, meeting—only two months after Lincoln had signed the Morrill Act—the trustees formed a committee "whose duty it shall be to procure the action of the legislature on the subject." The committee consisted of trustee president Watts, trustee A. O. Hiester, and trustee/congressman Hale.[32]

The first snag they encountered was presented by the governor, Andrew Curtin, ironically a Centre County native and an ex officio trustee of the college. Curtin sought to divert the Morrill land-grant fund away from the school and toward the provision of soldiers' homes, providing perpetual aid for disabled Civil War veterans. Pugh was livid. He told McAllister that Curtin was "too much of the politician" to support any movement "which does not reflect back upon him political power and influence and now that public feeling is turned upon wounded soldiers, the claims of Agl. Education for centuries to come must be sacrificed." Sensing, however, that the governor had "not committed himself very far in the wrong direction," Pugh asked McAllister to intercede with the governor.[33] Meanwhile, thinking that half a loaf was better than none, Watts drafted a bill directing that half the proceeds from the sale of scrip be dedicated to the college. He then handed the draft to state representative J. P. Rhoades, from his own Cumberland County, who referred it to the appropriate House committee. Watts quickly realized his folly, however, and rewrote the bill so as to give the college all of the money. As Pugh said, "he put the whole bill into better shape, talked to a number of members, found all friendly—put the Governor all right and thinks there will be no difficulty." Pugh copied Watts's rewrite and gave it to the chair of the Committee on Judiciary General. The bill was reported back to the House on February 4.[34]

The bill recognized the legislature's "high regard for the agricultural interests of the State" as demonstrated by the establishment of the Agricultural College of Pennsylvania, "and by making liberal appropriations thereto." This language set up the college as the only logical choice for designation as the beneficiary of Morrill Act proceeds. In its five sections, the legislature's act required the Commonwealth to accept the terms of the Morrill Act; provided for the disposition of the land scrip (Pennsylvania was entitled to 780,000 acres); set up a board of commissioners—the governor, auditor general, and surveyor general—to supervise the sale of the scrip and the investment of its proceeds; provided for the payment of annual interest to the Agricultural College of Pennsylvania; and mandated that an annual report of income and expenses be made to the legislature.[35]

Several innocuous amendments were made to the bill, but one change, passed unanimously by the House, would prove ominous: that the annual income would go to the Agricultural College "until otherwise ordered by the Legislature of Pennsylvania." Already, the political sharks were preparing to feast at the banquet promised by the Morrill Act, as Governor Curtin had proposed to do. Some representatives believed that it promised an unreasonable amount of money for a single fledgling school. One legislator offered to amend the bill to benefit multiple institutions—"and such other Agricultural College or Colleges in equal proportions as may hereafter be incorporated." Another wanted the act to go farther afield, benefiting the common (elementary) schools and homes for disabled soldiers. Nonetheless, a sense of urgency prevailed, driven by concern that the best federal lands would be claimed by other states if the assignees commissioned by Pennsylvania to sell the land dawdled. On February 26, 1863, the Pennsylvania House overwhelmingly approved H.B. 119, 82–9.[36]

Onto the Senate the bill went, being reported out to the full body by the Committee on Agriculture on March 11. Some changes were suggested, with most of concern being focused on setting a minimum price per acre for the sale of scrip, but better sense prevailed. Senator Henry Johnson, representing Lycoming County and parts of Centre County, took up the cudgels for the Agricultural College. He outlined the act's provisions, misunderstood by many, and argued that the potential income was not too large for any one college. In Johnson's view, the whole issue boiled down to one of two choices: either accept the grant and apply it to the Agricultural College, or accept it and build another like institution from scratch. "Those are the conditions under which we may accept this munificent grant . . . and we cannot accept it under any other conditions," Johnson said.

> And the question arising here is . . . whether we will appropriate out of the funds of Commonwealth, some two or three hundred thousand dollars for the erection of an Agricultural College accompanied with an annual expense thereafter . . . or whether we will avail ourselves . . . to the Agricultural College erected in the County of Centre, which is a State Institution, having been erected in part out of funds paid out of the Treasury of the Commonwealth, and in part by the contributions of citizens of this State—an institution which is in every particular just as such a one as is contemplated and described in this act of Congress.[37]

With that, the bill passed the Senate overwhelmingly, 21–7, on March 23.

The bill's passage in both chambers was helped to no small degree by the personal intervention of Congressman Hale. He visited the Pennsylvania legislature and "explained to members the necessity for a prompt acceptance on the part of the state." The result was an act directing that the fund "be temporarily devoted to the use of the Farmers' High School, we reserving to ourselves to say that it should remain there until otherwise ordered by the Legislature."[38] Pugh himself had spent considerable time in Harrisburg, advocating for the bill behind the scenes and watching as the Senate voted. McAllister and Watts had exerted their considerable influence in the Capitol as well.

Pugh reported the victory to Trustee McAllister in the late evening of March 23, letting him know that "our bill passed (thanks to the industry and influence of Judge Hale) this evening. It is all right and ready for the Governor's signature, which Judge Hale will secure as soon as he comes home. . . . I shall try and get Hale to go to Washington and see about securing the Land Warrants that the Scrip may go into the market at once."[39]

Pugh added that he was leaving at 2:00 a.m. to catch the train back to the college. "I trust it may never be necessary to so wholly neglect my duties at the College for so long a time again, but I think the friends of the College will under the circumstances pardon the neglect."[40]

The act was signed into law—pledging "the faith of the State to carry the same [the Morrill Act] into effect"—by Governor Curtin on April 1, 1863. Pugh and the trustees would plan no celebration, but they might have taken a measure of satisfaction in what had been accomplished over the course of the last twelve months: the passage of historic federal legislation, the Morrill Land-Grant College Act of 1862, and the state's relatively quick ratification of its terms that would, they hoped, usher in a new day.

CHAPTER 8

The Disruptions of 1863

THE SPRING OF 1863 may well have been high tide for Pugh and the Agricultural College of Pennsylvania. Through great effort, the Morrill Act had been passed nine months earlier and the state's acceptance of its terms, designating the college as the sole beneficiary, had been engineered successfully. Meanwhile, the college was thriving, with a record enrollment of 142 students, shoehorned into a building still under construction and not to be completed until the following December.

Some of those students were quite young. The academic year beginning February 1863 marked the introduction of the primary department—designed to enroll boys under the threshold admittance age of sixteen and to accommodate others who were not fully prepared for college work. Besides the twenty-four boys in the primary department, there were twenty-two in the fourth (freshman) class; forty-eight in the third (sophomore) class; twenty-nine in the second (junior) class, and a graduating (senior) class that had been whittled down to eight students. In addition, there were eleven "resident graduates" (graduate students). One student who received his Master of Scientific Agriculture degree in January 1863, C. Alfred Smith, Class of 1861, and another "resident graduate," John F. Miles, also Class of 1861, would wind up on the faculty later that same year serving as assistants in analytical chemistry. Pugh would claim that not only was 142 the largest enrollment in the college's short history but "it is also a larger number than have been during the same time in attendance upon any other Agricultural College in this country or in Europe."[1]

The faculty had also expanded, from five when Pugh arrived to eight by the end of 1863. And it was a faculty heavily weighted toward the sciences. In addition to the two aforementioned assistants in analytical chemistry, Pugh in the summer had persuaded his former fellow student and colleague George C. Caldwell, a Göttingen Ph.D., to join the faculty temporarily as professor of agricultural chemistry. In addition to Caldwell, J. S. Whitman served as professor of botany, physiology, zoology, horticulture, and gardening. T. R. Baker was professor of mathematics, astronomy, natural philosophy, and analytical mechanics. Vice President David Wilson covered the "classical studies" as professor of the English language and literature, moral and intellectual philosophy, and also served as superintendent of the agricultural department. Thomas Scanlan was the teacher of the new elementary (preparatory) department. And Pugh continued to carry his considerable teaching responsibilities as professor of chemistry, scientific agriculture, mineralogy, and geology.[2]

However triumphant the course of events may have seemed for the young institution in the spring of 1863, ill fortune was about to intervene. The summer months would bring a strange and dislocating pause to the life of the Agricultural College of Pennsylvania, interrupting four years of rapid progress under Pugh's leadership.

Rebecca Pugh and the Buggy Accident

The first disruption removed Pugh from the campus for nearly three months, depriving the college of its guiding light. In a bizarre twist of fate, Pugh and his fiancée, Rebecca Valentine of Bellefonte, were badly injured in a buggy accident on the night of June 16, 1863. Visiting William Shortlidge, a Pugh cousin, they left to return home and their buggy somehow toppled into the Logan Branch of Spring Creek in Bellefonte. Pugh's left arm was badly broken. Though he managed to free himself and extricate Rebecca, who was pinned underneath the buggy, he would never fully recover from the accident.

Although a bachelor when he came to the presidency, Pugh had an eye for the ladies and they for him, as he recounted from his time in England. He had always intended to marry, eventually, and start a family. Shortly after arriving at the Farmers' High School, he quite by chance met the love of his life. They courted for four years and, after both had healed sufficiently from the accident, finally tied the knot.

As Pugh wrote to Samuel Johnson in February 1864: "I neglected to tell you that about 4 years ago I visited the house of an old Quaker, an iron master,

FIGURE 19
*Rebecca Valentine Pugh,
1864.*

to talk about the reduction of iron ores etc. and that on first sight I *fell* in love with his daughter and that I have never recovered from the *fall* and hence the card I send you." Pugh noted that in the buggy accident, Rebecca "was worse hurt than I that she was carried home insensible and was not expected to live for several days." She eventually recovered; the couple married on February 4, 1864, and "consummated our 3 years engagement," making Pugh "a most happy man."[3]

Accounts of the accident vary, according to Penn State historians. In several versions, a thunderstorm came up and spooked the horse, which backed its human freight over an embankment into the stream. Other narrations omit the drama of the dark and stormy night—although it was dark, to be sure. The most descriptive account, however, is a story related by Elizabeth Shortlidge Walker, the daughter of the man Pugh and Valentine were visiting, and a witness to the evening's events. Walker's story was unearthed in 1949 when she was interviewed by the curator of the Penn State Collection in Pattee Library, Abbie H. Cromer. As Cromer transcribed the interview, Pugh and Rebecca had left Rebecca's home at Willowbank in Bellefonte to visit William Shortlidge, a cousin and friend of Pugh. The Shortlidge family lived in "Forge House," a large manse built in 1804 that still stands on the bank of Logan Branch of Spring Creek. After the couple arrived, the Shortlidge children—Elizabeth, then seven, and Annie, age five—were sent upstairs to bed, "but thrilled over the presence of the great College president in their home, they lingered over the upstairs rail and listened to the conversation."

Eventually, Pugh and Rebecca took their leave, the two daughters watching from an upstairs window on a "very dark night" as their parents saw the couple off. "Minutes later, from Spring Creek opposite Forge House, they heard a voice called 'Shortlidge, come help! Shortlidge, come help!' The buggy had gone off the ledge and into the stream below. The occupants were thrown out, and Evan Pugh's arm was broken in two places. With his one good arm he managed to lift the buggy and rescue Rebecca who had been rendered unconscious by the fall."[4] Walker's account of Pugh's nearly superhuman strength was no exaggeration. Even with his injury, Pugh had sufficient muscle power to rescue his fiancée. A former student recalled of Pugh, "I have never seen a stronger man. . . . I have seen him take a barrel of oil by the chines and put it into a wagon. Very tall, with immense chest and Samson build."[5] Today, a century and a half later, it is difficult to locate the exact spot where the accident took place. The distance Pugh and Rebecca traveled from her home at Willowbank, crossing the old Spring Creek Bridge in downtown Bellefonte, to Forge House is one mile. As described by the Shortlidge daughter, the accident happened very soon after the couple left Forge House. Pugh sought help at the nearest place and Forge House, then as now, was the only edifice in the vicinity; no other structures stood nearby.[6]

In Rebecca Valentine, Pugh had fallen for the most desirable woman in Centre County. Valentine was intelligent, beautiful, polished, and steeped in the ornamentals—the cultural knowledge and trappings, including music, poetry, literature, languages, art, sewing, and needlepoint—deemed essential for well-bred Victorian women. Her niece and namesake, Rebecca Pugh Lyon, described her as "clever, with a sense of humor, quick on the repartee and extremely attractive."[7] She was the cynosure of her affluent family, who, like Pugh, were Welsh Quakers. Her father, Abram, was the leading ironmaster of Bellefonte and an authority on the geology of Pennsylvania and Centre County in particular, which is why Pugh, who taught mineralogy and geology, was interested in meeting him. Also like Pugh, Abram Valentine and his family originally came from Chester County. The Valentine family became wealthy early on, moving into a large, elegant limestone mansion, named "Willowbank," astride Spring Creek proper. Although the Valentine family eventually sold Willowbank, the building still stands, albeit a mere shadow of its former glory; its interior has been subdivided into apartments and its exterior is in need of repair and restoration.

Rebecca has been described as "very intellectual." She could speak German and she loved poetry, Schiller's in particular—qualities that no doubt attracted Pugh. For her part, Rebecca considered Pugh to be "a genius" and she wanted him to "fulfill his destiny." They often spoke about England. She thought if he had remained there, or if he could return to England, "his chances for recognition would have been greater." The couple's marriage was short-lived, lasting not quite three months, Pugh dying by the end of April. Rebecca lived until 1921, but never remarried, though she had prominent suitors knocking at her door. Her niece recalled that, before she met Pugh, "no man had been able to hold her interest. After his death no other man ever seemed so interesting."[8]

Pugh's broken arm, which had been badly set, required more sophisticated medical attention than could be found in central Pennsylvania. Two weeks after the Battle of Gettysburg had concluded, he left the college for Philadelphia, arriving on July 18. There he consulted with Dr. George W. Norris of Pennsylvania Hospital, undergoing daily treatments. Norris was highly trained in his specialty. He had earned his A.B. and M.D. degrees at the University of Pennsylvania, had studied in Paris for two years, and in 1848 was appointed professor of clinical surgery at the University of Pennsylvania. His first publication was on the fracture and dislocation of the astragalus, one of the bones of the foot.[9]

As it turned out, Pugh's left arm was broken in only one place, but the bone was failing to fuse, a "non-union of the fracture." Norris's prognosis was that, with the arm "well secured" and with Pugh's remaining still and quiet, the arm would heal in six to twelve weeks, which, at the outside, would have kept Pugh from returning to campus until late October.[10] He stayed at his ancestral home in Oxford, Chester County, for recovery, making frequent trips into Philadelphia to see Norris. By the second week in August, Pugh was required to see his physician only once a week. On August 11, he reported to McAllister that the doctor thought he could detect the fracture getting stiffer, "and hence slowly uniting," expressing confidence that if Pugh gave the arm "absolute rest, it will unite."[11] Near the end of August, he reported that Norris had advised him not to attempt to travel to the college. "He says that if I save the arm at all it will only be by persisting in keeping it quiet."[12] On September 18, Pugh told Samuel Johnson, "My arm is slowly mending and will I trust come out all right."[13] By early October he had returned to the college. "We are getting on pretty well," he told Johnson. "My accident has put us back and I am still far from being fit for duty but must do something. My humerus has united but my elbow is very stiff as are all the joints below it."[14] By December, the injury had improved but was still causing some discomfort: "My broken arm is at work again quite stiff at the elbow but getting better," he told Johnson.[15] By then, Pugh had been through six months of physical pain and discomfort, not to mention the mental and emotional distress caused by his absence from the college and his fiancée from mid-July to early October.

Among Pugh's greatest concerns during his convalescence was finding a well-qualified replacement to teach his courses in chemistry and agricultural chemistry. He knew that upon his eventual return to campus, he would need to catch up on pressing college business and could not afford to return to teaching. He also learned that his advanced students were quite distressed that their educational progress was being delayed by his absence. Pugh needed to find a substitute professor, and fast, but he also needed to find one who would meet his standards. Thus he prevailed upon George C. Caldwell, a Göttingen Ph.D. who at the time was professor of chemistry at Antioch College in Yellow Springs, Ohio. Pugh and Caldwell had roomed together for a time as students at Göttingen and since then had kept their friendship alive. Pugh had the highest regard for Caldwell, investing him with nearly the same esteem he held for Johnson.

Pugh wrote to Caldwell before leaving for treatment in Philadelphia. The reply came on August 6, not from the professor, but from his wife. Caldwell had been suffering from illness all summer, made worse from overexposure while horseback riding. Nevertheless, he was willing to come. Pugh had only to say when he needed him. There was a complication, however: Caldwell had noticed in the local newspaper the night before that he had been appointed "'by the powers that be' to an office in the army of the United States—in other words drafted. I think he will be exempted."[16] Caldwell wouldn't get to the Agricultural College until the end of September, and he could stay for only the remainder of the academic year in December, as his call to duty would take him, with his scientific expertise, to a post with the U.S. Sanitary Commission in Washington, D.C. Pugh told Johnson in mid-October that Caldwell was "now here taking my classes while I am attending to neglected business details. He can remain only a few weeks." By the end of the semester, Caldwell had reported for duty in the nation's capital.[17]

Despite Caldwell's departure, Pugh continued to champion him for various positions at other colleges but especially for the position of chief chemist with the U.S. Department of Agriculture, the position that Pugh had twice turned down. He asked Johnson for help in that regard: "He is just the man for it and I am urging his appointment with all my might. . . . Dr. Caldwell is a most worthy fellow morally, mentally and *habitually* (by which I mean his habits of study and the amount he has studied)."[18]

Caldwell would return to the Agricultural College of Pennsylvania as professor of chemistry shortly after Pugh's death, persuaded to do so out of his sense of loyalty to his deceased friend and colleague. In doing so, Caldwell became the second consecutive Göttingen Ph.D. in the post, sustaining the continuum of high-quality instruction in chemistry and agricultural chemistry at the institution, at least for a time.

The Civil War and Its Effects on the College

Pugh's efforts to build the Agricultural College of Pennsylvania into the model institution of its kind took place amid the worst crisis in American history. However isolated the college may have been in its rural midstate valley, the Civil War was far more than a distant concern. Indeed, it intruded in ways both large and small.

When hostilities broke out in April 1861, during the institution's third year of operation, Pugh sought to keep the place from emptying out as war fever gripped the North. An alumnus recalled that, after Lincoln's initial call for 75,000 volunteers for three-month enlistments, the place nearly burst with excitement: "It seemed that nothing could hold the boys to their school duties, and that the Farmers' High School, was, for the time, doomed." Pugh called the students to the chapel and calmed things down somewhat. The alumnus, John I. Thompson, Class of 1862, could not recall Pugh's precise words but did remember Pugh's lines of reasoning. "One was that the war would not be fought out by 75,000 men just called, that it would not be ended in 90 days, that it was to be a struggle for years, and that all who were there assembled could remain and continue their education . . . and still have ample time to do their duty to their country in the mighty conflict just commencing." Pugh's other appeal was sentimental. Young men between sixteen and twenty were especially dear to their mothers; accordingly, "they should keep out of the war until they had passed the 20 years line."[19]

Notwithstanding his Quaker upbringing and the creed's pacifism, Pugh hated the Confederacy for its defense of slavery and dissolution of the Union. He wished the southern traitors dead and gone: "I have made up my mind to give the rebel leaders two years to repent before being hung, 6 mos. to leave Virginia, Kentucky, and Missouri, 6 more mos. to be beaten away from the Mississippi River and one additional year to run about dodging our army before they are hung. . . . I thank God that we now have a chance of killing men who I have long been satisfied never would be brought to reason in any other way."[20]

Nonetheless, Pugh did not want *his* students leaving for the "chance of killing men," but some of them left anyway. Pugh wrote to Johnson in early June 1861 that about fifteen students had gone off to war and that "had I not been here I would have been off—I would leave my quakerism at home till we could give those traitor scoundrels such a thundering thrashing as no people ever got before."[21] A couple of months later, he told Johnson that the school's first class was about to graduate and that he had just "shipped off ½ dozen to the war . . . who could not graduate."[22] Student departures continued throughout the early years of the war, though it was a trickle, not a torrent, never threatening to shut down the college. Even so, war fever was never far from erupting. In 1862 a number of students formed a military company and drilled on campus with ersatz wooden muskets.

In September 1862, as Robert E. Lee's Army of Northern Virginia invaded Maryland and the threat grew closer to home, the college's vice president, David Wilson, formed a volunteer company, based in nearby Boalsburg. Pugh was reluctant to see Wilson depart, as Wilson was away from campus all too frequently in Pugh's view. But he conceded the just cause behind it and the proximity of southern troops threatening Wilson's home. "If it is necessary we must give up all and go," Pugh told McAllister. "I do hope that there will now be no half way work about this matter, but that all who offer will be taken that we may move down upon these traitors 1,500,000 strong and finish the bloody work now and forever."[23]

At Antietam on September 17, 1862, Lee was turned back across the Potomac and the threat of southern invasion ended—for the time being. Ten months later, the threat was back in south-central Pennsylvania. The Army of Northern Virginia was coming off resounding victories at Fredericksburg in December 1862 and Chancellorsville in May 1863, and Lee's blood was up: It was time, once again, to bring the war to the North. On June 15, 1863, Lincoln issued a call for 100,000 volunteers—50,000 of them from Pennsylvania alone. Governor Curtin reiterated the call. On June 19, advance units of Lee's army had already crossed into Pennsylvania's lush Cumberland Valley, soon threatening Chambersburg, York, and Wrightsville, with a contingent entering the

Gettysburg area on June 26. Lee's original objective was to encircle Washington from the north, demonstrate southern invincibility, and compel the Union to sue for peace. But the plans were going astray, as the gathering storm in this small Pennsylvania town would prove.

Students of the Agricultural College of Pennsylvania responded in force to defend their native soil. Those who were of legal age, not requiring parental consent, enlisted immediately. Many went to their hometowns to join local volunteer militia companies. But thirty-one students united with other Centre County men to form a company of 100 under the command of Captain John Boal of Boalsburg, and were dispatched southwesterly into Somerset County, which bordered Maryland (rebel bands were reported to be roaming across Pennsylvania's southern tier). By June 27 the college had nearly emptied out, but it did not shut down. Still reeling from his unmending broken arm, Pugh feared that the ill-trained students would be less than effective as soldiers, especially going up against Lee's battle-hardened troops. Pugh told McAllister that he had sent a letter to the parents of the students who had left with the militia. He was anxious that they might be kept in service longer than ninety days, especially if the invasion were not countered. "We are going on as usual though with very diminished numbers," he said. He regretted that he had not made a greater effort to "hush up the wild and foolish excitement" that took so many students away. He doubted they would make "efficient soldiers" and worried that too many had left without the consent of their parents.[24]

As it turned out, the Union army would prevail at Gettysburg, ending the threat of southern invasion, and by late summer the college would come back to its usual life. But memories of those years would never fade. At the college's semicentennial celebration in 1905, alumnus John I. Thompson recalled with pride the college's response to the War of Rebellion: "From the time when Johnny Martin in 1861 laid down his life for his country—when gray haired Professor David Wilson in 1862 led a company to Chambersburg to assist in repelling the invasion of Maryland which threatened Pennsylvania, when all in the School who were old enough enlisted in 1863—to the time Tellico Johnson with his 100 days men marched away to the war in 1864—each student of the Farmers' High School stood ready for service at the beck and call of his country."[25]

Dissension and Political Intrigue during Pugh's Absence

The buggy accident, the invasion of Pennsylvania, the medical treatment in Philadelphia with the long absence from campus, and the effort to find a faculty member to teach his courses weren't all Pugh had to worry about in the summer and fall of 1863. Students had begun returning to campus in the weeks after the Battle of Gettysburg, as the volunteer emergency militias were discharged.[26] C. Alfred Smith, Pugh's assistant, noted that about 105 students were back on campus as of early August, including about a half dozen new ones.[27] Their numbers continued to increase as the weeks wore on, and soon nearly all of the students who had dispersed to fight the rebels had returned. But many of them, particularly the advanced students, were dismayed by the absence of their chemistry professor, which disrupted their academic progress. And Pugh's absence from his students weighed just as heavily on him. "I am very much concerned about our two oldest classes," he wrote to McAllister in mid-September. "I understand they are very much dissatisfied that they are not getting on in my own department." The students' complaints and that of their parents "disturbs my peace very much when I am unable to do anything to efficiently remove the cause of complaint."[28]

Caldwell didn't make it to campus until the end of September, about the same time that Pugh returned from his convalescence in Chester County. "It will be much better for you to remain away until you can return able to perform or at least to see that they are performed properly," Smith wrote Pugh in late September. "The students should feel unsatisfied to see you here and still unable to attend to them."[29]

But the more serious crisis involved a sub rosa attempt to turn the Board of Trustees against Pugh and have him removed from the presidency. Engineered by a certain "Doctor Thompson" of Centre County—not to be confused with Moses Thompson, the Centre Furnace ironmaster who was serving as secretary of the Board of Trustees—the coup attempt fizzled out soon after Pugh returned. But the plotting unnerved Pugh as he learned about it while still recovering in Oxford. His assistant Smith got wind of it, determined to learn more, and filled Pugh in via letter. Apparently, Thompson had handed a letter signed only by himself to trustee A. O. Hiester, the evening after the fall board meeting when Pugh was absent. The letter spoke of Pugh's incapacity to continue serving as president.

A few days later, Thompson was boasting to others that he was going to have Pugh removed from office, at which point Smith—always Pugh's most ardent champion—decided to intervene. Smith asked Thompson to visit him in the chemistry laboratory, and then confronted him about his intentions. Thompson was caught off guard. He did not deny Smith's accusation but tried to turn the matter into something "very funny and pleasant." Smith continued pressing him for motive. Thompson denied any personal malice, and said his effort was undertaken, only because 'it was not that I loved Caesar less but Rome more.'" Thompson told Smith that he did not wish to see Pugh removed entirely from the institution—that he could still teach chemistry—but he was unfit for the presidency. "He provoked me intensely," Smith said. "I talked to him pretty severely for sometime and I do not think he will trouble me with his presence very soon again." Apparently, Thompson also had given Hiester a list of prominent Centre County men who he said would corroborate the case again Pugh. "There is a very strong feeling against you," Smith told Pugh, advising him to talk to Hiester to learn more about how the trustees might have been influenced.[30]

However Pugh resolved the internal political threat, things began to improve as October progressed. Caldwell had arrived on campus and was carrying Pugh's teaching load, and Pugh himself, a formidable presence wherever he went, was back in resumption of his duties. By early November, campus life had returned to something resembling normality. But still weighing on Pugh was the completion of the college building. Though construction would be finished for the most part by the end of December 1863, the process had dragged on at least a year past the original deadline of November 1862 as shortages of labor and materials continually retarded progress. Pugh also suspected the contractor, George W. Tate of Bellefonte, was not pushing hard enough to get the project completed. In June 1863 he wrote to McAllister, demanding that the contractor be "hastened to finish."[31] After his return to the college in October, Pugh focused on getting the new kitchen ready for use and for the coming visit of the building inspector.[32] The privies also needed to be finished "at once." Painting remained to be completed. Pugh wanted to have as much work on the college building finished as soon as possible before the winter break in mid-December so as to "leave a good feeling" among the students before they departed. A few days before Christmas, Pugh complained to McAllister that the contractor had a "perfect opportunity" to finish up, given the absence of students, but was not taking advantage of it.[33]

The year 1863 ended not only with the departure of Caldwell but also with the resignation of Vice President David Wilson, whose last day in office was December 16. Pugh had never seen eye-to-eye with Wilson and periodically urged the trustees to ask for his resignation. The object of Pugh's ire was Wilson's frequent absences from the school. Wilson had never been able to get his wife to move from his home near Port Royal, Pennsylvania, and settle permanently at the college, and thus was making frequent extended trips

FIGURE 20   *The College Building after completion in 1863.*

home to tend to family affairs. Of course, Wilson, like Pugh, was quartered in the all-male college building, hardly a suitable environment for a wife. Therefore, Pugh was always looking for ways to build a house on campus for Wilson or at least have him living closer in Bellefonte. Wilson had been hired not by Pugh but by the trustees in May 1859, and thus it was the trustees, not the president, who held the authority to terminate his employment.[34] Pugh began asking McAllister to push the trustees to request Wilson's resignation as early as the summer of 1861 and would continue doing so as the situation warranted.[35] In June 1863 Wilson's wife fell ill and he left for home for an extended stay, seriously complicating Pugh's life in view of the buggy accident and the Confederate invasion of Pennsylvania.[36]

Despite the train of disruptions beginning in June 1863, Pugh managed to complete the college's catalog for the same year. He summarized the state of affairs positively, portraying a bright future for the institution. Noting the "interference" posed by the Confederate invasion of Pennsylvania, and the large numbers of students volunteering for service, he observed that they "returned in time to make very satisfactory progress in the studies of the

Session." (Pugh, however, made no mention of his injury or long absence from the college.) The imminent completion of the college building meant that "the process of completion will no longer interrupt the progress of the students." Especially noteworthy, the institution had a reached a record enrollment. "It is also a larger number than have been during the same time in attendance upon any other Agricultural College in this country or in Europe," he observed.

Concluding the report, Pugh predicted that the Morrill Act would provide the means to put the college on a sound financial footing, but not immediately. "It will be some time yet before the College will derive any pecuniary aid from this source, but it will ultimately enable the trustees to employ competent professional aid to fully develop all its several departments, and thus elevate the standard of industrial education to the scientific character of that of the best educational institution in the world."[37]

Pugh's Master Plan for American Industrial Colleges

Trying as 1863 was, 1864 would bring even bigger battles to Pugh's doorstep—battles for the continued life of his school and, ultimately, for his own life. During his convalescence, Pugh and the trustees got wind of a building interest among certain state legislators and private colleges to rescind or revise the state's act of acceptance of April 1, 1863; the intent of these adversaries would be to use the Morrill Act fund in other ways—principally to benefit other Pennsylvania colleges.

To counter the growing insurgency, Pugh produced a sweeping manifesto, his masterwork as a champion of industrial education: *A Report upon a Plan for the Organization of Colleges of Agriculture and the Mechanic Arts, with especial reference to the organization of the Agricultural College of Pennsylvania in view of the endowment of this institution by the land scrip fund donated by Congress to the State of Pennsylvania*. Ostensibly, the plan was addressed to the trustees and presented to them during their meeting in Harrisburg on January 6, 1864. But there was a much larger audience in mind, and the trustees immediately authorized the printing of 3,000 copies, to be widely circulated.[38] Particularly notable in this document is the quick pivot of Pugh and the trustees in advocating for *industrial* colleges (including the mechanic arts or engineering) and no longer for purely agricultural colleges, in conformance with the broader intent of the Morrill Act.

In creating a detailed framework for industrial higher education, Pugh's organizational plan became the most far-sighted document of his day. The seminal land-grant historian Earle D. Ross called Pugh's plan an "elaborate report" constituting "the most complete and understanding contemporary statement of the financial and educational requirements of land-grant education. . . . The most thorough and understanding early analysis, both informing and interpretative."[39]

Pugh called for industrial colleges to be organized on a large scale, of a size comparable to that of Harvard, Yale, and Columbia, then the leading American institutions of higher learning. Even so, these three institutions did not constitute the competitive set Pugh envisioned for American industrial colleges. Even the best American colleges and universities were inferior to those of Europe, he stated categorically. And the reason he gave was that America's best, despite their comparatively large faculties and endowments by national standards, were far underfunded and undersized compared with their European counterparts. Pugh's gold standard was the European university, not the American, and he wanted the nation's industrial colleges to equal if not exceed the quality of Europe's best.

Relying on Child's *National Almanac for 1863,* Pugh presented statistical data for the roughly 220 extant American colleges and universities. Categorizing them on the number of faculty members, Pugh showed that there were 41 institutions with two to five faculty; 97 with six to ten; 20 with eleven to fifteen; 6 with sixteen to twenty; 4 with twenty-six to thirty; and 3 with more than thirty-six. Selecting institutions with at least 15 faculty members, endowments of at least $400,000, and annual expenses of $12,000 or more, he drew up a set of 18 such institutions: Bowdoin, Dartmouth, Harvard, Amherst, Brown, Yale, Columbia, University of New York City, New York Free Academy, Union, Rochester, Vassar, Princeton, Penn, Philadelphia [Central] High School, Girard, Michigan, and Illinois (the normal school, not to be confused with the present-day University of Illinois, which was not operational until 1868). He found that the average number of professors was twenty-five and the average endowment $600,000. Despite their resources, Pugh characterized them as deficient. In all of them, he found "an absence of that *thoroughness* which characterizes the highest order of study. With very few exceptions, we will find Professors obliged to teach *too many* different things to teach *anything* very thoroughly, or to keep themselves posted on the progress of knowledge, in their own department, in the learned world."[40]

He looked at the three institutions with the greatest annual expenditures—Harvard, Yale, and Columbia—and then focused on Harvard, whose annual expenses at $153,431 were twice that of the other two. Harvard's income was provided by three sources: endowment, which at $1,613,884 was second only to Columbia's slightly larger such fund ($1,650,666) and provided the largest source of income, about $89,000 (5.5% in earnings); tuition, which supplied $50,782; and "sundries," which brought in $12,753.

Pugh proceeded to show how even that amount—$153,000 for the year—was penurious for what Harvard was trying to accomplish. He talked first about faculty salaries, reporting that the annual instructional budget was $44,680, divided among forty-three individuals. Nearly all, he lamented, received lower salaries "than men of the same degree of attainments and application would receive in any other profession." Although Harvard was America's greatest college, its "educational standard is much below that of the best Universities of Europe." The institution spent about $14,400 annually for its scientific school, "yet the graduates of this school are constantly going to Europe to complete their scientific education" (7–8).

And if Harvard was lagging far behind its European counterparts, the rest of the American field was doing much worse, "for want of additional funds" (9). With that, Pugh had found the opening he needed to criticize "the avidity with which, in some States, they have grappled for the proceeds of the Land Grant by Congress." Pugh was particularly appalled that "none of these Institutions before had attempted to develop departments for Agriculture and the Mechanic Arts, and many of them had taken especial pains to show, that substantial education must be based upon classic culture, and that the modern idea of tending towards a substitution of scientific education for the study of Latin and Greek, was a pernicious result of the too utilitarian spirit of the age" (10–11).

Next, Pugh turned to the resources he deemed necessary to support industrial colleges. He began his analysis, however, by addressing the philosophical issue of whether industrial institutions should be elevated to the highest educational standard or left to merely subsist as inferior schools. In Pennsylvania, he noted, the question had already been answered in appropriating the Morrill Act funds to the Agricultural College. He argued that industrial education must be predicated on principles and laws, embracing the "entire range of human industry . . . and almost the entire range of human thought."

The American system of industrial education must be scientific in character, he added, encompassing "the entire range of the Natural and Physical Sciences" and supported by endowments "equal to those of the best educational Colleges in the country." Finally, he observed that the class of students industrial education is designed to reach "are generally persons of *small income*:

The education they receive is calculated to benefit *society in general more especially* than themselves in particular" (11–12).

To organize an industrial college properly, Pugh called for a faculty of professors, including the president, and assistants, numbering at least twenty-nine. The president, he said, should be a "scientific man . . . because the expenditures for *material*, as *auxiliaries to study* in a Scientific College must always be great, and they are such as can only be properly *regulated, encouraged* and *controlled* by a scientific man" (15). The major faculty would include professors of mathematics and the higher mathematics and astronomy; civil engineering and applied mathematics; pure chemistry; agricultural chemistry and geology; metallurgy, mining and mineralogy, and chemical technology; anatomy, physiology, and veterinary; natural history, especially zoology, comparative anatomy, and entomology; botany, horticulture, and entomology; practical agriculture; English language and literature; modern languages, particularly German and French; and—"though not indispensable to a system of industrial education"—Latin and Greek languages and literature; military art, science, and tactics; and a treasurer, bookkeeper, and librarian. Ten assistant professors and two superintendents would bring the number up to twenty-nine—the minimum number that might be employed, not the maximum, as Pugh stressed (18).

College facilities would include not only the necessary classrooms and lecture halls but also much more in the way of "auxiliaries to study," as Pugh called them. Of necessity, an industrial college, as opposed to a literary college, must have "much more space devoted to Natural History collections, museums and store-rooms for models of tools and machinery, and for scientific apparatus, laboratories, and rooms for scientific investigations, etc." In addition, he observed, the industrial college should be able to accommodate between 400 and 800 students—quite large by the standards of the day, but essential to realize economies of scale (18).

Pugh said industrial colleges must emphasize research as much as instruction. In every academic department, they must be "experimental Institutions, no less than for teaching what is already known in science." The faculty must be researchers as well, not content to teach "what is known in their several departments," but "who could extend this knowledge by their own researches, and they should be provided with means for this purpose" (22).

Pugh called for industrial schools to incentivize student achievement and provide financial aid. He advocated for prizes acknowledging meritorious academic performance, a beneficiary fund for indigent students, and free scholarships based on merit. He also described the particular challenges of academic requirements for admission—"since there are no subordinate schools to prepare students for Industrial Colleges as there are Academies to prepare them for Literary Colleges." The solution, he offered, was to establish elementary or preparatory departments at industrial colleges, "in which students can be prepared to enter the regular College course" (24).

Students should be given some choice, within limits, on selecting their final course of study. But this would occur only after becoming conversant with the basic branches of all the natural and physical sciences. The student, in his advanced years, "should be taught the method of original research." And, ideally, the student's education should not conclude with the conferral of the bachelor's degree. Rather, he should be encouraged "to continue longer in the institution, as a resident graduate, and make original scientific investigations upon such subjects as well most directly bear upon the special industrial operations of life to which he expects to be devoted" (25).

Pugh recommended four major programs of study: (1) a course of agricultural science and practice, such as "that now pursued at the Agricultural College of Pennsylvania"; (2) a course of engineering and architecture, embracing a higher and lower course, according to mathematical ability; (3) an industrial course, relating "more particularly to a practical and scientific knowledge of those industrial operations which are the offspring of the Natural Sciences . . . Metallurgy, Technological Chemistry, Pharmacy"; and (4) "a purely practical course," for students who are "too old, or may not have time, or who are too delicate to stand the close discipline of a more extended course," as well as for "grown up men" who may not have had the advantages of a scientific education and who want to gain such knowledge. Pugh also called for two ancillary programs: a commercial course, "to make students familiar with the laws of trade and commercial intercourse"; and, in the spirit of the Morrill Act's retention of classical studies, a literary department bent not so much to Latin and Greek but instead to modern languages. The standard classical studies such as logic, rhetoric, moral philosophy, and political economy would be offered not as college majors but as adjuncts to the other departments. If students wanted to work toward a literary degree, they "could easily do so afterwards by going to a Literary College" (25–28).

As for endowments, Pugh stressed that, because their students are less affluent, industrial colleges "require as large endowments, as do Literary Colleges, if not larger." An industrial college endowment should generate, minimally, $27,000 in earned income annually. To this would be added tuition, which he estimated would bring in $20,000 based on 400 students paying $50 per year. The income from these two sources, $47,000, would support: sixteen professors at $1,500 per year—$24,000; ten assistants at $400 per year—$4,000; a farm superintendent, $700; janitor and helpers—$1,000; additions to museums, scientific apparatus, and library—$5,000; scientific investigations—$5,000; indigent students, soldier's orphans, free scholarships—$7,000; and building repair—$1,000. Accordingly, these total annual expenses would amount to $47,700. Even with that, Pugh argued, the industrial college budget was hardly adequate. Faculty salaries were not as high as they were at literary colleges (29).

The central question for Pugh was whether an endowment income of $27,000 per year could be generated from the sale of land scrip. He had his doubts. "Owing to the general depreciation of public lands this land scrip will not bring nearly as much as was anticipated at the time the bill was drawn up and hence the income . . . will be less than half what it otherwise would have been," he said. Pugh judged that annual income from the sale of scrip at the Agricultural College of Pennsylvania would fall between $10,000 and $20,000. That was not enough to allow the institution to develop as fully as Pugh had described, but it would allow it to succeed to the point where, he hoped, philanthropists would provide gifts to lift the endowment higher (30).

In his conclusion, Pugh excoriated private literary colleges for not only failing to meet the needs of the rapidly industrializing nation but also insisting that the only proper education for practical duties in life was to be found in the study of Latin and Greek. "The idea of Industrial Education," he continued, "was turned into ridicule, and Industrial Colleges were denominated visionary ideals of impracticable men." The Morrill Act's purpose, Pugh said, was to endow entire industrial colleges, not simply to establish industrial chairs in literary colleges. "That Literary Institutions should, with such undignified haste, grasp at resources (secured for the endowment of Industrial Colleges) to which they had not the *slightest legitimate claim*, is a melancholy illustration of the terrible extremities to which they are driven in the struggle for existence."

Pugh questioned the ability of literary institutions to implement industrial education in any legitimate way. "Can they with their half dozen professors, do the work which fourteen first class scientific men are required to do, in addition to teaching all their literary studies? No! They would only degrade Industrial Education to the standard upon which they have heretofore looked with merited contempt" (31–32). Pugh also questioned why the state's literary institutions waited so long to act in clamoring for a piece of the Morrill Act's bounty. They had made no attempt to obstruct or influence the legislation during its congressional gestation. They knew full well that the only actors in supporting the legislation were "the friends of the Agricultural College" (33).

After Pugh's organizational plan had been presented to the trustees on January 6 and sent to the printer in Philadelphia, a bill was moved in the Pennsylvania legislature stipulating that one-third of the land scrip be designated for Allegheny College in Meadville. Pugh rushed to the printer an addenda protesting the move, arguing seven points: (1) the land-grant fund would hardly yield enough to endow one industrial college; (2) two or more colleges would not be able to provide industrial education efficiently and effectively; (3) the Agricultural College was a state institution, the state having already appropriated $100,000 for its support; (4) the Agricultural College could not effectively use its property without the land-grant endowment; further, the College abstained from asking the state for an endowment in view of the pending success of the land-grant bill; (5) the friends of the Agricultural College secured the passage of the land-grant bill; (6) the Agricultural College had no other endowments and, if it should be removed, the institution would be more dependent on the state; and (7) Allegheny College was not a state institution; it had no idea as to how to provide industrial education. Pugh defined it as a "local denominational literary school" (33–35).

However cogent and forceful his argument, Pugh would not carry the day. New attempts at kindred legislation benefitting additional private colleges and other causes would soon pose a formidable threat, consuming Pugh's attention and adding to the stress that would hasten his death.

CHAPTER 9

The Battle Royal

PUGH'S ORGANIZATIONAL PLAN FOR industrial colleges of January 6, 1864, presaged a bitter battle in the state legislature during the ensuing winter and spring. Private colleges and their champions in the legislature would vigorously contest the designation of the Agricultural College of Pennsylvania as the sole beneficiary of the Morrill Land-Grant College Act—a designation granted by that same legislature the year previous but with a proviso allowing for a change of mind.

These efforts at recession revealed misunderstandings of the Morrill Act that were naive in some quarters, intentional in others, as legislators proposed a variety of "uses" for the land-grant fund. Various political interests attempted to modify, repeal, and even annul the state's acceptance of the terms of the Morrill Act. Attempts were made to split the fund to benefit additional colleges; to divert it to a fund to educate the children of Civil War veterans; to use it for the common schools of the Commonwealth; and to establish new, separate schools for agriculture, the mechanic arts, and military science.

Not a little of the opposition to the Agricultural College derived from the strong bias in favor of private denominational colleges and against any kind of incipient public institution of higher learning. That bias, in fact, extended across the northeastern United States, where private colleges had proliferated, dominating the educational landscape. Toward the end of his life in 1906, George W. Atherton, the seventh president of the Pennsylvania State College, wrote a personal memorandum that referenced the private college bias that persisted well into the 1880s: "The idea of State support for Higher Education was then practically, if not theoretically, dead in Pennsylvania, but the maintenance of the State College has now come to be accepted as one of the regular objects of the care of the Legislature. Only those who have labored in this field, in the older States east of the Allegheny Mountains, can have any conception of the amount of labor involved in bringing about such a change."[1]

In addition to the first bill, favoring Allegheny College in Meadville, six other bills were introduced to the House and Senate during the spring session—a veritable land-grant rush. Oppositional legislators seized upon language in section 4 of the act of April 1, 1863, which stated, "That until otherwise ordered by the Legislature of Pennsylvania, the annual interest accruing from any investment . . . is hereby appropriated . . . to the Agricultural College of Pennsylvania."[2] They interpreted the words "until otherwise ordered by the Legislature" as being provisional and temporary, using the Agricultural College as a placeholder until they could apportion the funds elsewhere. The other major line of objection had to do with the disposition of the land scrip—when to sell it, and for how much. There was talk in early March that the land scrip would probably fetch about 30 cents an acre; oppositional legislators wanted to set a minimum price below which the land scrip would not be sold—80 cents, even $1.05 per acre, seemed to be the minimally acceptable amount.

The State House representative from Centre County, Cyrus T. Alexander, reported to trustee McAllister that he had been watching "the movements of the land thieves that infect this capital." The House committee, he said, is "likely to report in favor of dividing it into three parts," for Allegheny College, the Polytechnic Institution, and the Agricultural College. Alexander felt fairly confident the bill could not pass the Senate but was not so sanguine about the House, where he suspected a "strong effort . . . to procure passage of the bill." He advised McAllister or Pugh to come to Harrisburg to lobby against the effort.[3]

Ultimately, the most significant House bill (H.B. 809) would apportion the fund to five institutions in addition to the Agricultural College: Allegheny College, the University at Lewisburg (Bucknell University), Pennsylvania College (Gettysburg College), the Western University of Pennsylvania (University of Pittsburgh), and the Polytechnic College of the State of Pennsylvania. Of the two dozen or so private colleges in the Commonwealth, the only other institution that might have had some legitimate claim on the land-grant fund was the Polytechnic College. Founded in 1853, and privately endowed, this Philadelphia institution had carved a name for itself in the mechanic arts and engineering, the other half of the Morrill Act's purpose. The

Polytechnic was the first college in the nation to grant bachelor's degrees in mechanical engineering (1854) and mining engineering (1857).[4] Nonetheless, Pugh and the trustees had quickly and smartly pivoted in the fall of 1863 and winter of 1864 to position the Agricultural College as ready to embrace the mechanic arts and everything "industrial education" encompassed. They also pointed out that the Polytechnic had ventured into scientific agriculture and failed miserably. That much was true. As the historian of higher education in Pennsylvania wrote, "Although a department . . . of agriculture had been announced from the outset, its instruction, for want of farming facilities, was almost wholly theoretical." By the early 1890s, the Polytechnic College had closed its doors forever.[5]

Preoccupied as he was with countering the opposition, Pugh finally found time to marry his fiancée, Rebecca Valentine, now sufficiently recovered from the buggy accident of June 1863. They planned their ceremony during the college's vacation period, which would last until mid-February, and were wed on February 4, 1864, at her Willowbank home in Bellefonte. The newlyweds departed for a brief honeymoon in Philadelphia. They also planned to visit Samuel Johnson and family in New Haven, Connecticut, but had to cancel that trip as Pugh had to return to the college and prepare for the legislative battles ahead.[6] Upon their return, Pugh continued to reside in the main building, biding his time until the president's house on campus could be finished and present a suitable home for the couple. Rebecca, in the meantime, continued her residence in the family home at Willowbank—twelve miles distant from campus. Still, they managed to see each other and, as he told Johnson, he was now "a most happy man."[7] The open question is whether this might have been the first commuting marriage in American higher education.

Whatever marital bliss Pugh might have enjoyed did not last long. Upon his return, he became engaged in two major efforts to defeat the proposed legislation that would remove or alter the Agricultural College's exclusive claim to the land-grant fund. The initial effort was to invite members of the Pennsylvania legislature to campus to see, firsthand, the institution that, despite the war, was thriving with a record enrollment of 146 students. In addition, the college building had been substantially completed in December, so Pugh and trustees deemed it time to showcase the college for the lawmakers. Their discussions about the desirability of a legislative visit began in November 1863 and their decision to proceed was made amid a fair degree of ambivalence. "I think it would be wise to ask the Legislature to visit . . . with the Understanding that no Whiskey be furnished on the occasion," trustee

A. O. Hiester said. He added, however, that trustee president Watts would not approve of inviting them because "he has no very exalted opinion of them, and . . . all that we now require is to be let alone." The larger fear was that if they became more familiar with the college, "they may be disposed to tinker with the management of the institution."[8] Trustee Daniel Kaine, himself a former legislator, also expressed strong reservations: "I think you had better *not do it*," he told Pugh. "Your report will be laid before them, and those who feel any interest in the institution will inform themselves, without going there. From my own experience in Legislative visitations, I am not in favor of them."[9] Eventually, the trustees determined to go ahead with the visit. The invitation, dated February 26, came from Watts to all members of the House and Senate, asking them to "appoint an early day to visit the institution."

Senator Henry Johnson, who represented Lycoming, Clinton, and Centre counties, and who would be the college's most ardent champion in the Senate, read the invitation to the upper chamber on March 1. Johnson then asked for a resolution appointing a committee of three to meet with House representatives, who had passed a similar resolution the night before, to figure out a suitable date for the visit. The response was surprising. The resolution passed, but by only one vote, 16–15, prefiguring the battle lines that would stay in force all spring long.[10]

The visit took place on March 18–19, but no record exists of precisely who attended. It was, however, reported to be "a goodly number." Tellico Johnson, then a student at the college, said, "We had everything put in ship shape, fires in all the furnaces lighted, laboratory stoves and furnaces running full blast, everything in the way of apparatus on display, a big dinner prepared, turkey, ice cream, everything the best and plenty of it. . . . The members of the Legislature and their wives and State officials inspected everything and then sat down and ate their fill. Dr. Pugh told me he was afraid the dinner would cost more than the College would get out of it."[11]

It is difficult to sort out what effect, if any, the visit had. It may have done nothing more than harden existing opinions on either side of the issue. In all the debates of the spring, there are only two references to the campus visit. Senator Henry Johnson, the college's champion, said every senator who had visited concluded that the college "required and demanded for its continued and successful operation the further aid and assistance of this State." The college's special advantage for the Commonwealth, Johnson emphasized, was that it was "calculated to accommodate a very large number [of students] at a lower rate than in any other institution." Senator James L. Graham of Allegheny County, chair of the Education Committee and an opponent of the college, voiced an antithetical view: "The opinion of some of the gentlemen . . . was that it was a failure, and that this grant to that college ought to be revoked, and these lands distributed over the State for the benefit of the masses of the people."[12]

The second major effort of the spring, preceding the legislative visit, was Pugh's appearance on March 3 before the House Judiciary Committee in Harrisburg. The testimony Pugh gave was afterward printed and circulated widely, with an addendum that addressed the several points of criticism from certain lawmakers to the original statement.

Pugh's argument boiled down to a defense of why all of the interest from the sale of land scrip should be devoted to a single institution, as opposed to having it split among several. One proposal submitted to the committee called for dividing the fund among three or four institutions, letting each one establish a professorship of agriculture and the mechanic arts and a professor of military tactics. Another proposed dividing the funds among a large number of private colleges—"literary institutions," as Pugh called them—that would be required to apply for the funds. A third proposal envisioned establishing three separate schools in three different locations—one a school for agriculture, another for mechanic arts, a third for military science.

"Any proposition to combine industrial education with such professional education, as is given in Literary Colleges, is impracticable, because so widely different must be the habits, the tastes and the aspirations of the students of one class, from those of the other class, that they cannot possibly be properly educated together in harmony," he asserted. It would be impossible to juxtapose industrial students required to do manual labor with literary students who would "spend the hours of manual labor in idle recreation."[13]

Pugh objected even more strongly to the proposal to use the fund to establish three separate institutions. Instead, agriculture and the mechanic arts should be combined in a single institution because of their complementarity. "Both are branches of industrial education, both associate the idea of manual labor and study, and both represent interests so inseparably connected." The strongest reason for conjoining the two, he added, is to economize the educational resources of each, "since many of the professorships would be common to both." Last, he argued that the land-grant fund would be barely sufficient "to endow one first-class Industrial College," much less several (2–3).

Then, Pugh laid out the case for the ideal industrial college, building on the organization plan for industrial colleges published just two months earlier. In that plan, Pugh had estimated that the annual cost of sustaining such a school would be $47,000—covering sixteen professors and ten assistant professors, as well as several departmental superintendents, in addition to the costs of maintaining libraries, museums, laboratories, equipment, and other essentials. Pugh qualified that number as being the bare minimum of required faculty; even so, he added, they would be at extreme disadvantage because the faculty members "have at least twice as much assigned to them as would be assigned to the same Professor in a German University, and yet the natural sciences in a German University are not taught more thoroughly than they should be in an Industrial College" (3–4).

Pugh argued instead for a "medium" number of faculty members to staff a competent America industrial college. He called for thirty professors and twenty assistants, as well as a large number of superintendents. Again he pointed to Europe, where the universities "of the highest order have much more thorough and efficient courses of instruction than American Institutions," with concomitantly larger faculties. He cited Leipzig and Göttingen, which each had about 110 professors, and Berlin with 168. The European advantage lay not so much in their buildings, laboratories, or facilities, he pointed out, but rather "in the large number of their Professors and the profoundness which necessarily results from this large number and from their unceasing devotion to the subjects they teach" (4–5).

Industrial colleges, Pugh emphasized, must go far beyond teaching; they must also promote scientific research, and their faculties must be of adequate number to allow each faculty member to engage in such work. "The scientific Professor or Professor of Natural Sciences, as he is generally called in those [American] Colleges where one man must teach all the sciences, has no time to keep himself posted on the progress of science, much less to make investigations." Research was especially important at industrial colleges, he added, "because they are devoted to subjects which need much more investigation before they can be taught with entire satisfaction" (5).

Pugh was making the case for a critical mass of faculty members, students, and resources at industrial colleges, in proportions that far exceeded the average size of the two dozen or so private colleges in Pennsylvania. In many respects, he was envisioning the modern research university, which, in America, lay decades in the future. The annual operating budget for his "medium" ideal college would be $87,800 per year—$56,000 in faculty salaries and $31,800 for scientific research, museums, indigent students, and building maintenance. Even at that, his budget represented "a little more than half the annual expenditure of Harvard University" (6).

After making the case against a division of the land-grant fund, he turned his argument to why the Agricultural College of Pennsylvania should be the exclusive beneficiary. The institution was the only state institution "especially devoted to the object for which the Land Scrip Fund was donated to the State." The demonstrably public character of the Agricultural College, in contradistinction to the private, sectarian character of the two dozen literary colleges across the Commonwealth, was paramount. It was, in fact, the only college of its kind "belonging to the whole people of the State and controlled by them, as its property is held in trust by a Board of Trustees elected by delegates from all the county agricultural societies in the State, together with the Executive Committee of the State Agricultural Society." In addition, the Agricultural College had been in operation "longer and more successfully than any other Industrial College ever has in the United States. It has had a larger number of students, and hence enjoys a higher degree of confidence than any other." Its only other need was "an endowment to enable it to fulfill its entire mission of usefulness" (7).

Pugh reminded the legislators that the college had promised not to ask the state for an endowment, anticipating instead that the Morrill Act would provide that resource. "The Agricultural College . . . cannot exist without this fund, and unless it can be shown that this Institution should cease to be a State Institution, and should cease to be an Industrial College, and should have none of the Fund, it should have it all." If another state institution should be established, and have a stronger claim, then the entire land-grant fund should go to it. "The Agricultural College of Pennsylvania, like the Hebrew mother before Solomon, would rather see her child given undivided to a usurper, and die herself for want of its support, than share with them the mutilated fragments of what could only effect the object of its existence by being undivided" (7).

Citing both the $200,000 investment the state had already made in the Agricultural College and the school's $40,000 debt, Pugh cut to the heart of the matter: Unless a better industrial college were to be established, why should Pugh's institution be allowed to "struggle in poverty" sinking ever deeper in debt (7)? "You will either give to them [the people of Pennsylvania] one Grand Institution like Harvard University, or the world-renowned Educational Institutions of Europe, which will unite all the interests of Industrial Education in our State; or you will transit to them a number of petty Institutions, jealous of each other, who will come up to succeeding Legislatures to exhibit their poverty, and dispute with each other about whatever means of support may seem to be within reach of their needed hands" (8).

Pugh's repeated references to European universities apparently rankled some members of the legislature. To address their criticism, he attached addenda to his published remarks that were circulated immediately following his appearance before the House Judiciary Committee:

To the objection that he was trying to build a German-style university in central Pennsylvania, Pugh said decidedly not, "except in the *one item* that it will teach all those sciences which *relate* to agriculture and the mechanic arts *as thoroughly* as they are taught in the German University."

To the objection that the system does not educate "the masses," Pugh responded that a division of the land-grant fund "prevents the education of any body properly, and deprives all of the means and results of scientific investigation, without which all scientific teaching must be very poor and inefficient."

To the objection that the Agricultural College was far removed from factories and industrial operations of a city, Pugh said that was true to some extent, "and yet within easy access to the students we have furnaces, forges, rolling mills, woolen factories, foundries, machine shops, iron, coal, lead, and zinc mines . . . and all in one of the richest fields for geological students in the world,—at the same time that we have such advantages for farm practice . . . as the student never can have except he lives in the country." Here, Pugh may have been stretching the point, as many of the industrial facilities he mentioned were small in scale with some of them obsolescing.

To the objection that each religious denomination should have some of the fund to use in their own colleges, Pugh said the same objection "might be made to the making of appropriations to normal schools, to military schools, to asylums, to the army, and to many other great public enterprises. . . . Let not the only chance of this state having an efficient system of industrial education be defeated by *sectarian prejudice*."[14]

However well constructed, however forcefully presented, Pugh's testimony before the House Judiciary Committee argument would not stay the efforts to divide the land-grant fund. Over the next few weeks, into early April, it did seem as if the matter had been tamped down somewhat, with the various bills still in committee but not reported out to either House or Senate. It was the proverbial calm before the storm. "We have had a long hard fight on the Land Grant Fund—we have outflanked the enemy and spiked his guns but the infernal guerrillas still hover around in the shape of anonymous correspondents," Pugh wrote Samuel Johnson on April 1; ". . . I still have some fears though they are very much allayed. I have been honored with a little ill will and vile criticism for my services but hard words break no bones."[15]

Then things erupted. On April 14, Senator William J. Turrell of the Education Committee and a fierce opponent of the Agricultural College, introduced S.B. 809. This bill fixed a minimum price for the sale of land scrip at 80 cents an acre. More ominously, it ordered that the fund be split into six equal portions benefiting six institutions: Allegheny College in Meadville, Polytechnic College at Philadelphia, Agricultural College in Centre County, Pennsylvania College at Gettysburg, University at Lewisburg in Union County, and the Western University at Pittsburgh. Furthermore, the bill stipulated that the colleges were to advance the money to the Commonwealth at 80 cents per acre for their respective shares, until such time as the scrip had been sold and the land-grant endowment was generating interest. Annual reports were required and tuition was to be free "for the sons of the citizens of Pennsylvania." The colleges were required to accept the terms of the act, and any failing to do so within a year would be removed as a beneficiary with the remaining lands divided among those colleges that did accept the act.[16] S.B. 809 infuriated Pugh, and it was in protest against this measure that he would write his last words eight days later. But ultimately the act was not called up, debated or voted upon. In the meantime, it weighed heavily on Pugh's mind.

At the time, the situation was deemed serious enough that Centre County's congressional representative and Agricultural College trustee, James T. Hale, arrived in Harrisburg to confer with Senator Henry Johnson, whose district included Centre County. Hale had lobbied effectively in the Pennsylvania legislature the year before for the passage of the act of acceptance, and was concerned that things were getting out of hand. "I have been looking after our bill and think the prospect fair for its defeat," Hale wrote to McAllister on April 15. The Senate committee had reported out the bill for a six-way division, while the House committee simultaneously reported out against taking any action on the bill during the current session. "So that while the Senate bill passes and goes to the House there is no danger and I do not think it will pass but a little attention may be necessary."[17] As things turned out, the House would not be nearly as docile as Hale had predicted.

Instead, the Senate turned its attention to S.B. 617, "An act repealing portions of an act of 1863, in regard to the distribution of the proceeds of the public lands for educational purposes." S.B. 617 had been in gestation for weeks. It was introduced out of the Senate Education Committee on April 5, called up by Committee Chair James L. Graham of Allegheny County on April 19, and debated at length. Senator Henry Johnson argued to keep the bill in committee, to no avail. Senator Hiester Clymer, of Berks County, a leading proponent of repeal, delivered the consensus of the opposition. "Those of us who were here last winter will recollect that it was well understood that this grant was merely temporary," Clymer said. "No other institution seemed to be in a position to comply with the terms required by the act of Congress." Clymer conceded that the Agricultural College might be entitled to a share of the fund, but because it had already received comparatively large amounts of state funding, it was time to split the new bounty "between three institutions."[18]

S.B. 617 did not designate the particular colleges to which it would direct the funds, but it repealed sections of the legislature's acceptance act of April 1, 1863, removed the Agricultural College as the sole beneficiary, fixed a minimal price for the sale of land scrip, and set the stage from which the Senate could designate specific beneficiaries in a future session.

One of the issues was whether passage of the bill to repeal would somehow invalidate the legislature's act of April 1, 1863, to accept the terms of the Morrill Act. Senators favoring the Agricultural College argued that a repeal would invalidate the original act. Those opposing argued otherwise. Senator Morrow Lowry of Erie, an opponent of the Agricultural College, said, "[W]e chose to do it [designate the Agricultural College as the recipient] at the time we accepted the grant; but we surely reserved intact the power to alter the destination of that fund . . . and today we say that we revoke that disposition of the lands. We have four years in which to appropriate them. We do this to preserve the great benefit of this fund to the State, leaving it to ourselves to say how it shall be distributed hereafter" (745). To drive the point home, Senator Clymer introduced a proviso to S.B. 617 that said that nothing contained within the bill "shall be so construed as to revoke, annul, or in any manner invalidate the acceptance by the state . . . as provided by the act of General Assembly."

Some argued for a legislative addendum that would order the committee charged with the disposition of the land scrip—the governor, the auditor general, and the surveyor general—to sell the land immediately so that appropriations could be made to various other institutions. Others opposed such interference, preferring to allow the committee to use its best judgment as to whether and when the sales should take place, according to market opportunities. Senator Turrell noted that a sister bill (S.B. 809) purported to distribute the fund to "four or six institutions," provided that those institutions would pay 80 cents per acre. "If this fund so raised, were distributed to a large number of institutions it would be more beneficial than if confined to one" (746).

Despite attempts by proponents of the Agricultural College to postpone a second reading of S.B. 617, the body voted 18 to 13 to consider it further.

The bone of contention in the ensuing debate was whether and where to set a minimal price for the sale of the entitled public lands, although, as one opponent of the Agricultural College, Senator William Hopkins of Washington County, reminded his colleagues, "I trust that we will not suffer our eyes to be closed to the main question—the repeal of so much of the act of 1863, as gives to this college the entire proceeds of the sale of this land" (747). Ultimately, two amendments to set the price for sale of the lands were defeated, 22 to 9 and 25 to 7.

During the debate, Senator Johnson made an impassioned plea not to repeal the previous year's act until such time as the disposition of funds in regard to other recipient institutions could made—which Johnson doubted could ever take place: "this Senate should refuse to repeal the act until a bill making an alteration in the disposition of this fund among a number of institutions . . . shall have been fully considered." It would be an act of treachery for the legislature to deny the Agricultural College's claim to the fund, Johnson charged. The legislature would be depriving the college not only the needed money but also its reputation, in essence declaring that that the college "is not entitled to our confidence" (748).

The Senate debate continued the next day, April 20, and Clymer again thundered against the Agricultural College. Estimating that the sale of the land scrip at 80 cents per acre would yield a fund worth about $640,000, he said, "It is perfectly apparent that this fund is too large for any institution, unless that institution should center within herself all the different educational interests of the State. Now, it is admitted that the Farmers' High School does no such thing" (771). Clymer's argument then degenerated into accusations of local interest: "I appeal to the Senator [Johnson] whether it is the part of duty, generosity or interest to demand that this whole sum shall go to his district, especially when it has already received one hundred thousand dollars for educational purposes, and we are to give it twelve thousand dollars a year more." Johnson held his ground, appealing to the Senate not to repeal the act until it found a more qualified institution: "You have opened the doors of these halls for a general scramble. . . . And . . . leaving the matter open for future consideration . . . is a bid to the institutions of this State to come here and importune Senators . . . to make this a mere scramble for the spoil."

Johnson got some help from his allies. Senator William Wallace defended the Agricultural College as a state, not a local, institution: He accused Senator Lowry of Erie of characterizing the situation as nothing more than a donation to Centre County to enhance a local institution. To Wallace the issue was "whether we are to have an institution of the Commonwealth, not a county institution, but an institution which, devoted to the purposes of the act of Congress, shall be co-extensive with the State, and in every sense of the word, a State institution." As for dividing the land grant among several institutions, Wallace cited the example of the New England states. Harvard and Yale emerged as great institutions, he claimed, because "the States that created them have nourished them and extended their aid to them as State institutions; they have made magnificent bequests to them, while we have seen fit to divide out to north, south, east and west these magnificent bequests. It is wrong in theory, wrong in principle and vicious in practice" (772).

But Johnson, Wallace, and their allies did not win the day. The Senate voted 20 to 12 to accept the Clymer amendment for repealing the act so as to eventually divide the land-grant fund. The amended bill, however, was to be given a "third reading" and acted upon. The next day, April 21, the bill was introduced with Clymer's amendment, repealing sections 3, 4, and 5 of the acceptance act of April 1, 1863. Section 4 had directed that the interest from the fund be apportioned entirely to the Agricultural College. Section 5 had required the college to make an annual report to the legislature. In addition, the amendment repealed section 3, which had given the commission carte blanche in the matter of disposing of the land scrip; the amendment now required the commissioners to dispose of the land scrip at not less than 80 cents an acre, the proceeds to remain with the state treasury until otherwise ordered. As Clymer explained, his amendment left the original act intact, except for repealing "the disposition of the fund made to the Farmers' High School." Further, he argued, the commission's power to market the scrip was left intact except for the new proviso "that they shall not sell the land scrip for less than eighty cents per acre."

Senator James Graham of Allegheny County put the nail in the coffin of the Agricultural College: "It must have been apparent to every gentleman who has noticed the course of argument . . . that if the proceeds of the sales of these lands are to be taken from this Agricultural College they must be taken now." Graham characterized the college as a failure and wanted "these lands distributed over the State for the benefit of the masses of the people." In what may be considered as the ultimate insult to Pugh, he added that any college offering chemistry might "lay claim" to the fund (776).

Johnson tried to parry the amended bill one more time, emphasizing that no other institution of the Commonwealth qualified for the fund. He proposed that a special commission be appointed to examine all other institutions in Pennsylvania to judge their qualifications, and if any exceeded those of the Agricultural College, he would be willing to accept the results. His motion was voted down, however, 22 to 10. Clymer's amended bill to repeal the Agricultural College's exclusive designation as the land-grant recipient and to set a minimal per-acre price for the sale of the land was passed by an overwhelming margin, 23 to 9. But the Agricultural College had not lost the fight quite yet; Senate approval was only the half the battle, the House the other half—and then, of course, the governor's concurrence.

As an eloquent, forceful advocate for the Agricultural College, Henry Johnson may have lost the battle in the Senate, but he would score a profound legislative victory on a different front during that same fateful year. Born in 1819, and nearly a decade older than Pugh, Johnson graduated from Princeton in 1837 and practiced law in Muncy, Pennsylvania, near Williamsport in Lycoming County. Elected to the state Senate in 1861 as a Republican, he afterward enlisted as a private in the Pennsylvania militia and took part in the Antietam campaign of September 1862 and then mustered out. To help get Lincoln re-elected in the November 1864 general election, he pushed through a bill that lowered the voting age in Pennsylvania to eighteen for those in "actual military service." That allowed Pennsylvania soldiers to vote, and vote they did for Lincoln, providing 14,000 of the 19,000 votes by which the Great Emancipator carried the Keystone state and thus won re-election.[19] Johnson could win the day for Lincoln but not for the Agricultural College.

Word of the Senate's deliberations beginning April 14 and extending through April 21 got back to Pugh quickly and turned him livid. The following day, Friday, April 22, from the desk in his chemical lecture room, Pugh wrote a howling protest against S.B. 809 (which, as it turned out, didn't gain consideration by the Senate). He didn't mince words: "The effect of the bill is virtually to squander the entire proceeds for all time to come of the magnificent grant of public land from Congress to this state for the purposes of industrial Education." Incredulous that a majority of the Senate would agree "to sacrifice this munificent gift," he called on the state's agricultural and industrial constituencies "to visit a speedy rebuke" upon the responsible parties. Should the legislature's action stand, "we may well despair of any progress amongst the industrial classes of our country."

Pugh detailed the flaws in the bill. To the section requiring that the scrip be sold for not less than 80 cents per acre, Pugh said it would prevent "a single acre from being sold until New York (now selling about 1,000 acres per day at 73 cents per acre) sells nearly a million of acres." If other states followed suit,

FIGURE 21 *Chemistry Room where Pugh gave his last lecture.*

the competition would preclude Pennsylvania's selling any land for years to come. "Had the author of the bill by malicious design intended to frustrate the sale of the scrip he could not have done it better than by the 1st section of the bill." As for the distribution of the fund equally among six colleges, five of them were "not only private but merely local in the sphere of their operations and sectarian in character." The Agricultural College of Pennsylvania, Pugh insisted, was "a bonafide state Institution, originating under state patronage, built by the State and now owned by the State as truly as are the Legislative halls in which this monstrous act of legislation was passed. . . . We are mistaken if the Agricultural constituencies of the State don't see equally clearly the manner in which this Legislature attempts to swindle them & the State out of the only means they have of sustaining the only state institution in the State. . . ."[20]

There the jeremiad trailed off. These were the last words Pugh would ever write. He was seized by a violent chill, followed by fever. Still suffering, he rallied to present a lecture to the senior class in the chemistry room, but afterward became too sick to do anything more and went to his bed in the college building. The following day, he was persuaded by C. Alfred Smith, his closest friend at the college and his chemistry assistant, to go to Bellefonte "and enjoy with his wife the rest and care which he could not hope to obtain at the college." Smith said that Pugh "made light of my solicitude as to his condition and his last remark as he took a seat in his buggy was, 'I am tired, my brain is tired, but I have a body that will stand everything.' That strong body only served to feed the fever which consumed him."[21]

Friday, April 22, was fateful for another reason. S.B. 617 as amended was now gaining traction in the House. At issue was whether to remove the bill from the purview of the Judiciary Committee and put it before the full House for resolution. The clock was ticking. The legislative session in both chambers was originally slated to end on Saturday, April 30. S.B. 617, at least before amended, was a virtual replication of the bill that had been originally introduced to the House as H.B. 993. In the House, the bill was assigned to the Judiciary Committee, before which Pugh had testified on March 3. In the Senate, it was assigned to the Education Committee.

Actually, the House was where more of the action had been taking place, specifically in the Judiciary Committee. Over the course of the session, six bills had been referred to the committee dealing with the redistribution of the land-grant fund among several institutions. A seventh bill, the most recent to be introduced, sought to distribute the fund for the education of orphans of war veterans, with the remainder going to the common schools.[22]

With the House Judiciary Committee now considering S.B. 617 as amended the day before, the enemies of the Agricultural College made no bones about their intentions. They wanted to get it out of committee and onto the floor for debate and vote. Representative Bryan A. Hill said,

> I dare assume that more than one half of the gentlemen on this floor doubt whether it [the land-grant fund] will be properly and economically expanded, if it be left where it is. There is a kind of recklessness of expenditure about the manner in which that institution is conducted which . . . has driven me to the conclusion that, if it be left where it is, the whole thing will be squandered with very little profit to the people of Pennsylvania. Two hundred thousand dollars, we were told by the president of that institution, have already been expended up there; the institution is forty thousand dollars in debt, and that debt is accumulating every year.

Hill accused Pugh of telling the committee in March that "eighty thousand dollars or eighty five thousand dollars annually . . . would be insufficient to sustain such an institution as he was ambitious to build up in Centre county. When I heard that remark, I deliberately made up my mind that it was a most visionary affair, and that it would not be safe to leave the proceeds of this vast fund at the disposal of those who managed that institution." Hill was also distressed that Pugh had told him "that the land scrip was not worth more than thirty cents on the acre. That was named as a reason why the Centre county college should have the whole of it. . . . Now . . . some of the institutions of the State have offered to take at eighty cents per acre any portion of it that this Legislature may put at their disposal, and to pay the money in advance."[23]

Like Johnson in the Senate, Cyrus T. Alexander, the House representative from Centre County, would take up the mantle of championing the Agricultural College in the lower chamber. Born in 1836, Alexander was considerably younger than Johnson, however. He graduated from Dickinson Seminary in 1853 and joined the Centre County bar in 1859, while also pursuing business interests in a limestone quarry and later becoming part owner and editor of the *Democratic Watchman* newspaper in Bellefonte. An ardent Democrat, he was elected to the state House in 1863 and to the state Senate in 1879.[24] On April 22 Alexander jumped into the fray: "He [Hill] was surprised at the 'reckless extravagance' of this Agricultural College, or as he chose to term it, the 'Centre county institution'—with a kind of sneer upon his tongue as he uttered it," Alexander said. "It is not a Centre county institution! . . . It is a State institution, in which the people of the county of Erie have as much control as the people of the county of Centre; because the directors of that institution are elected by representatives chosen by every agricultural society in the Commonwealth."

Representative Cyrus L. Pershing, another opponent of the Agricultural College, took a more temperate view of the matter: "I was last session favorably disposed to a proper division of this fund. The act of Congress itself plainly contemplated that some of the States might have more than one institution in which the branches prescribed in that act should be taught." While Pershing favored appropriating the fund "for the time being" to the Agricultural College, he felt that "its location was such that it could not accommodate all those who might seek the benefits of such an education as that prescribed by the act of Congress."[25] Representative Hill wanted quick action on the bill so that land could be sold immediately: "Before the next meeting of the Legislature, a large amount of this land will, in all probability, be thrown upon the market by other States. Is Pennsylvania to tie her hands and sit down with folded arms until the market is flooded with the land donated to other States?"

The vote to discharge the bill from the committee was approved 48 to 36 and the subsequent motion to put it onto the floor was approved by an even wider margin of 49 to 34. The bill was then read to the full House, with another proposed amendment pegging the sale of land at $1.00 per acre. Alexander jumped back into the debate, this time filibustering by reading parts of Pugh's earlier reports recounting the history of the institution from 1853 to the present, and also reading from more recent documents about the institution's mission, purposes, and ambitions. As he ended his remarks, one representative asked him, "What is the meaning of these words in the act, 'one or more colleges'?"

"The State can establish one or more agricultural colleges if it sees proper, and divide the fund among them after it sells this land scrip and has a fund to divide," Alexander responded. "But at present it has only one institution of the kind designated by the act of Congress, and until it does establish such other institutions the Agricultural College of Pennsylvania is entitled to it all." The other institutions laying claim to the fund "should have waited until this scrip was sold, and then if it proved too much for the endowment of one institution, they could ask of the State to donate them the surplus as a charity."

Alexander also tried to tamp down expectations that the scrip would produce a veritable bonanza: "Owing to the present inflated currency and the spirit of speculation, it may net you forty cents per acre, or, for the whole, three hundred and twelve thousand dollars, the interest of which will be eighteen thousand seven hundred and twenty dollars. But this fund cannot all be realized for a number of years, as it should not all be thrown upon the market at one time" (926–27).

Alexander's forceful speaking carried the day, or at least the evening. He concluded his final remarks at 10:00 p.m., when the speaker discharged the weary House. On Thursday, April 28, however, the House resumed its work. Under the business item of committee reports, the Judiciary Committee came out with negative recommendations for all of the bills regarding the division of the land-grant fund save the current S.B. 617 as amended. This committee report began with a negative recommendation to the "act to appropriate to Allegheny College, in the county of Crawford, a portion of the land scrip fund held by the State of Pennsylvania." It was followed by a negative recommendation for two supplements to that same bill as well as negative recommendations for four more related acts involving the other colleges (928).

Still in play, however, was S.B. 617 as amended, which would remove the land-grant designation from the Agricultural College and establish a baseline of 80 cents per acre for the sale of scrip. Then came a pause in the action. In deference to Representative Alexander, who asked to be excused so he could attend Pugh's funeral, the House postponed consideration of S.B. 617 as amended until Wednesday, May 4, when it voted by the slimmest of margins, 45 to 44, to consider the bill (1044). Once again, Alexander seized the day, this time deploying a practical argument about the inability of the land scrip sales process to produce any money in the immediate future: "not an acre of this land scrip has been sold. . . . Though these commissioners may do the best they can, they cannot get this land scrip in the market sooner than four or five months from this time. They will then be required to invest the proceeds of the sale in of United States stocks. It will be six or eight or ten months longer before any interest will accumulate upon that investment, so that before the next annual meeting of the Legislature, the State Agricultural College will not receive any benefit from this land scrip." Alexander could see no use in passing the bill "at this time." Doing so would not benefit the other institutions laying claim "because it is conceded on all hands that the bill dividing this fund cannot now pass both Houses this session."

Alexander offered an amendment that would authorize the commissioners to sell the land scrip for a minimum of 80 cents an acre and to hold the proceeds in escrow in the state treasury "until otherwise ordered." The Agricultural College was retained as the beneficiary, but it would not gain benefit of the interest until and unless the legislature approved such a measure. Alexander's amendment was not agreed to, but he nonetheless had hit the soft underbelly of the House. Time was running out. Representative George H. Wells offered an amendment simply to prevent the sale of the scrip until the next meeting of the legislature, in the meantime removing any assignment of it to any college, including the Agricultural College. The offered amendment went nowhere, however.

Then procedural issues intervened. For any legislation to pass into a signable law at the end of a session, the rules required a two-thirds vote for both the House and Senate. Even if that might have been theoretically possible, another rule required that "no bill or resolution to which the signature of the Governor may be required, shall be passed by either house on the day of the final adjournment." And the day of final adjournment was Thursday, May 5.

With those procedural barriers looming larger by the minute, Representative Arthur G. Olmsted moved "that further consideration of the bill be postponed indefinitely." The House approved the motion, 47 to 44, and there the matter ended, at least for the time being (1045). The Agricultural

College of Pennsylvania did not receive a positive vote to continue as the sole beneficiary of the land-grant fund, but it narrowly avoided a negative vote that would have rescinded its status.

On the following day, however, Thursday, May 5, the last day of the session, the college's opponents made a last-gasp effort. Representative Wells sought to get a vote on a motion of "expression of opinion" that the land scrip not be sold for anything less than $1.00 per acre. The motion would carry no authority, but would at least convey the "sense of the House" if passed. Representative Robert A. McMurtrie put an end to it:

> I thought that we had yesterday finally disposed of this question, but it seems that the friends of different colleges . . . are determined . . . to gobble up this money which should legitimately go to the Agricultural College in Centre county. . . . We yesterday voted to postpone the question indefinitely. . . . I think that the classical colleges and their advocates ought to absent themselves from this hall for at least the remainder of this session. We have had them here all this session annoying the Legislature about the land scrip. Yesterday . . . they received a quietus, and I trust that we shall not this morning revive their drooping energies.

After further debate, Representative Alexander called for a vote on the resolution "for the expression of opinion." It was defeated, 40 to 35 (1058).

With that, the legislative session of 1864 ended, though the issue in question would come back to haunt the Agricultural College again in subsequent sessions. For the time being, however, the Agricultural College retained the full benefits of the Morrill Act endowment, although no land scrip had been sold and not a penny earned. At best, it was a Pyrrhic victory, the college having lost its forceful young leader in the climactic heat of the battle royal.

CHAPTER 10

Death and Aftermath

The Senate's work on Senate Bill (S.B.) 617 had ended in its passage the evening of Thursday, April 21. The House took up the bill the following Friday morning, just as Pugh was writing his protest against the Senate's S.B. 809. Before he could finish his tirade, he suddenly was overcome with chills and fever. Taken to his wife's home, Willowbank, in Bellefonte, on Saturday, April 23, Pugh would linger abed, his condition worsening as the week wore on. Toward the end, he slipped into delirium, but even in that state, he kept "working," talking profusely to relevant audiences.

His admiring protégé, C. Alfred Smith, traveled to Willowbank on Thursday, April 28, and stayed until the end. Smith knew Pugh "as perhaps no other person could have known him. He stood to me somewhat in the relation of a father and I looked up to him and loved with the tender regard of a son." Smith stood by his bedside and "saw his eyes close in death." It was 10:15 p.m. Friday, April 29, exactly two months after Pugh's thirty-sixth birthday. "That voice which, for many hours, in the midst of delirium argued before an imaginary audience of Legislators or before College Classes, lectured upon Chemistry, was forever hushed in death," Smith recalled. With his passing, the Agricultural College of Pennsylvania and the land-grant college movement lost "a soul utterly unselfish, a man whose life was a period of unswerving devotion to the welfare of his fellowman."[1]

What killed Evan Pugh? The ostensible cause, according to various historians, was typhoid fever, a disease caused by the *Salmonella typhi* bacterium and

FIGURE 22
*Pugh's grave in Bellefonte's
Union Cemetery.*

spread through contaminated food and water or close contact with a carrier. Now rare in the United States and the developed world mainly because of improved public sanitation and antibiotics, typhoid fever, also called typhus, was a scourge of nineteenth-century America. The disease presents itself through fever, malaise, abdominal pain, and constipation. Untreated, typhoid fever is "a grueling illness that may progress to delirium, obtundation, intestinal hemorrhage, bowel perforation," and a relatively quick death.[2]

But those who knew Pugh attributed his demise to other causes as well, a concatenation of the trauma of a badly broken arm, sheer overwork, and the crescendo of stress he encountered upon his return—stress culminating in the near passage of legislation that threatened to undo everything he had fought for. Smith cited the accident and its aftermath as having contributed to what would be described today as a weakened immune system. One can only imagine Pugh's frustration and despair in those final hours of lucidity, before

the delirium set in, as he foresaw the prospect of his life's work—the first successful, scientifically based agricultural college in America—being destroyed
by the Pennsylvania legislature. He would not live to see the final vote in the
House only six days later, which preserved, for the time being, the status of the
Agricultural College of Pennsylvania as the sole beneficiary of the land-grant
endowment.

The buggy accident of June 1863 had taken an insidious toll. In his letters to Johnson and McAllister, Pugh presented an improving picture of his
broken left arm, despite the very slow process of the bone's reuniting itself.
But he was taken out of circulation, removed from the college for two and a
half months, and was never quite the same. As Smith recalled, "Nearly eleven
months after the injury, the arm was still nearly useless." From the consequent
strain on his system, Pugh "never fully recovered, and in this accident was laid
the foundation of the disease which finally terminated his useful career."[3]

As for stress, there was more to it than the unrelenting political battle of
the winter and spring; there was the chronic stress of building and leading
a new experimental college. In today's parlance, Pugh would be dubbed a
workaholic, typically working past midnight yet rising every morning at 5:45
a.m. to take on the daily torrent of demands and obligations, from the profound to the ridiculous. Pugh once said his ideal amount of sleep was seven
hours—"With less I can't do and more I don't want"—but as president he
seldom had the luxury of so long a nightly slumber.[4]

Pugh did just about everything required to build a college from scratch.
He was at once the head teacher, researcher, curriculum organizer, student
recruitment officer, personnel officer, business and finance officer, promoter,
publicist, lobbyist, strategist, disciplinarian, procurer of supplies, superintendent of the physical plant, construction supervisor, and much more.
From today's perspective, he might have been labeled a micromanager, but
he was determined to build a successful institution and would leave nothing
to chance. Indeed, he poured his fortune, such as it was, into the institution—$500 per year out of his $1,500 annual salary to purchase laboratory
supplies and equipment and an additional $1,000 out of the same salary to
build the president's house that was never finished during his lifetime.

The completion of the college building was a preoccupation. The construction project took more than four years from the time Pugh set foot on
campus in October 1859 until it was substantially finished in December 1863,
just four months before his death. The nearly $50,000 building appropriation
that Pugh and the trustees won from the legislature in 1861 meant not only

the difference between life and death for the college but also between life and death for an entire movement, absent its capstone institution. Without proper accommodations for students and facilities for the educational programs, the college couldn't grow and achieve its efficient scale of 400 students. And there were other facilities, besides the college building, that Pugh brought on line. By the winter of 1863–64, the college boasted a large barn, blacksmith and carpenter shops, a granary, and other outbuildings, not to mention orchards, fields, fences, and the other concomitants of farm life.

In all of this work, Pugh had a source of constant support in trustee Hugh N. McAllister of Bellefonte. Indeed, McAllister was of special help to Pugh, in part because of his proximity but much more because of his willingness to do anything and everything to support the college. Trustee president Frederick O. Watts, of Carlisle, Pennsylvania, also was key in providing guidance and support for Pugh. Never did they waver in the confidence they had placed in him.

As for research, Pugh had great interest but little time to devote to it. He did manage to conduct analyses of commercial fertilizers as time allowed, typically engaging students in the investigations. Pugh was on a lifelong crusade to rid the market of the many fraudulent fertilizers developed by manufacturers looking for cheap and easy profits. Through his chemical analysis, Pugh exposed numerous "quack" products—generally made from cheap blends of leached ashes, common loam, and a little gypsum and falsely labeled as rich in superphosphates, which barnyard manures lacked. Pugh published his results in *Farmer and Garden* and other popular farm journals and urged the state and national governments to develop uniform standards for labeling such products. Prompted in part by moral outrage over the ways in which farmers were being cheated, Pugh deemed this work of utmost importance in demonstrating to the farming community the practical benefits of scientific agriculture.[5]

Rebecca Valentine Pugh, a bride of less than three months and a widow for fifty-seven years, contended that the college had killed him, through overwork and stress. She would not return to campus until 1890, when she consented to be part of ceremony in which the Class of 1861 presented an oil portrait of Pugh to the college. She also is reported to have visited the college in 1905, during its semicentennial celebration.

Rebecca never fully recovered from her husband's death. She never remarried, though she had more than a few eminent suitors seeking her hand. Rebecca's niece said Rebecca's long life was "unhappy" after her husband's death. "Her grief over the loss of Evan Pugh was always with her." For the rest of her days she always wore, on a chain, the watch Pugh had given her as a wedding gift.[6]

Rebecca eventually moved out of Willowbank, the family home where Pugh died. She bought a house, still standing, on West Curtin Street in Bellefonte, where she spent the remainder of her life, and where she died on July 7, 1921, at eighty-nine years of age. Rebecca was buried beside Pugh in the Valentine family plot in Bellefonte's Union Cemetery. The Bellefonte *Democratic Watchman* eulogized her as having lived "a beautiful and useful Christian life . . . she was noted for a beauty of feature and brilliancy of mind that attracted men of prominence and education."[7]

Occurring quickly and unexpectedly as it did, Pugh's death came as a shock to everyone, not least his students. On April 30 the student body quickly drafted a resolution, which was sent to newspapers across the Commonwealth: "To his unwearied and cordial devotion to our interests, and his quick and clear perception of our needs, is largely due the success which has thus far attended us," they said, recognizing that their future would be impressed with "the stamp of his character and his labor." En masse, the students attended Pugh's funeral in Bellefonte on May 3.[8]

Bellefonte's *Democratic Watchman* ran the obituary on May 2, calling the loss to the institution "almost irreparable." Describing the manifold difficulties the college had faced in its opening years, "through the energy and untiring efforts of Prof. Pugh, all this was overcome and it is now considered a fixed institution worthy to be copied after."[9]

Another testimonial stated, "He had before him a career second to that of no one associated in name and labors with the progress of American Agriculture, and his untimely death is a loss, not to the farmers of Pennsylvania only, but to those of the whole country, and to the friends of agricultural education in every state."[10] Thomas P. Knox of the Pennsylvania State Agricultural Society wrote to McAllister that Pugh "was a man of rare abilities, a scholar, and one of nature's noblemen . . . his place will not be easily filled."[11] Dr. Alfred L. Elwyn, the trustee with whom Pugh had corresponded from Germany nine years earlier about the prospect of a position at the Farmers' High School, sent his testimonial far and wide. Pugh, he said, "had to go through the almost desperate struggle . . . of attempting to place a new idea before indifferent and unprepared minds . . . we could never perceive that he had a selfish purpose, or any purpose but that of making the Agricultural College the first institution of its kind."[12]

The Board of Trustees, which had not met since January 6 in Harrisburg, convened on June 15 in the college building, some six weeks after Pugh's death. The trustees resolved, "That we now appreciate more highly than ever the value of his devoted attachment to the interests of Agriculture, his disinterested services to the Institution over which he so ably presided and the industry with which he prosecuted his noble purpose to elevate the public mind in its appreciation of the agricultural science."[13]

In England, in the Hertfordshire newspaper, an obituary appeared on August 2. "Evan Pugh has made us feel a much stronger interest in and regard for that country from which he sprung, in that nation whose son he was so proud to be called. . . . Our loss is indeed irreparable, and to us his place can never be filled."[14]

The *American Journal of Science and Arts* published Pugh's obituary in its September 1864 issue, calling him "one of the most able scientific men of this country." Written by his colleague and confidante Samuel W. Johnson, the obituary listed his four major scientific publications and his nitrogen fixation experiment at Rothamsted.[15] "The Agricultural College of Pa., the first institution of the kind established in this country, was attaining a high degree of success and usefulness, as a result of the rare combination of scientific and practical knowledge with administrative energy which characterized its lamented President. His death is a loss to Pennsylvania and to the nation," the *Journal* concluded.[16]

Months after Pugh's death, John Lawes of Rothamsted wrote to Rebecca Pugh, telling her how greatly he was grieved. "Although I had my fears that he was taxing his powers too greatly, I was watching his course with the greatest interest as I felt certain that if he lived he would be the founder of a great College. While working in my laboratory he received many cautions from me upon his mode of living, working, as he died, almost day and night and abstaining from wine and animal food." Volunteering to establish an annual prize in Pugh's name for student achievement in agricultural chemistry, Lawes said he would be "proud to become a contributor in honor of a man whose character and abilities I so greatly admired."[17]

In sum, the consensus of opinion characterized Pugh as the indispensable leader in the success of the Agricultural College of Pennsylvania and the advancement of scientific agricultural education in America. In regard to the Agricultural College, at least, the events of the next eighteen years would prove that opinion accurate.

The Pugh Aftermath

Penn State's three institutional historians—Erwin Runkle (1933), Wayland Dunaway (1946), and Michael Bezilla (1985)—have characterized the eighteen years between presidents Evan Pugh (1859–64) and George Atherton (1882–1906) as an era of experiment and drift. That's putting it politely. Despite eventual success in retaining its designation as the sole beneficiary of the land-grant fund and having the entirety of that endowment assigned to it, the institution lost its way. Over five troubled presidential administrations, the institution failed to serve the cause of industrial education. In the 1870s it effectively abandoned its land-grant mission, devolved into a backwoods classical college, was subjected to increasing criticism and threats of investigation, and nearly closed for good. By the dawn of the 1880s, it was almost as if Pugh had never lived.

It was, indeed, a time of "strange transmutations," as C. Alfred Smith described it. "When I returned to the College in 1877 as Professor of Chemistry and Physics, I realized how completely the Institution had become a 'mere literary College.'" The scientific course was nominally in place, but lacking "enthusiasm," with only one laboratory that could accommodate no more than twenty students. There were no specialized laboratories, and a portion of what once existed was now stored in the basement with the other part cut into kindling wood and burned. "In answer to my surprise, President Calder said, 'If Prof. Smith remains with us he will find that we are not devoting as much time to Chemistry as in the old years.'"[18]

But it didn't start out that way. In the weeks after Pugh's death, the trustees had the good sense to gauge the interest of Yale's Samuel W. Johnson in the presidency. At the same time, there was interest in William H. Allen, the recently retired president of Girard College in Philadelphia. Trustee President Watts knew something of Johnson from Pugh, but told McAllister that he had "a young man employed in my office who graduated two years ago at Yale who says that Prof. Johnson was very highly estimated as a practical chemist."[19] Watts sent his inquiry to Johnson on May 10, simply to learn whether he "might be willing to give direction to its destinies . . . the scope of my information presents no name more likely to command the confidence of our friends than yours."[20]

There's little question that Johnson could have sustained Pugh's standards scientifically and educationally, but he demurred. While feeling "honored" to be considered, he was aware of "the many difficulties" the college had endured before emerging as "a bright example of success and usefulness." Johnson replied to McAllister on May 14. "I wish my strength were equal to my will. But I am not strong enough for a situation of such responsibility. I am too easily tired out by brain-work and care to dare to attempt the work of carrying out the plans of your college."[21] It is more than likely that, from his many years of friendship with Pugh, Johnson knew full well how crushing the job was; in any event, he was far more interested in science than institutional leadership and administration.

The trustees' pursuit of William Allen was successful, however, his appointment becoming effective June 15, 1864. A graduate of Bowdoin College, Allen had served as professor of chemistry and natural history at Dickinson College for ten years and then assumed the chair of Mental Philosophy and English Literature. In 1850 he became president of Girard College, retiring in early 1863. He served two years at the Agricultural College, facing enormous difficulties from the start. Finances were a pressing issue, as the institution remained $50,000 in debt and the $100-per-student tuition revenue was insufficient to cover operating costs. The commission charged with selling the land scrip remained inactive until early 1865, when sales proceeded, albeit slowly. Only 27,000 of the 780,000 acres had been sold by the end of the year, dimming prospects for revenue from that source. In April 1866, however, the trustees convinced the legislature to approve a college bond issue for $80,000 as an emergency measure.[22]

Culturally, however, Allen was mismatched. He and his wife had long enjoyed the amenities of civilized life in Philadelphia; although they resided in the now-completed house that Pugh had designed, partly financed, and helped to build, they quickly became disenchanted with the primitive conditions and rustic environs. A professor remarked that Allen and especially his wife "seemed dissatisfied with their life at the college, apparently regretting that they had moved there." Allen left the Agricultural College, moved back to Philadelphia, and was re-elected president of Girard College in 1867, serving in the post till 1882.[23]

Although Allen was mismatched as president, the man appointed to assume Pugh's professorial responsibilities was not. Soon after Pugh's death, George C. Caldwell was persuaded to return to the Agricultural College of Pennsylvania to take up Pugh's mantle as professor of agricultural chemistry. Caldwell found it difficult to leave his post with the U.S. Sanitary Commission. "But knowing that it would be so much in accordance with the wishes of my good friend that I should take his classes, at least till a better person can be found, and feeling much honored by your invitation as well as a deep interest in all such institutions as yours I have concluded to come to your aid for the present."[24]

Shortly after his arrival, however, Caldwell protested Allen's appointment. "It seems to me a matter of the greatest importance that a *scientific* man should

FIGURE 23
George C. Caldwell,
professor of chemistry,
1863–68.

be placed at the head of the Institution—and if such a man cannot be found
. . . then the one chosen should have a *just* and *hearty appreciation* of the
importance of science in the management of the College—and you know as
well as I how strong Dr. Pugh would have insisted upon this," Caldwell told
McAllister.[25]

Nevertheless, Caldwell would stay for four years, striving to maintain
Pugh's standards. Predictably, he was increasingly dismayed by the direction
in which Allen was taking the College—away from the rigorous scientific curriculum of Pugh's invention—but he soldiered on well past Allen's tenure. In
1868, however, Caldwell was recruited by Ezra Cornell and Andrew White to
join the faculty at Cornell, which was opening for instruction that same year.
He jumped at the opportunity. Caldwell spent the rest of his career at Cornell,
establishing and heading the Department of Chemistry. In 1869 he wrote the
first English-language textbook on agricultural chemistry, titled *Agricultural
Qualitative and Quantitative Analysis*. His national reputation increasing with
each passing year, Caldwell was elected president of the American Chemical
Society in 1892.[26] In Pugh and Caldwell, the Agricultural College of Pennsylvania
for nearly a decade had leadership in agricultural chemistry provided by two

William Henry Allen
1864-66

John Fraser
1866-68

Thomas Henry Burrowes
1868-71

James Calder
1871-80

Joseph Shortlidge
1880-81

FIGURE 24   *The five presidents (1864–81) between Pugh and Atherton.*

Göttingen Ph.D.s, bringing to the remote school perhaps the highest standard of instruction in that subject available in American higher education.

In September 1866 Allen was succeeded in the presidency by his fiercest opponent on the faculty, John Fraser, professor of mathematics and astronomy. Fraser, in fact, had mounted a campaign against Allen that resulted in a no-confidence vote by the faculty. Fraser tried to restore the industrial education model, adding engineering to the curriculum. Financial difficulties thwarted his ambitions, however. Enrollments also continued to decline, only thirty undergraduates being in residence in 1868. The trustees consequently deemed his curricular reorganization to be a failure, and Fraser resigned in early 1868.[27] Of the five presidents between Pugh and Atherton, Fraser demonstrated a vision that was most in line with Pugh's intent and the land-grant mission; by the end of his short tenure, however, the institution was locked into a downward spiral.

The trustees then turned to a once-familiar face, David Wilson, who had served as vice president of the institution from 1859 to 1863. Wilson declined with regret, "as I feel a deep interest in the success of that great enterprise, and I have an unfaltering faith in its ultimate triumph over all prejudice and opposition."[28] After six to eight months of searching, the trustees found a successor to Fraser, an educator with exceptional credentials: Thomas H. Burrowes, former state superintendent of the common schools, and the founding editor of the *Pennsylvania School Journal*, which he continued to edit to his death. Burrowes also is credited with drafting the legislation to create the state's system of normal schools. Notwithstanding his reputation, Burrowes's appointment stirred anger in Pennsylvania's agricultural circles. "You have no idea of the almost universal prejudice against the college, among the farmers of eastern Penna. Our Agricultural papers are constantly denouncing it; the political Press take up the cry and seem to vie with each other in the bitterness of their denunciations," J. Lacey Darlington wrote to McAllister in December 1868. "The appointment of Mr. Burrowes has furnished them with another occasion for attack, and while they all acknowledge his eminent fitness for any educational post, they unite in predicting that his administration will be a failure—as the college is practically dead, past resurrection."[29]

Nevertheless, taking office in November 1868, Burrowes tried to return the Agricultural College to its roots, focusing on practical agricultural education, foregoing the mechanic arts, and returning to the old daily manual-labor regimen. He embarked on a publicity campaign to restore confidence in the institution and initiated the "Harvest Home" festival, designed to showcase the college. Enrollments increased somewhat but failed to meet the needed threshold, with only forty-six students attending in 1869 and seventy-six the following year. Age sixty-three when hired, Burrowes took his students on a winter camping and hunting expedition, suffered afterward from the effects of cold and exposure, and died on February 25, 1871, the second of four presidents to succumb in office.[30]

The trustees moved in a different direction with their next selection. James Calder was serving as president of Hillsdale College in Michigan, one of the nation's first coeducational colleges, and possibly one of the reasons for his selection, as the trustees had authorized the admission of women in 1870. A native Pennsylvanian, Calder was a Methodist minister and former missionary. Under his direction, the curriculum was again reorganized, this time into three four-year programs: agricultural, scientific, and classical. He brought several women students with him from Hillsdale when he arrived in 1871, and in 1874 changed the name of the institution to the Pennsylvania State College, a name it would retain until 1953. The change was made partly to reflect a broader, more traditional curriculum, attractive to a wider array of students. But he also wanted to erode the perception that the college existed mainly for the education of farmers to the exclusion of all else.[31]

With the land-grant fund finally intact and producing income, as this chapter will explain later, Calder eliminated tuition. Enrollments increased to about 150 per year, roughly equal to the student population during Pugh's last years. But under Calder, the bulk of the growth occurred in the preparatory department rather than the undergraduate population. The academic program drifted away from any emphasis on agriculture and the mechanic arts, such that the traditional classical curriculum became dominant. The trustees and certain state political leaders noticed the institution's seeming indifference to its Morrill Act mission, and the state agricultural society registered a complaint as well. The legislature appointed a special joint committee in the spring of 1879, which, after a cursory inspection, declared that, "while evidence does not show actual fraud or disclose corrupt management, the institution has been very badly managed." A bill was introduced to halt payments to the college from the state treasury until the legislature was satisfied that the agricultural and mechanic constituencies of the state were being well served. The bill failed by a slim margin, but the writing was on the wall. Calder announced his intention to resign at the end of the 1879–80 academic year, but was out of office by January 22, 1880.[32]

The final president in this eighteen-year drift was an unmitigated disaster: Joseph Shortlidge, president of the Maplewood Institute, a private academy in Chester County. Ironically, Shortlidge was a cousin of Pugh and the younger brother of William Shortlidge, whom Pugh and Rebecca Valentine had visited on the evening of their buggy accident. Joseph Shortlidge brought with him neither higher education experience nor political acumen. He quickly criticized the legislature for its lack of adequate funding and alienated the faculty and the student body, introducing corporal punishment for disruptive young scholars. The state's agricultural community remained up in arms over the absence of agricultural focus. A faculty committee finally took matters into its own hands and recommended substantial changes to the curriculum, especially to include engineering, as well as arguing for Shortlidge's removal. Serving less than a year, Shortlidge submitted his resignation, which was eagerly accepted. He was gone by April 8, 1881.

FIGURE 25 *George W. Atherton, president, 1882–1906.*

An internal trustee committee investigated the institution as well, and another committee of the legislature was formed to begin its own inquest in the fall of 1881. The trustees, at their June meeting, adopted the curriculum changes recommended by the faculty, adding courses in natural history, chemistry and physics, and civil engineering, to the three standard courses in agriculture, classical studies, and general science. Substantial laboratory work was reintroduced as well. But only forty-seven undergraduates remained in residence.[33]

Such was the fate of the college absent Pugh's vision and leadership. After abandoning its land-grant mission and then, at the eleventh hour, moving to reinstate it through substantial curricular reform, the Pennsylvania State College narrowly escaped the "death penalty"—the very real potential for closure or discontinuation through action by the Pennsylvania legislature. A slow, careful search for a new president began in the fall of 1881. The man the trustees found, George W. Atherton, then the Vorhees Professor of History, Political Economy, and Constitutional Law at Rutgers and a land-grant college advocate of national reputation, would preside for twenty-four years, like

Pugh, dying in office (in 1906). Penn State's second founder, as Atherton is called, would breathe new life into the college; reconcile it to its land-grant mission; stabilize and build it up considerably in enrollments, faculty, and facilities; and set it on course for growth and success in the twentieth century.

The Continuing Battles over the Land-Grant Designation and Disposition of Scrip

Aside from issues of leadership after Pugh's death, the Agricultural College of Pennsylvania faced a continuing struggle to retain its exclusive designation as the state's land-grant college and thus realize the proceeds of the endowment created from the sale of land scrip. The legislative session of 1865 started much like the session of the previous year, when Pugh was still alive. Numerous bills appeared, proposing to repeal the state's act of April 1, 1863, which designated the Agricultural College of Pennsylvania as the sole beneficiary. Because of the volume of legislation and the residual uncertainty of whether a partial repeal would result in complete revocation, the House resolved to print 500 copies of the state's land-grant act so members could become familiar with its directives. The legislative record mentions two bills, one of which aimed at the same redistribution among the same six institutions as was proposed the year before in S.B. 809: the University at Lewisburg (Bucknell), Allegheny College, Pennsylvania College (Gettysburg), the Polytechnic College in Philadelphia, the Western University of Pennsylvania (Pitt), and the Agricultural College.

It was the second bill, S.B. 120, however, that would be most feverishly debated. In the manner of its predecessor the year previous (S.B. 617), it repealed sections 4 and 5, removing the Agricultural College as sole beneficiary. It also directed the Board of Commissioners (constituted by the third section of the act) to dispose of the land scrip now on deposit in the office of the Secretary of the Commonwealth, at a price not less than 80 cents per acre, with the proceeds to remain in the treasury of the Commonwealth until further ordered.

Personal attacks filled the air, as they did the year before. Friends of the Agricultural College cited the inappropriate influence of the literary colleges and their religious denominations on various legislators. Said Senator Louis Hall, an advocate for the Agricultural College,

> The college in the Meadville district, for instance, a Methodist institution, bringing its influence to bear upon the Senator from Erie, (Mr. Lowry),

the Washington and Canonsburg college, a Presbyterian institution, calling not in vain on the Senator from Washington, (Mr. Hopkins), the one in Gettysburg holding its former protégé and pupil, the Senator from Bedford, (Mr. Householder), under its wings, those in western Pennsylvania, having an eye single to their Senators, all these institutions under the care of religious denominations can, I am fully aware, bring a very powerful influence to bear upon the legislature, because members are not likely to look far outside what seems to be the peculiar interests of their own constituents.[34]

Then a more purely ideological battle ensued, as the tension between the two sides revealed differing conceptions of what industrial education should entail. The Agricultural College interests said that the land grant should be allocated to an institution that primarily focused on agriculture and the mechanic arts, as Pugh had argued so forcefully the year before. Trustee president Watts sent a memorial on behalf of the college to the legislature, attaching a statement from Ohio governor John Brough describing the type of education envisioned by the Morrill Act. Brough said that the act implemented "a new and distinct species of education" whose purpose was to promote the agricultural and mechanical interests of the nation. This new model of education necessitated a new type of institution, a college whose primary objective was to teach the industrial sciences. Brough observed that traditional literary institutions were incapable of providing this education, because they had to completely change the nature of their institutions and subordinate all other types of education to the industrial sciences.[35]

Advocates of the repeal argued that the land grant should be used "not to propagate a new system of education" but to disperse practical agricultural and mechanical knowledge to as many people as possible. The two sides also differed on the value of manual labor. Agricultural College advocates deemed manual labor necessary to elevate the legitimacy of industrial sciences and nurture students' capacity for the hard work attendant to agriculture and engineering. Repeal proponents argued for a softer approach to student life, suggesting that the student experience be "pleasant and agreeable" (117).

Senator Hiester Clymer of Berks County broke the standoff with an amendment to assign one-third of the land grant to the Agricultural College in perpetuity and replace the remaining two-thirds in the state treasury, This, he believed, would appease both sides, as literary colleges still would remain in position to apply for shares of the larger fund. The bill passed the Senate on May 8, 1865, and the one-third restriction was codified into law the following year. Several measures to redistribute the land grant would appear in the legislature until 1880, but S.B. 120 marked the last time that the Agricultural College's status as sole beneficiary was in serious jeopardy—although, of course, no one knew it at the time.

Ten months later, on March 2, 1866, the Agricultural College presented a memorial to the legislature, this time adopting a very different strategy. Rather than offering a strong defense of the college's right to the fund, or criticizing competing institutions for their interest, the Agricultural College discussed its financial difficulties and warned of dangers of further postponing the sale of the scrip (118). Time was of the essence. In 1864, only a few states managed to sell their scrip, and those that did were able to command about 80 cents an acre—the price floor set by the Pennsylvania legislature. But with the end of the Civil War, the market for public land was suddenly and severely depressed. There was so much of it that supply far exceeded demand, a dynamic exacerbated by the end of hostilities. The federal government sold land to anyone for $1.25 per acre. The Homestead Act of 1862 granted 160 acres of land to an adult head of household who would settle on it and improve it for five years. The market also was flooded by about 10 million acres of soldiers' land warrants and millions of acres of unused lands apportioned to the transcontinental railroads (121).

The Board of Commissioners charged with disposing the scrip held its first meeting on July 14, 1864, ten weeks after Pugh's death. Unfortunately, the board had no resources to market the sale of the scrip and the Morrill Act itself forbade the use of any portion of the fund to aid expenses related to marketing and sales. Despite the attempts on the part of the legislature to "fix" the price of the scrip at 80 cents per acre, that price would not obtain over time. Speculators had entered the market, and they discounted the price due to the costs of locating the land, and registering and clearing land titles—tedious, time-consuming, difficult work for college or state authorities to undertake.

Nonetheless, the Board of Commissioners pressed ahead with sale of Pennsylvania's scrip. In December 1864 they decided that 85 cents was a suitable minimum and accepted twelve bids for about 12,500 acres at that price. Disappointed with lackluster sales, the board lowered the price to 75 cents per acre, which generated the sale of 3,000 more acres. Only 764,500 more acres to go! (122).

The disposition of land throughout the rest of 1865 and 1866 slowed down, as land speculators refused to pay high prices and the commission did not have the resources for marketing. Thus the board focused on selling land to small purchasers in Pennsylvania who were willing to pay higher prices than the large speculators and whose proximity obviated the expenses of advertising. By February 8, 1866, the board had sold only 22,400 acres in all for a total of $18,258, or 81.5 cents per acre. On April 11, 1866, the legislature finally passed a bill that authorized funds to cover expenses related to the marketing and sales of the Agricultural College's guaranteed one-third share of the scrip. Reinvigorated by the legislature's action, the board now solicited large bids.

On February 19, 1867, the legislature finally threw its support to the Agricultural College by passing House Bill (H.B.) 215. This act appropriated the income and interest from the sales of the remaining scrip, in its entirety, to the Agricultural College (123). Though Pugh had been dead nearly three years, his life's work was finally vindicated. There was debate, of course, along the same lines of argument as had been used before. Adversarial senators proposed measures to stall further consideration of the bill, recommit the legislation to another committee, establish a minimum price per acre, and apportion a third of the funds to Allegheny College. House debate followed suit. But it was, at best, a last-ditch effort. Observing that other colleges had not taken steps to comply with the Morrill Act, Senator George Connell of Philadelphia acknowledged that the Agricultural College had firmly established itself as the sole beneficiary by stating that "the feeling of the public has been gravitating toward the institution." On February 14, the House passed H.B. 215 over-whelmingly, 58 to 16, and on February 19 the Senate followed suit.

The Board of Commissioners moved quickly to sell the remaining 520,000 acres of land, receiving 275 bids on lots ranging between 160 and 520,000 acres—the entire amount. The prices ranged from 10 cents to $1.00 per acre, the majority of bids coming in at around 55 cents per acre. In all, the sale of the allocated 780,000 acres of public land brought in $439,186, or 56 cents an acre on average (123–24). The sales of scrip were completed by September 17, 1867. In 1872, during Calder's administration, the Agricultural College benefited from an act of the legislature, voting to add $61,000 to the proceeds of the scrip sales to bring the college's land-grant endowment up to an even $500,000, a sum that as invested generated annual earnings of about $30,000.[36]

Though it took three years to finally resolve the issue of the Agricultural College's exclusive right to the land-grant fund and five years beyond that to get an additional grant from the legislature to augment the corpus of the endowment, it is good things happened as soon as they did. Again, the clock was ticking. Section 3 of the Morrill Act required the states accepting its terms to "provide, within five years from the time of its acceptance, at least not less than one college . . . or the grant to such State shall cease." In Pennsylvania's case, that five-year term would have ended on April 1, 1868. And, too, it is fortunate that the state's additional grant of $61,000 to increase the endowment came very early in Calder's administration, before the institution's drift toward classical education was as pronounced and noticeable as it had become by the end of the 1870s.

CHAPTER 11

Epilogue

IN SUNDRY WAYS, Evan Pugh retains his place in Penn State's institutional memory. There is the Pennsylvania Agricultural College (PAC) Herbarium, housed in Whitmore Laboratory, with more than 110,000 botanical specimens, including the original 3,000 specimens Pugh brought back from Germany to start the collection. In addition, the large poster he used in presentations to illustrate his Rothamsted experiment is on display in the Physical and Mathematical Sciences Library in Davey Laboratory. The Evan Pugh Papers—totaling more than 5,000 pages, and exceedingly well organized, are housed in the University Archives of the Eberly Family Special Collections Library, where Pugh's writing desk is also kept on display. On the university's Allen Street Mall is a historical marker—one of more than eighty-five such markers sponsored by the Penn State Alumni Association—that denotes Pugh's national significance. Another historical marker describes the president's house he designed, helped to fund, started to build, but never occupied; the house is preserved, protected, and utilized as part of the Penn State Alumni Association's Hintz Family Alumni Center. And one of the main north-south thoroughfares in State College is named Pugh Street.

But it is in Old Main, the neoclassical building that houses the university's administration, that Pugh looms largest. Rebuilt in 1929–30, using the same stone from the original edifice, Old Main occupies approximately the same footprint as the original college building that was completed by Pugh in 1863 but torn down sixty-six years later because of structural problems.

FIGURE 26   *The Land-Grant Frescoes by Henry Varnum Poor, Old Main.*

On the upper walls of Old Main's lobby are the famed Land-Grant Frescoes by the distinguished muralist and American master of the fresco medium Henry Varnum Poor (1888–1970). The three large panels featured on the central staircase depict both figuratively and literally the origins and growth of the university and the land-grant college ideal. Commissioned by the Class of 1932, Poor completed the triptych in 1940, and was called back in 1949 to add side panels depicting the more particular work of the University in pursuit of its land-grant mission.

On the original triptych panels, beside the central towering figure of Abraham Lincoln, sit several students of thoughtful mien around a table, receiving instruction from their expounding professor, Evan Pugh, robed like a biblical prophet. Then again, on the first of eight side panels painted in 1949 is a panel Poor called "The Old Boys," featuring a group portrait of ten early leaders, Evan Pugh foremost (and tallest) among them.

Flanking the central staircase are two pedestals, with bronze busts and memorial plaques of the two early presidents to which the university owes

FIGURE 27 *Land-Grant Frescoes panel, "The Old Boys," with Pugh at center.*

its existence: Evan Pugh (1859–64), the founder, and George Atherton (1882–1906), the second founder. These two leaders are, at the institutional level, roughly analogous to George Washington and Abraham Lincoln on the national level. Just as Washington set the standards, precedents, and expectations for the U.S. presidency, and just as Lincoln reconciled the nation to its founding purpose, so too did Pugh and Atherton achieve similar ends for Penn State. Pugh set the high academic standard, built the nation's model agricultural college, and won the land-grant designation. After the institution endured eighteen years of retrogression, Atherton arrived and brought the college back into alignment with its land-grant mission. To the Penn State community, the Old Main lobby is hallowed ground. In 2014, the university completed a multimillion-dollar restoration of the Land-Grant Frescoes and installed climate controls to preserve their quality evermore.

Hanging on the Old Main lobby's first floor wall are oil portraits of Penn State presidents and recent chairpersons of the Board of Trustees. The oldest portrait is that of Evan Pugh, painted in 1890 by the American artist William A. Greaves (1847–1900). The portrait was a gift to the college from Pugh's first graduating class, the eleven members of the Class of 1861, the first students in the nation to graduate with the Bachelor of Scientific Agriculture degree. At the class's reunion on June 25, 1890, the portrait presentation marked the first of the intermittent Evan Pugh memorial events over the years.

The centerpiece of the 1890 ceremony was a memorial address by Pugh's protégé, C. Alfred Smith, who also received the first graduate degree offered by the school—the Master of Scientific Agriculture (M.S.A.) in January 1863. Smith's address ran twenty-three typewritten pages, and passages from it have been presented as appropriate throughout this book. It is an intimate, sentimental, and at times sycophantic portrait of Pugh as man and leader, recollected by one who knew him perhaps better than anyone save his wife. In fact, Rebecca Valentine Pugh attended the 1890 memorial service, her first return to campus after Pugh's death some twenty-six years earlier. Recounting Pugh's accomplishments, Smith noted his disappointment that in the college catalogs for 1864, 1865, and subsequent publications, there was "no mention of the work of its greatest President, nor even the mention of his death. It has been a wish very dear to my heart through all these years to see some memorial of our beloved President Pugh."[1]

The next Pugh retrospective was held as part of the college's semicentennial celebration in June 1905. Smith again presented an address, a recycling of what he delivered in 1890, but with some new elements of remembrance.[2] The semicentennial reunion attendees also heard an address by George G. Pond, who had been serving as professor and chair of chemistry at the college since 1888 and dean of its new School of Natural Sciences since 1895. Pond had taken his bachelor's degree at Amherst College; he then studied chemistry and mineralogy at the University of Göttingen but because of a family emergency returned to America before completing his studies. He went back to Amherst as instructor in chemistry, and in 1888, as he was about to leave for Penn State, his alma mater awarded him the honorary Ph.D. A legend among students and well respected by his peers nationally, Pond would remain at Penn State until his death from pneumonia in 1920. Adding faculty and modern facilities, he rebuilt a department that had been on hard times in the era of drift between

Pugh and Atherton. One of Pond's early protégés was William H. Walker, Class of 1890, who went on to earn his Ph.D. at Göttingen and in 1894 became instructor in chemistry at Massachusetts Institute of Technology. At MIT Walker designed the first chemical engineering program in the United States and was later enshrined as the "father of academic chemical engineering."[3]

Pond's semicentennial address was on "Dr. Pugh's Career as a Chemist," and he sought to remind his audience of the founding president's stature and influence in the sciences. Born in 1861, Pond never knew Pugh personally, but his address might have suggested otherwise. Harkening back to Pugh's studies in Germany, Pond observed that "there was at that time a wave of agricultural chemical investigation extending through all the Universities of Germany, and Pugh's interest was enlisted, together with that of several Americans who were destined later to become prominent agricultural investigators and teachers." Pond was particularly taken with the "omnivorous character" of Pugh's scholarship: "It is common to find in one note book, such a sequence of subjects as a discussion of the theory of polarized light, followed by an outline of a copper smelting process, a scheme for the destructive distillation of coal, a criticism of a work on Plant Anatomy and Physiology, studies in Advanced Algebra, and notes on a pendulum apparatus." But it was about Pugh's research on nitrogen fixation at Rothamsted that Pond waxed most enthusiastic. He said that Professor William H. Brewer of Yale, "who had kindly furnished many facts about Dr. Pugh and his investigation, visited Rothamsted during the progress of this work, and reports in superlative terms, even at this remote day, on the extreme thoroughness and attention to every detail which characterized this whole inquiry."[4]

In 1928, on the centenary of Pugh's birth, the university was the site of a major event to memorialize Pugh. Organized under the auspices of the Central Pennsylvania Section of the American Chemical Society, the event was held on February 29, the leap year date of Pugh's birth 100 years prior. The event's principal organizers and players were Penn State professors Erwin Runkle and R. Adams Dutcher.

Runkle came to Penn State in 1893 as instructor in philosophy and ethics and served as the part-time college librarian from 1904 to 1924, when he was named head of the new department of philosophy. In 1905, for the college's semicentennial, Runkle assembled a raft of materials related to Penn State's history and, in conjunction with his work as college librarian, organized the forerunner of the University Archives, the "Statiana Alcove" in Carnegie Library. He was named the university's official historian in 1926, and in the early 1930s wrote the university's first history, *The Pennsylvania State College, 1853–1932: Interpretation and Record* (1933).[5] The manuscript was never published, remaining on fragile onion-skin paper in the university archives, where it was made accessible to researchers. With the support of the University Libraries, the Nittany Valley Society published Runkle's manuscript in book format in 2013.

Dutcher came to Penn State from the University of Minnesota in 1921 to serve as head of the Department of Agricultural and Biological Chemistry, remaining at Penn State until 1951. He was internationally known for his work on vitamins, and "much of his early work laid the foundation for later discoveries in human and animal nutrition."[6] At the time of the Pugh Centenary, Dutcher was chairman of the American Chemical Society's Central Pennsylvania Section.

Runkle provided the major address for the event, his remarks soon afterward published in expanded form by the *Penn State Alumni News*. Runkle characterized Pugh as a man with vision far ahead of his time, evident in his early plans for the foundation of the Agricultural College and kindred institutions. Pugh's vision was such, Runkle emphasized, that "practically all of his plans have been instituted not only at Penn State but in most of the land grant Colleges and Universities of the country." Two of his plans, in particular, were carried out after his death and "meant more to the nation's agriculture then perhaps anything else," Runkle said, "the establishment of agricultural experiment stations and the dissemination of information to farmers through free bulletins."[7]

Dutcher prepared a radio address, which he delivered on February 29, as well. It was akin to a royal celebration. As Dutcher set the stage: "At 8 o'clock there will be a gathering of faculty, students, members of the [American Chemical] society, friends and relatives of Dr. Pugh in the chemistry amphitheater on the campus. At this meeting there will be exhibited a collection of books, letters, photographs and chemical apparatus and other effects used by Dr. Pugh in his student days and as the first president of the college." Dutcher cited Pugh's contributions as a scientist and pioneer in the agricultural experiment station movement, but also characterized him as "the first historian of the College . . . possessed of genuine literary as well as scientific abilities." Dutcher ended by calling Pugh "without doubt the brainiest man of all our presidents."[8]

Another outcome of the Pugh Centenary was the publication, in the March 1930 issue of the *Journal of Chemical Education*, of "European Laboratory Experiences of an Early American Agricultural Chemist—

Dr. Evan Pugh (1828–1864)." The author was Charles A. Browne, chief, Bureau of Chemistry, U.S. Department of Agriculture and historian of the American Chemical Society. As a young man, Browne had been a laboratory assistant at Penn State.[9]

The article came about when Runkle sent a copy of his *Alumni News* article on the Pugh Centenary to the journal's editor, Neil Gordon, who, "much interested," commissioned the piece.[10] Browne gained access to the Pugh papers, and focused on the letters from Pugh to Samuel Johnson during the 1850s in addition to a few of Pugh's newspaper articles. Browne was impressed. "Had his brilliant young life been spared we are confident that by the force of his leadership the great movement which began in the eighties for the promotion of agricultural chemistry and scientific agriculture, would have been advanced by at least a decade," Browne concluded.[11]

No major Evan Pugh events took place over the ensuing two decades, but work on his legacy continued quietly. In 1945 Mrs. C. Otis "Abbie" Cromer was appointed as the first curator of the Penn State Collection in Pattee Library. Serving until 1952, she cataloged the Pugh Papers as a major part of her responsibilities in organizing the Penn State Collection. In 1949 she staged an Evan Pugh Memorial Exhibition in the foyer of Pattee Library.[12]

In 1953 Margaret Tschan Riley, Class of 1932, was hired as a part-time research assistant in the Penn State Room of the library. She took up the cudgel for Pugh, producing several articles on the founding president and making other contributions to preserving his memory.

As the 1960s approached, scholars, archivists, and administrators began to turn their attention to the centennial of the Morrill Act. Anticipating the occasion, Riley produced an article on "Penn State's First President: Scientist, Educator, Administrator" for the January 1960 issue of *Penn State Alumni News*. She followed that with a scholarly article on "Evan Pugh of Pennsylvania State University and the Morrill Land-Grant Act" for the October 1960 issue of *Pennsylvania History*.[13] The University Archives in conjunction with the Department of History approved a graduate student, Jacqueline M. Bloom, Class of 1958 (now Jacqueline Bloom Struble), to write her thesis for an M.A. in history on "Evan Pugh: The Education of a Scientist, 1828–1859." Completed in 1960, it remains a highly valued scholarly contribution, but it ends as Pugh leaves England for Pennsylvania.[14] Finally, at about this same time, the university came into possession of the wooden door from the Chester County farm of Evan's grandfather, Jesse Pugh. Pugh carved his name on the door in 1839, at age eleven.[15]

In February 1962 Penn State anticipated the 100th anniversary of the Morrill Act with an address by alumnus David D. Henry, then the president of the University of Illinois. As a Penn State freshman in 1922, Henry confessed, "In my undergraduate days . . . it never occurred to me that here was a man no older than many graduate students of my own time, who fashioned a plan for an institution's growth; who tenaciously fought for its establishment with the vigor of a great civic soldier and inspired others to do so in a way that sustained the college's faint grasp on life until better days should come." Pugh's greatest contribution, Henry concluded, "was in giving institutional structure to the Land-Grant idea."[16]

The events surrounding the Morrill Act centennial in 1962 and the impending centennial of Pugh's death (1864) prompted interest in erecting a historical maker in Pugh's memory. Archivist Margaret Riley provided the impetus, working with interested parties in Chester County. Actually, two Pugh markers were erected that year. The first, sponsored by the Pennsylvania State University, the Chester County Chapter of the Penn State Alumni Association, and the Chester County Historical Society, was erected on the site of the Jordan Bank farm, near Oxford, where Pugh grew up. The second, sponsored by the Pennsylvania Historical and Museum Commission was dedicated at the Jordan Bank Elementary School in Oxford. In 2003 the state historical marker was replaced by a newer version. Margaret Riley's daughter, Anne Riley, a past president of the Penn State Alumni Association and a Penn State trustee, spoke on the university's behalf, noting how honored she was to be a part of the ceremony replacing the marker her mother had helped to dedicate some thirty-nine years earlier.

In addition, a smaller bronze plaque, sponsored by the Oxford Area Historical Society and the Penn State Alumni Association, was dedicated inside the Jordan Bank Elementary School. Of all the Pugh markers, this one presents the best synopsis:

EVAN PUGH, Ph.D.

(Feb. 29, 1828–April 29, 1864)

"Man can wear out his body in no nobler effort
than in instructing his mind."

Evan Pugh was born just a few miles south of this school on farmland bordering Jordan Creek. He founded and conducted Jordan Bank Academy from 1849 to 1853 before spending several years in Germany, France, and

England pursuing his education and passion for science. While there, he earned his Doctorate in Chemistry and, with his experiments, provided the evidence that is the basis for today's ammonia and nitrate fertilizers. He was a passionate student and became an equally passionate educator when he returned to the U.S. to accept the principalship of what is now the Pennsylvania State University in 1859. The University's first and youngest president embarked on a crusade to save the school from bankruptcy and to make it the leader in the new field of agricultural science. He also fought for laws such as the Morrill Land-Grant Act, which gave the profits from the sale of public land to colleges to support instruction in agricultural, engineering, and other practical fields of study. In 1864, after five years of tireless labors on behalf of Penn State, Pugh died from typhoid fever at the tender age of 36. Although his leadership of the school was brief, his efforts gave it a firm foundation, and his accomplishments are timeless.[17]

The most enduring tribute to Pugh, however, was the university's establishment of the Evan Pugh Professorships, beginning in 1960. The designation is the highest distinction that the university can bestow upon a faculty member. Nominated periodically by a panel of seven eminent faculty members at Penn State, candidates must be acknowledged founders and developers in their fields of research or creative activity. Evan Pugh professors are provided an annual salary supplement and unrestricted grant to support their programs. Only sixty-eight faculty members have held the designation of Evan Pugh Professor from 1960 to 2015.[18]

Oddly, a century and one-half since his death, no building at Penn State has been named for Pugh. Buildings have been named for other Penn State presidents, deans and department heads, distinguished faculty members, philanthropists, and Pennsylvania governors, but nothing of like tribute is dedicated to the founding president. His legacy, however, cannot be buried by history: a profound scientific research accomplishment providing the foundation for the modern ammonium nitrate fertilizer industry; the successful introduction of scientific agriculture to American higher education, manifested by the nation's first successful state-sponsored agricultural college to be based on the highest scientific standards; advocacy for agricultural research on a grand scale to be conducted through a national system of agricultural experiment stations; advice and counsel to the federal government on the aborning U.S. Department of Agriculture; influence on the passage of the

1862 Morrill Act coupled to rapid success in gaining the state's designation for the Agricultural College as the sole beneficiary; and a visionary plan for structuring and financing the new institutions of agriculture and the mechanic arts that would become the American land-grant colleges.

Had Pugh lived beyond 1864, his influence on the land-grant college movement, on American agriculture, on American science, and on the whole of American higher education, would have been substantial. And Pugh's national model—the Agricultural College of Pennsylvania—would have developed more quickly and fully as a paragon of industrial education, minus those eighteen lost years following his death.

But one surmises that he might be pleased, at least provisionally, with what the Agricultural College of Pennsylvania, now the Pennsylvania State University, had become by the second decade of the twenty-first century: One of the nation's top 20 research universities, according to the National Science Foundation; among the top 100 global universities (out of a field of more than 27,000 colleges and universities worldwide), according to numerous international rankings and ratings; among the national leaders in scores of academic disciplines, according to various rating organizations, including the National Research Council's 2010 assessment of doctoral programs; more than 750,000 alumni since the first graduating class of 11; and with nearly 100,000 students, 45,000 faculty and staff, and 24 campus locations across the Commonwealth, the realization of the grand, efficient scale that he wanted for his model agricultural college.

Accordingly, Evan Pugh's legacy may be more appropriately defined by the epitaph of the seventeenth-century London architect Christopher Wren, in Saint Paul's Cathedral: "si monumentum requiris, circumspice." "If you seek his monument, look around you."

A Report upon a Plan for the Organization of Colleges for Agriculture and the Mechanic Arts with Especial Reference to the Organization of the Agricultural College of Pennsylvania

A REPORT

UPON

A PLAN FOR THE ORGANIZATION

OF

COLLEGES FOR AGRICULTURE

AND THE

MECHANIC ARTS,

WITH

ESPECIAL REFERENCE TO THE ORGANIZATION

OF THE

Agricultural College of Pennsylvania,

IN VIEW OF THE ENDOWMENT OF THIS INSTITUTION BY THE LAND SCRIP FUND,
DONATED BY CONGRESS TO THE STATE OF PENNSYLVANIA;

ADDRESSED

To the Board of Trustees of the Agricultural College of Pennsylvania, Convened
at Harrisburg, January 6, 1864:

BY DR. E. PUGH, PRESIDENT OF THE FACULTY.

HARRISBURG:
SINGERLY & MYERS, PRINTERS.
1864.

INDUSTRIAL COLLEGES.

The Pecuniary Resources and Educational character of the Colleges and Universities of the United States.

There were, previous to the rebellion, over two hundred and twenty Colleges and Universities in the United States, in addition to a number of Schools for law, medicine and theology.   No other class of Institutions bearing a common name, differed more widely in the value of their pecuniary resources, and in the extent of their operations than did these Colleges and Universities.

A large number of them were without any endowment whatever, and were obliged to rely wholly upon the fluctuating resources of their income from students ; others were moderately endowed, but had their class rooms almost filled with students owning perpetual scholarships, the original sale of which secured the endowment fund ; while a few were sufficiently well endowed to enable them to employ a large number of professors and teachers with the proceeds of the Endowment fund alone.

The number of Professors, in these Institutions, varied from as low as *two* in some of them, to forty in others, while the number of students varied from twenty to eight hundred, as may be seen by referring to the statistical tables of Child's National Almanac for 1863.

The examination of so large a number of Educational Institutions, all of which aim at finishing the education of students, must afford valuable data for the consideration and guidance of those who would found Industrial Colleges; for, although the course of instruction, in an Industrial College, must be radically different from that of a purely literary Institution, yet there will be important points of identity between them, in matters of organization and the pecuniary resources required to give them efficiency.   The difference in the number of Professors, which Educational Institutions are enabled to employ, is one of the most marked sources of difference in the extent of their operations.

It is a difference which, with few exceptions, corresponds to the income of the College, and to the extent and efficiency of its course of instruction.

4

A glance at the statistical tables referred to above exhibits the greatest difference amongst these two hundred and twenty Colleges, in regard to the number of Professors they employ.

So far as they afford the data, the following sub-division, of American Colleges, dependent upon the number of Professors in each, has been made, to wit:—

Colleges with from   2 to   5 Professors.. 41
Do.   do.   6 " 10   do.. 97
Do.   do.   11 " 15   do.. 29
Do.   do.   16 " 20   do.. 6
Do.   do.   26 " 30   do.. 4
Do.   with over   36   do..... 3

Were we to arrange them in the order of the amount of their endowment, or of their income, or the number of their students, we would find the differences quite as marked as those just given, for the number of their Professors.

Had we time to examine closely the internal organization, and the subjects taught, and the means of teaching in each of these Colleges, we would find that all those with a small number of Professors, and with a limited income, were laboring under a great many disadvantages.

But without stopping to dwell upon these disadvantages, we will consider the resources and the operations of some of the most prominent amongst them.   For this purpose those in table I have been selected.   They embrace, with a few exceptions,

First.—All Institutions with 15 or more Professors.
Second.—All with $400,000 or more endowments.
Third.—All, the annual expenses of which are over $12,000.

5

TABLE I.—*Showing the Educational Resources of the more prominent American Colleges.*

COLLEGES.	No. of Profs	No. of Stud'ts.	Am't paid Profs. and Teachers	Amount of Endowment.	Annual Expenses.	No. of Volumes in Library.
Bowdoin College..............	18	181	....	*$182,000	....	30,595
Dartmouth College............	20	307	$13,000	217,667	$17,907	35,402
Harvard University...........	56	833	68,000	1,613,884	153,431	149,000
Amherst College.............	17	229	....	*590,000	18,500	30,000
Brown University............	12	202	....	220,000	36,000	37,000
Yale College.................	40	617	....	....	78,000	75,000
Columbia College............	43	689	52,000	1,650,666	79,269	18,000
University, City of New York..	36	488	....	*250,000	14,011	10,000
New York Free Academy.....	25	916	42,000	†	52,580	10,000
Union College................	17	276	19,400	658,000	30,000	18,000
Rochester University.........	11	160	10,950	123,224	13,408	7,000
Vassar Female College........	....	....	....	408,000	....	....
Princeton College......	13	221	....			22,200
University of Pennsylvania...	28	642	....	306,654	26,844	8,000
Philadelphia High School.....	19	502	....		23,430	....
Girard College................	13	400	....	2,000,000	85,000	....
University of Michigan........	27	286	....	600,000	40,000	8,000
University of Illinois..........	38	.....	....	427,625	....	....

The attention of the Board is respectfully invited to a careful consideration of the data afforded by the above table.   The average number of Professors in these Colleges is twenty-five, while the average amount of endowment fund is over $600,000.   The figures in all the columns are remarkably suggestive of the resources required to carry on Educational Institutions of even moderately high character.   Had we time to examine closely into the details of the working of these Institutions, as exhibited in their annual reports, we would find, in all of them, the most indubitable evidence of the insufficiency of their resources, for the accomplishment of the mission they are laboring to fulfil.   Whether we examine their Linguistic, their Literary, or their Scientific Departments, or any one of the several Professional Schools which some of them have, we will find, in all of them, an absence of that *thoroughness* which characterizes the highest order of study.   With very few exceptions, we will find Professors obliged to teach *too many* different things to teach *anything* very thoroughly, or to keep themselves posted on the progress of knowledge, in their own department, in the learned world.   If confirmation of the insufficiency of their resources were needed, we have it in the constant efforts that nearly all of them are making to secure additional pecuniary aid.

In order to examine more closely the manner in which the pecuniary resources given in table I, are applied to the purposes designed by them, the

---

* In these, some property which does not afford any income is included.

†This Institution is wholly supported by the city of New York.

6

following table has been prepared from the recent Treasurer's reports of the three colleges named :

TABLE II.—*Showing Source of Income and Expenditure for Harvard, Yale, and Columbia.*

ITEMS OF INCOME FROM	ANNUAL INCOME OF		
	Harvard.	Yale.	Columbia.
Funds invested, rents, &c...........	$89,039 47	$28,066 62	$63,652 52
Tuition.................	50,782 35	40,563 15	9,955 33
Sundries................................	12,753 89	4,411 00	....
Amount total........................	152,575 71	73,040 77	73,607 85

ITEMS OF EXPENDITURE FOR	ANNUAL EXPENDITURE OF		
	Harvard.	Yale.	Columbia.
Salaries in academical depart't....	$44,650 00	$24,268 38	$47,239 18
Salaries in other departments......	23,158 96	11,619 16	5,206 79
Beneficiary fund, free scholars'p, &c	7,591 12	4,873 40	*
Library...............................	13,894 64	3,328 80	1,012 50
Museum and apparatus..............	4,815 33	954 15	100 86
Scientific department................	11,368 72	3,987 50	....
Sundries........................	47,951 73	29,151 02	25,710 34
Amount total........................	153,431 50	78,182 41	79,269 67

As an example of the source of the several items of income above given, we quote from the recent Treasurer's report of Harvard University :

Fund appropriated to Academical department.... .... $183,440 24

Do.	do.	to Scholarships......................................	60,326 54
Do.	do.	to different Professorships.....................	338,970 96
Do.	do.	to Library........	27,582 16
Do.	do.	to Law School........	22,943 63
Do.	do.	to Observatory.............	110,665 74
Do.	do.	to Theological School......	110,650 19
Do.	do.	to Scientific School............................	130,711 55
Do.	do.	to Medical School....	37,447 79

---

* Columbia College gives gratuitous instruction to a number of students.

7

Fund appropriated to special purposes			$519,796 93
Do.	do.	to conversion of Indians	15,290 04
Do.	do.	to Minister and School Master	4,558 34
Do.	do.	to Zöological Museum	51,348 38
Total			1,613,884 11

Persons who are not familiar with the expenses involved in carrying on first class institutions, might be filled with amazement at, what would seem, the prodigality of spending the large sum of $152,575 11 annually in one educational institution. And when such persons contemplate the sum of $1,613 884 as the *invested endowment* of such an Institution, they are unable to comprehend why an Educational Institution can want so much property; and yet when we come to examine the expenditures in the different departments of Harvard University, we find the strictest economy exercised in all of them. Every dollar that is spent goes out of the treasury to bring in some *essential* element of power, upon which the success of the great Educational Establishment is partially dependent.

If we examine the details of the expenditure of the $44,680 which is paid for instruction in the Academical Department, we will find it divided among forty-three Professors, Assistants, and Superintendents, nearly all of whom receive lower salaries than men of the same degree of attainments and application would receive in any other profession than that of teaching.

Among them we find Agassiz, the greatest living comparative anatomist and zöologist, whom Louis Napoleon offered a large salary, and a seat in the French Senate, would he honor the French court by his presence in Paris.

Professor Pierce, the greatest mathematician in the world.

Professor Gray, the greatest American botanist, and other such men receive less salaries at Harvard than the income of many second class professional men in the country towns of our State. If we follow these men to the respective fields of their labor in the University, we will find all their services needed to give Harvard the high character as an Educational Institution which it maintains. And although Harvard may justly claim the right to stand at the head of the Educational Institutions of America, yet with all its resources, its educational standard is much below that of the best Universities of Europe.

The present President, who is justly accounted one of the finest of American scholars, in his recent inaugural address to the overseers of the College, says, in considering the affairs of the University, that "while gratified to note the evidence of her prosperity, he is even more forcibly struck with the opportunity still offered for an advantageous employment of still larger means."

8

"No department," continues he, "either in the college or professional schools, can be said to stand above the need of improvement, and few if any can court comparison with the most thoroughly furnished schools of Europe."

The sum of $11,368 12 is applied to the scientific school of the University, and yet the graduates of this school are constantly going to Europe to complete their scientific education, in the more extensive course of instruction in the Universities of Germany and France.

Several thousand dollars are annually appropriated, as may be seen by table II, to organizing and filling up libraries and scientific museums, and yet these are far behind their prototypes in the old world, or what every scientific man must recognize as complete collections of the objects to which they relate.

The sum of nearly $8,000 is annually expended for the education of meritorious, indigent students, and yet this fund is inadequate to the demands upon it.   The recent President *pro tem.* of the University, in an address to the Trustees, says, "we have now 37 scholarships for indigent students.   It is impossible to over-estimate their beneficial influence upon the College.   They attract to the University a large number of the very best of our students, who otherwise would seek less expensive Colleges.   They have raised to a degree which those not connected with the school can hardly appreciate, the general standard of scholarship and of character; they might be multiplied with added advantage to the Institution."

"Many of these students submit to severe privations, struggle on with depressing poverty, and incur a burden of indebtedness which must weigh heavily on them for many subsequent years."

He then goes on to urge the necessity of securing the means to increase the number of scholarships.

And thus it will be with all the items of this $153,430 53, expended annually to support Harvard University; instead of the amount being too large for an Educational Institution of the highest character to employ advantageously, a close examination will show that it is not large enough.

In like manner we might examine into the details of the annual expenditure of the $79,269 47 by Columbia College, and show that all this large sum is used for indispensable purposes in the educational system of that Institution.   The fact is worthy of note, that notwithstanding the College has an income of over $60,000 from endowment, and that its price of tuition is $50 per annum for students, yet during the year 1861 its expenditure exceeded its income by $5,660 62.

No less decisive are the facts shown by the receipts and expenditures of Yale College.

9

Of about $78,000 expenditure by that institution, nearly one half is derived from endowments, and no one familiar with the internal workings of the educational system of Yale, would fail to see, as at Harvard, the necessity for a larger expenditure of means.

One prominent feature in connection with all these Educational Institutions, of large pecuniary resources, is the fact, that they are still the subject of more liberal donations than any other Educational Institutions in the country.

Year after year the repeated solicitations of the friends of these Institutions, for an extension of their pecuniary resources, have been met by liberal appropriations and princely endowments, from men who are thoroughly acquainted with the necessities and the workings of them.   The fact that shrewd business men, of extended information, who are well acquainted with the workings of these Institutions, are willing to subscribe liberally to their further endowment, is an indubitable evidence that the large sums spent annually for their support are really required for the maintenance of Educational Institutions of high order.

Table III gives the annual income and expenditure of several prominent colleges, including the three to which table II is devoted.

Particular attention is invited to the amount of income from endowment, to the amount paid to Professors for tuition, and to the last column of gain or loss.   The values are taken from recent Treasurers' reports of the Institutions given.

After what has been said in relation to the inadequate resources of Harvard, Yale and Columbia, it is needless to remark, that all the smaller Institutions of table III must labor under great disadvantage, for want of additional funds.   A comparison of their course of instruction, with that of the Colleges just named, no less than the balance sheets of their Treasurers, and the repeated acknowledgment of their friends, all point to the inadequate nature of their resources.

10

TABLE III—*Showing balance sheet of several Colleges.*

COLLEGES.	Profs	Stud'ts.	Income.	Expenditure.	Gain or Loss
Dartmouth College...............	18	181	$17,104	$17,906	—$802
			4,260*	14,000**	....
Harvard University...............	26	833	152,576	153,431	—855
			90,000*	71,000**	....
Yale College....................	40	617	73,041	78,182	—5,041
			30,000*	30,000**	....
Columbia College...............	43	689	78,607	79,269	— 5662
			64,000*	50,000**	....
Union College	17	276	30,000†	30,000†	....
			18,000*	19,400**	....
1861–2			28,600	22,102	6,498
1862–3			17,326	22,086	—4,760
Hamilton College...............	12	156	11,697	19,798	—8,101
			5,500*	14,818**	....
University of the city of New York,	36	488	13,018	12,787†	221
			8,335*	11,297**	....
University of Rochester...........	11	160	11,199	13,408	—2,209
			5,000*	10,662**	....

Had we time to dwell upon the hard struggle for existence of smaller institutions, and to show how many of them have broken up under the pressure of the war, while Harvard and Yale have flourished with their endowments, the value of extended pecuniary resources would appear still more obvious.

Their necessities are attested by the constant efforts of those interested in them, to secure additional pecuniary aid from every possible source, as also by the balance sheet of their Treasurers. Their want of means is strikingly illustrated by the avidity with which, in some States, they have grappled for the proceeds of the Land Grant by Congress to the several States, for the endowment and support of Colleges for Agriculture and the Mechanic arts. No sooner had the friends of Agricultural Education, after the persevering efforts of years, secured the passage of the Land Grant bill, with a view of founding Agricultural Colleges in their respective States, then they found members of existing Colleges prepared to dispute their right to what they had thus secured from Congress, on the ground that they, too, had just established Agricultural Departments in their Colleges which needed endowment. This is all the more remarkable, because none of these Institutions before had attempted to develop departments for Agriculture and the Mechanic arts, and many of them had taken especial pains to show, that all

*These numbers give the amount of income from endowment—those above them the total income.

** These numbers give the amount paid for teaching—those above the total expenditure.
†These values, with the next below them, are given for Union before the war—the other values are for total expenditure, 1861–2, and 1862–3.

11

substantial education must be based upon classic culture, and that the modern idea tending towards a substitution of scientific education for the study of Latin and Greek, was a pernicious result of the too utilitarian spirit of the age.

An apology is due to the Board for this attempt to demonstrate so obvious a truth as that the large sums of money, expended by these Educational Institutions, are essential to give them the high character they maintain.   An apology is, most especially, due in view of the fact that the Board is already committed upon the subject of the means required to endow a first class Industrial College, by their prolonged and persistent efforts to secure the passage of the congressional Land Grant bill, for the endowment of the Agricultural College of Pennsylvania.   I have devoted this much space, however, to the subject, because many persons, seemingly not aware of the expense involved in first class Colleges, have expressed great surprise that the friends of the Agricultural College of Pennsylvania should want all the endowment which they procured from Congress for the development and maintenance of this Industrial College.

Resources required to sustain Agricultural and Industrial Colleges.

Having briefly examined the resources expended in sustaining the literary Colleges of our country, we are prepared to consider what may be required to found and sustain Industrial Colleges.

The first question that arises, in this consideration, relates to whether it is desirable that Industrial Colleges should be elevated to the highest possible educational standard, with the greatest range of scientific and practical subjects, within the scope of their teaching, in the class room; or whether they should be Institutions of an inferior grade, with contracted limits to the variety and extent of the subjects taught in them.   This question has already been settled in this State, by the action of the State Legislature, in conjunction with the citizens of the State, in appropriating and subscribing money to found the Agricultural College of Pennsylvania, upon a basis capable of being successfully carried out, only upon a large scale, with an efficient course of instruction.   But as the extent and character of the course of instruction might still seem open to discussion, the attention of the Board is respectfully invited to its consideration.

First.—A complete system of industrial education must afford the means of making known to students all that can be known of the Principles and Laws, according to which the industrial operations of life are regulated.   If the system does not do this, it fails to afford the student all that he may wish to know, and obliges him to look beyond it, to other systems, to complete his education, in the *very sphere* to which the Industrial College is

12

especially devoted. If he must look beyond it for the *highest kinds* of knowledge it claims to teach, he will lose his respect for it, and ultimately seek elementary instruction in the same source to which he is obliged to go for his profounder studies, and thus industrial education is left to obtuse minds, without aspiration for thoroughness, and the whole system falls to the ground disgraced.

Again.—By no system of education can elementary principles be perfectly taught without there being somewhere in the system a clear understanding of all that is known in the advanced studies of these principles. The purely practical Mathematics of elementary instruction would be a contemptible part of education, were it not that they rest upon sublime truths that are demonstrated and understood in the higher grades of mathematical study.

Second.—A system of education which embraces all that can be known of the Principles and Laws, according to which the industrial operations of life are regulated, must be a very extensive system. This follows from the fact that the industrial operations of life embrace the *entire range* of human industry, and almost the entire range of human thought. The fundamental difference between man as a savage and man as an enlightened being, consists in the *difference in the extent of his industrial operations*. The characteristic peculiarities of the present age, by which it is distinguished from preceding ages, consist in its more extended industrial operations. The Principles and Laws which lie at the basis of all industrial operations, must, therefore, be at the basis of human progress, and the study of them as important and as extensive as is human progress itself.

Third.—This extensive system of industrial education must be of a *scientific character*. The industrial operations of life are carried on through the instrumentality of Matter and the laws which govern it. They extend to Matter in all conceivable forms, and in all known places, and for the systematic and intelligent consideration of Matter under all these circumstances, we must call to our aid the entire range of the Natural and Physical Sciences.

Fourth.—A system of scientific education, embracing the entire range of the Natural and Physical Sciences, can only be carried out efficiently upon a large and liberal plan, supported by endowments equal to those of the best educational Colleges in the country. This is proven, no less, by a consideration of the subjects to be taught, than by the fact that no American College, however well endowed, has yet succeeded in establishing a complete system of scientific education, and even the European Universities, with which the President of Harvard College says that University dare not court

18

comparison, do not pretend yet to have, at any one of them, a complete course of scientific instruction.

Such then will be the magnitude of the demands of industrial education in Industrial Colleges. We cannot expect to meet them in the present generation, but with their collossal proportions before us, let no man say that endowments, equal to half of those of our best literary Colleges, are too much for our industrial Colleges. But rather let their endowments be doubled and tribled, that America may become in industrial education, as she already is in the industrial operations of civil and military life, the *first country* in the world—that the nations of Europe may be taught in our industrial Colleges, as they now are taught by the industrial operations of our stupendous military system.

One other consideration—while the expenses of an industrial system of education are thus great, *those for whom that education is designed* are generally persons of *small income.* The education they receive is calculated to benefit *society in general more especially* than themselves in particular. It does not, like a professional education often does, elevate them from an humble position in life to lucrative posts, in which they can retail out to community the knowledge they have acquired; but it enables them more effectually to perform the several duties of their industrial operations, and thus leads to an ultimate improvement of all those means by which, as before remarked, civilized man is distinguished from the savage; hence not only the necessity, but the justice to the industrial classes, of endowing industrial colleges.

The Organization of an Industrial College.

Having shown the extent of the resources of some of the best American Colleges, and endeavored to show that Industrial Colleges have need of resources quite as ample, the attention of the Board is now invited to the consideration of the organization of an Industrial College. For the sake of simplicity, I would present this subject under several different headings:

1st. *Officers and Assistants.*—Under this heading is embraced the consideration of the number and kind of men required to carry on all the varied operations, and perform all the duties of the Industrial College.

2d. *College buildings and out-buildings—the number, kind and quality.*

3d. Apparatus, and natural history collections, museums, and library, and reading room.

4th. Means of scientific investigation.

5th. Prizes, beneficiary fund for indigent student, free scholarships, &c.

6th. Plan and course of instruction.

14

7th. Endowment of Industrial Colleges.

8th. The Land Scrip Fund donated by Con gress, its object, and the proper manner of using it.

OFFICERS AND ASSISTANTS.

These will embrace a Presiding Officer, Professors, assistant Professors, Tutors and Superintendents. I would here beg leave to remark, that in the consideration of the qualifications of the several persons to whom the above titles refer, I have labored to look at the subject as a *purely intellectual question,* divested entirely of any personal feeling or prejudice, which, as one of the parties named, I might be supposed to have in the matter. If I have erred in my estimate of the character and quality of the duties of each of the officers and assistants, I trust the Board will have the forbearance to attribute my error to a mistake in judgment, rather than to a selfish bias in favor of my own course of action. To commence then with the

PRESIDENT OF AN INDUSTRIAL COLLEGE.

The Presiding Officer of any large educational Institution occupies one of the most responsible positions to which it is possible for man to attain. To use the language of one of the most distinguished friends of education in America, when speaking of the late President Felton, of Harvard University:

"Over every department he is expected to exercise a superintending care. He is the representative of the college, before the public. Every parent or guardian who has a son or a ward at the college, looks to the President for information as to his condition, and holds him responsible for his moral welfare, and intellectual progress. Towards every student he is expected to sustain the relation of a parent, a kind, sympathising, watchful and interested friend."

He should not be a recluse, inaccessible to the student on the one hand, nor should he listen to childish complaints and unmanly petitions on the other. His intercourse with students should be characterized by the most punctilious justice and equity in the enforcement of moral government, and the most unwavering firmness as to the privileges he would grant or refuse to students. He should be willing and able to concentrate all his powers upon the immediate sphere of his duties, rather than seek duties beyond the interest of the College. And lastly, he should possess *as much knowledge as is possible for one man to possess,* of all the *leading branches* to which the educational system of the College is devoted. As a President of a Literary College, he should be well versed in language and literature; as a President of a College for civil and military Engineering, he should be well acquainted with mathematics and the physical sciences, and as a President of an Indus-

15

trial College, he should, as far as possible, be thoroughly acquainted with the natural and physical sciences, and their practical application to the industrial operations of life.   It is *more important* that the presiding officer of a Scientific College should be a scientific man, than that the same officer in a Literary College should be well versed in literary studies, because the expenditures for *material*, as *auxiliaries to study* in a Scientific College must always be great, and they are such as can only be properly *regulated, encouraged* and *controlled* by a scientific man.   No scientific Institution ever has been, or ever can be successful as such, the control of which, either *directly* or indirectly, is not vested in a scientific man.   An appeal to experience, no less than a consideration of the intrinsic nature of the question will demonstrate this fact.

The Presiding Officer should be familliar with the entire plan according to which all the departments of the Institution are carried out, and with the manner in which it is being carried out, and he should be able to take charge of some of the prominent branches taught to the advanced classes, and to cousult with individual Professors as to plans of scientific research.

PROFESSORS AND ASSISTANTS REQUIRED.

1st.—A Professor of pure Mathematics and the higher Mechanics and Astronomy.—A man capable of reading the works of Newton, Laplace and Pierce on Mathematics and Mechanics, and who could teach Descriptive Geometry, Perspective and Drawing.   A serious fault with American teachers of mathematics, is an inability to give geometrical and stereometrical shape to their mathematical ideas, a consequence of their knowledge of drawing not having kept pace with their study of mathematical analysis, and this again is the result of the great neglect of drawing, throughout our whole educational system, from the common schools to the University.   Every Professor of pure or applied mathematics in an industrial College, should be free from this source of inefficiency.   This Professor should have one assistant, to take charge of the elementary classes.

2d. *Professor of Civil Engineering and Applied Mathematics.*—A man familiar with all the details of Civil Engineering, Architecture, mechanical Drawing, Topography, map-making, &c., so that he could not only teach the students the mathematical demonstrations of the class-room, but could make them good practical engineers, capable of delineating with accuracy the topography of a Country, the route of a Railroad, or the construction of an Edifice.   He should have one assistant, who should be a good draftsman, and who could show the student how to work up the details of a survey.

3d. *A Professor of Natural Philosophy and Astronomy, Mechanics and Physics.*—A man familiar with all the recent extended investigations upon

16

light, heat, electricity and optics, an accomplished experimenter, and a good mathematician.

An assistant, to prepare experiments for lectures, and to teach classes in the physical laboratory, where students would learn the art of experimentation with philosophical apparatus.

4th. A PROFESSOR OF PURE CHEMISTRY, who would give a course of lectures upon the science in general, and who would have charge of the laboratories and of chemical investigations.

An assistant, to help prepare lectures and look after classes in the laboratory.

A sub-assistant, to take charge of the chemicals, and to help in the laboratory, with no other salary than free tuition. A chemical department, embracing laboratory instruction, cannot be efficient with less aid than one professor and two assistants.

5th. A PROFESSOR OF AGRICULTURAL CHEMISTRY AND GEOLOGY, who would give lectures upon these sciences, and have charge of a laboratory for agricultural chemistry and chemico-agricultural investigations, in the field and in the laboratory, and who would instruct students in the science of field experimentation, in connection with the professor of practical agriculture.

An assistant, to help with field experimentation, and work in the laboratory.

6th. A PROFESSOR OF METALLURGY, MINING AND MINERALOGY, and Chemical Technology, who would give practical laboratory instruction in all the processes of Metallurgy, and a course of experimental lectures upon all the leading processes of applied chemistry in the industrial arts.

An assistant, to prepare lectures and help in the laboratories.

7th. A PROFESSOR OF ANATOMY, PHYSIOLOGY AND VETERINARY, under whom students could be made familiar with the laws of health and disease of animals, and who could carry out investigations in animal physiology. Such a man should be able to make anatomical and pathological preparations of domestic animals, corresponding to those of the human subject used for demonstration in Medical Colleges. This is a very important Professorship, and one hard to fill properly. A candidate for it should be a successful graduate of a Medical College, who had subsequently studied at least two years in the Veterinary Schools of Europe, and hence would be familiar with the French and German literature upon the subject.

8th. A PROFESSOR OF NATURAL HISTORY, MORE PARTICULARLY OF ZÖOLOGY, COMPARATIVE ANATOMY AND ENTOMOLOGY.—A great part of the time of this professor would be consumed making collections, organizing museums, and carrying out investigations, as is the time of Prof. Agassiz, at Harvard, and Glover, at Washington.

17

9th. A PROFESSOR OF BOTANY, HORTICULTURE AND ENTOMOLOGY, who would be devoted to purely botanical instruction, and to the practical application of Botany to Horticulture, and who would take charge of the botanical gardens, green-house and Horticultural Department, and who would give instruction in vegetable Anatomy and Physiology.

One assistant, to take charge of the green-house, and give field instruction in Horticulture, and a *gardener*, to take charge of the garden.

10th. A PROFESSOR OF PRACTICAL AGRICULTURE.—The man who fills this position should be thoroughly acquainted with the history of Agriculture and with its present condition the world over. He should not only have been a man of close study and observation at home, but of extensive travel abroad. He should be able to judge, from having observed and studied agricultural practice in all its departments all over the civilized world, as to how far the agricultural practice of each country is capable of being improved by the adoption of new methods. He should be familiar with the whole subject of stock-raising and feeding and keeping, with the cultivation of crops, and with the use and improvement of tools, implements and machines, from the rude agricultural implements of the savage, to the latest improvement of an American reaper. He should bring this accumulated knowledge before the student in the class-room, and he should unite with the Professor of agricultural chemistry in scientific experimentation in the field.

As assistant, he should have a practical farmer of the highest attainments in his art, and the latter should be assisted by two good farm hands, and by all the students in the College.

11th A PROFESSOR OF THE ENGLISH LANGUAGE AND LITERATURE, with the teacher of the elementary department for an assistant.

12th. A suitable Professor to take charge of a Commercial Department, embracing book-keeping, farm accounts, banking business, together with the science of commercial intercourse and domestic trade, as developed in domestic, political and National Economy.

13th. A Professor of Modern Languages : or a number of partial Professors, could take charge of this department. The modern languages, or more particularly the German and French, should be introduced, in order to enable the student to complete his studies by consulting scientific works in those languages.

To the foregoing Professors the following should be added, though not indispensable to a system of industrial education.

14th. A PROFESSOR OF THE LATIN AND GREEK LANGUAGES AND LITERATURE.

15th. A PROFESSOR OF MILITARY ART, AND SCIENCE AND TEACHER OF MILITARY TACTICS.

16th. A TREASURER, BOOK-KEEPER AND LIBRARIAN, who could help teach

2

18

in the commercial department;—a Janitor and general superintendent of the halls, rooms, grounds and furnaces.

The organization of the Culinary Department may be omitted here as not requiring any new plans.

SUMMARY.

We then shall have President and Professors.................................... 16

Librarian and Treasurer.................................... 1

Assistants 10

Superintendents.................................... 2

Total... 29

We thus have an aggregate of twenty-nine Professors, Assistants and Superintendents for the complete organization of an Industrial College; and after devoting much thought, during the last ten years, to this subject, I think this is the smallest number of men with which a complete system could be efficiently organized, and any person familiar with the duties to which each of these men would be devoted, will see that nearly all of them will have a wider field of labor, than is assigned to men, in the same departments, of those institutions in the country that have established scientific schools. In the Scientific Departments of the Universities of Europe such duties as have been assigned to a single Professor, in the above scheme, are divided among two, three or four men, and no class of teachers in the world are more devoted to their professions, or labor harder at the duties of them, than do these Professors. But as the means at the disposal of the best endowed Industrial Colleges must for a long time be limited, I have, in the above plan of organization, given the *minimum* number of Professors and Teachers required, rather than the *maximum* that might be advantageously employed.

College Buildings and Out-Buildings, &c.

Under this head should be discussed the size and form of the College buildings best adapted for the purposes of *instruction* and *moral government*. As the form best adapted to secure good order and moral discipline, though a question of the highest importance, is not different from that of other colleges, it need not be discussed here. The kind of building best adapted for the purpose of instruction, in an Industrial College, will differ from that of an ordinary College, in its having much more space devoted to Natural History collections, museums and store-rooms for models of tools and machinery, and for scientific apparatus, laboratories, and rooms for scientific investigations, &c. As these will be considered under the next sub-division of our subject, they may be omitted here. It hardly need be remarked here that the size and extent of the College buildings should be such as would afford means of instruction for from 400 to 800 students.

19

The out-buildings should embrace a *barn*, wagon house, tool house, black-smith shop, and all the associated parapharnalia for efficient farm practice, in addition to a special department adapted to experimentation in agricultural field practice and stock feeding.

Apparatus and Natural History Collections and Museums.

These may all be classed under one head, as *auxiliaries to study*. Like the character of an Educational Institution, the scientific collections within its walls can only be brought to a high standard of perfection by prolonged years of industrious effort on the part of all those interested in it; most especially cannot these things, adapted to a new course of instruction, be bought in any market of the world; they must be developed out of the *ideas* and the *ideals* of the Professors of the Institution; and the extent and character of them will depend on the number and the attainments, and will represent the industry of their Professors. Even the kind and quality of philosophical apparatus, in an Educational Institution of the highest order, is more dependent upon the *character* of the Professors who would use it, than the man who makes it, or the science it illustrates; so that the material for the scientific collections, adapted to the necessities of an Educational Institution, can only be accumulated after years of patient effort. Yet there should be a general plan, conceived at the origin of an Industrial Institution, according to which the labor of collecting and arranging this material should go on.

Prof. Agassiz, with $200,000, at Cambridge, has commenced a Zöological Museum, which he estimates will take over two million of dollars, and many years labor, to complete. Corresponding to all the scientific Professors in the list already given, there should be extensive scientific collections.

The *Professor of Mathematics* should have geometrical and stereometrical figures, to illustrate all the abstract ideas of mathematics that are capable of representation by lines and surfaces, and not simply a few sections of a cone to which illustration is too often limited. The mathematical figures of the Professors of the schools in Paris would more than fill an American coal wagon.

The Professor of Chemistry should have complete laboratories for beginners, advanced students, and for special investigations; that students may experiment themselves, rather than look at the Professor making experiments. There should also be a complete set of apparatus adapted to illustration in chemical lectures, and a full set of rare and common chemical substances to illustrate the science.

The Professor of Agricultural Chemistry and Geology should have extensive collections of all the Proximate constituents (as starch, sugar, &c) of plants, and means in the laboratory of showing the student how to prepare them. He should have collections of different soils, plants, ashes, manures, and all other materials that are important in agricultural practice.

20

He should have field experiments, involving all questions in vegetable physiology carried out upon the College Farm, and in an experimental barn and stable, have experiments going on upon the nutrition of animals, the value of cattle foods, and the manufacture and preservation of manures. He should have a good geological and mineralogical collection, and a museum of Economic Geology, in connection with the Professor of Mining and Metallurgy. Very good museums of this kind exist in London and Paris, and one is being inaugurated in the scientific department of Yale College.

The Professor of Metallurgy and Mining, and Mineralogy, to have complete models of all kinds of smelting furnaces, fluxing furnaces and refining furnaces, and every thing else required to give a clear, connected idea of the entire process of taking ores from the earth, and preparing their metals for use. He should also have furnaces, muffles, &c., with which to teach the science of Metallurgy, and, with the Professor of Geology, should have a museum of Mineralogy and Economic Geology, and Technology.

The Professor of Veterinary should have such an anatomical museum of the domestic animals as our medical schools have of man, in addition to a collection of all the preparations of Veterinary Pharmacy, and all the instruments for the operations of veterinary surgery. He should have an anatomical dissecting room, and a laboratory for making anatomical preparations. The finest veterinary collection in the world is at Alfort, near Paris, but even it is susceptible of much improvement for educational purposes.

The museum of Natural History may be of almost any size, since there is no limit to the extent of such museums. It should be one, something of the style of the museum of the Academy of Natural Sciences, of Philadelphia; except that it should be collected and managed more with reference to systematic teaching, and not so much as a repository of individual specimens as that grand collection is. In an adjoining laboratory, students should be taught the art of taxidermy.

The Professor of Civil Engineering should have, in addition to all the apparatus for out-door and in-door work, a complete set of models of different styles of architecture, and specimens of the different kinds of material out of which structures can be built. The schools of mining and engineering in Paris afford the best examples for imitation in the number and variety of their auxiliaries to the study of these branches.

The Professor of Natural Philosophy and Astronomy should have several thousand dollars worth of philosophical apparatus. With the limited resources to which the most wealthy Industrial Colleges must long be confined, it would not be well to attempt to establish Astronomical Observatories in connection with them, but they should possess all the apparatus requisite for a much more extended series of illustrations than are given in any American College. There should be, in connection with this collection, a Physi-

21

cal Laboratory, in which students would learn the art of experimentation in physical science. Such is the case in the highest scientific schools of Europe.

With the Professorship of Botany, Horticulture and Entomology, there should be as full a collection of dried plants as could be obtained. There should also be a special collection of Medicinal plants. Another of weeds and useful plants; another of different parts of plants exhibiting the anatomical structure, and embryonic and advanced forms of growth; also microscopic preparations of plants; and a botanical laboratory, with several microscopes, in which to teach students the habit of microscopic investigation in vegetable anatomy and in entomology. There should also be a Botanical Garden with all kinds of plants in it that would grow in the climate, and an Economic Garden for medicinal and useful Plants and Weeds; a nursery in which students could learn everything about nursery practice; and a green house and a collection of different kinds of wood, to illustrate their economical value, and lastly, a museum of insects injurious to vegetation.

The Professor of Practical Agriculture should have a collection of Models of all kinds of machines and implements used by agriculturists all over the world. He should, as far as practicable, have full sized machines and implements of each kind, of the *very best* pattern. Such a collection may be seen in the Royal Agricultural College of Hohenheim, in Germany; and it might, in part, be selected from the immense mass of agricultural models in the Patent Office at Washington. He should have a complete collection of all kinds of grains, root crops and other agricultural productions, as cotton, wool and flax, &c., exhibiting each article in all the different states through which it passes, between the points of its original production and ultimate consumption. Such a collection is in part to be seen in Paris, and one of a popular character was, a few years ago, being established in London.

Such is a brief outline of the colossal work of bringing together all the auxiliaries to study required in an Industrial College. As extensive as the lists of items may seem, there are none that it would not be desirable to have, and the most of them are indispensable to success in an Industrial College.

Means of Scientific Investigation.

The characteristic distinction between man as a savage, and man as an enlightened creature being, as already remarked, the difference in the extent of his industrial operations, it follows that all those agencies, by means of which the field of industrial operations is widened, are of the utmost importance to the human race. But these agencies are all within the domain of Science, and hence they operate in proportion to the extent to which scientific investigations are successfully carried out. This proposition is too generally recognized to need demonstration. The spirit of the present age has been moulded to its

22

present form by the investigations of science.   Not only our physical comforts, but our *mental* and *moral* peculiarities, are in no small degree the result of the discovery of some obscure scientific man, known only to the few who are devoted to his profession.   The almost rebellious spirit of impatience with which we look, each day, for news of events happening the day before, all over our entire continent, and which our forefathers would have waited patiently for a month to learn, is due to the fact that in the last generation an obscure scientific investigator in Sweden discovered that a current of electricity passed around an iron bar rendered it magnetic. And the just indignation with which a modern lady contemplates the necessity of using a tallow candle, on learning that the village gas works have been allowed to get out of order, is a state of mind due to a desire cultivated by a luxury which originated in the investigation of an obscure English chemist.

The spirit of the age proclaims the necessity of scientific researches in every department of industrial pursuits, from the peaceful operations of the Agricultural Bureau at Washington, to the death-dealing avengers of treason, now in Charleston Harbor.   Our Industrial Colleges, to meet the demands of the age, must be experimental Institutions, no less than for teaching what is already known, in science.   It would prolong these remarks too much to dwell upon the character of the experimentation required.   Suffice to say, that all the foregoing Professors should be men who are capable, not only of teaching all that is known in their several departments, but who could extend this knowledge by their own researches, and they should be provided with means for this purpose.

There is scarcely any limit to the amount of means that may be advantageously spent in scientific investigations, in all the experimental sciences. As examples, for illustration, we might cite Mr. Lawes, of England, a shrewd scientific *practical* man, who spends from $5,000 to $10,000 annually in agricultural investigations, the Smithsonian Institution at Washington spends a much larger sum for general scientific investigation ; and a consideration of the expenditure of Harvard College, appended to this report, will show an expenditure of several thousand dollars for scientific research.

Prizes, Beneficiary Fund for Indigent Students, Free Scholarship, &c.—A most important item in the organization of a College is the establishment of a well chosen set of prizes as the reward of merit.   Whatever may be said in favor of impressing upon the student the necessity of study as a duty, or of teaching him to study for the love of study, the fact is undisputed that suitable prizes offer an additional motive for study.   The best regulated Educational Institutions, the world over, have admitted the necessity of prizes, and they grant them to all grades of students, from the mere child, in the elementary school, to the accomplished scholar of the high-

23

est Professional Departments of the best Universities.   Nearly all our more prominent American Colleges have adopted, more or less, extensive series of prizes.   Thus Harvard University gives about fifty prizes for meritorious effort, varying from an appropriate book of moderate value to money-prizes of $10, $15, $30, $40, $50 to $100, and sometimes even as high as $250.   Columbia College is even more liberal than this in the distribution of prizes, and Yale is committed to the same policy by a long established custom.   This subject is recommended to the Board as one of the highest importance, as soon as the resources of the Agricultural College of Pennsylvania will allow of the distribution of a series of prizes commensurate with the extent and character, and object of the Institution.   So important do I deem these prizes, that nothing but a consciousness of the fact that the pecuniary resources of the College will not admit of it, prevents me from suggesting a plan for the distribution of them at once.

A Beneficiary Fund.—Several Educational Institutions in this country and Europe have funds from which they can give or loan money to meritorious students, whose resources are inadequate to meet the expenditures in College.   Harvard University thus distributes from $2,000 to $3,000 per annum, and the sum at the disposal of the College is much less than the necessities of meritorious students require.   As such students, struggling in poverty, realize to a higher degree the necessity for industrious effort than do their more favored companions, they give a tone and general character to the classes they attend, which elevates their standard of excellence to a degree unattainable without the influence of their example.   This was most strikingly illustrated, in my own observation, during the year and a half which I was a student in the University of Leipsic, Germany, which had about three hundred students deriving gratuitous aid from the University.   It was from these students, much more than from their wealthy associates, that the succeeding great men of the University were derived.   The pecuniary ability, on the part of Colleges, thus to assist meritorious students, who would otherwise be obliged to leave College for want of funds, is therefore an inestimable source of power for good, both within the Institution and beyond its walls.

I am reminded by a recent circular, sent to me from the "Institute of Reward," for orphans of Patriots in New York, of a very large class of students who will hereafter appear at our Industrial Colleges, asking for an education, while they point to the graves of their fathers upon the battle fields of the Nation, as the melancholy evidence of their claims upon our regard.   Already we have had numerous applicants, from such that it seemed almost unpatriotic and ungrateful to reject, but our pecuniary resources forbid our affording them the aid they required.   The propriety of devoting a part of the income of the College to this purpose, as soon as its

24

financial affairs will admit of it, is respectfully submitted to the Board. No less important is the subject of free scholarships; a large number of them is granted by Literary Colleges to meritorious, indigent students, and the beneficial influence of such scholarships is similar to that of the Beneficiary Fund.

Plan and course of Instruction.

Having given the number and character of the Professors, Teachers, Superintendents and Assistance, for the organization of an Industrial College, it now remains to point out the qualifications and the course of study of the students of such Colleges.

First. Then as regards the qualifications of students, it will not be possible, in justice to those for whom such Colleges are intended, to fix upon any definite educational standard of admission, since there are no subordinate schools to prepare students for Industrial Colleges, as there are Academies to prepare them for Literary Colleges.

I took particular care to converse with all the prominent teachers of Industrial education in Europe, during my six years residence there, and the invariable response to my inquiries was, that they labored under great disadvantages in not being able to properly class many of their students as soon as they entered the Industrial College, owing to there being no subordinate schools in which to bring them up to a fixed educational standard.

The same difficulty will be experienced in America, even to a greater extent than in Europe, and it can only be obviated by having Elementary Departments, in connection with Industrial Colleges, in which students can be prepared to enter the regular College course.

These Elementary Departments may be of two kinds; they may be either sufficiently extensive to prepare the students to enter at once upon the purely scientific studies of an Industrial College, or they may be devoted simply to finishing up the deficiencies of a good common school education, leaving higher English branches to be taken in connection with the scientific studies of the Industrial course.

Of these two plans, the latter would seem decidedly the best adapted to the necessities of American students, and hence it only will be discussed.

How much of the course of an Industrial College all students should be required to study, and what parts they should be allowed to exercise a choice of studying, is a question of vast importance, though not peculiar to an Industrial College.

If the standard of admission of an Industrial College does not require familiarity with all the branches of a good English education, its course of instruction should embrace these, and no student should be allowed to graduate without having acquired them.

There are also certain branches of science, embracing the consideration

25

of the physical and physiological laws of life, with the elementary branches of which every student should be familiar.

There are also the great fundamental principles, of Morality and the Christian Religion, which should be taught to all students.

Hence all should be required to study these things, no matter what their taste and inclinations, or their intentions for future activity, may be.

But beyond these the student should be allowed the exercise of choice, within certain limits, as to the studies he would pursue for the purpose of graduating. But this first study, preliminary to the period of his making choice of the final course he would pursue, will make the student familiar with the elementary branches of nearly all the natural and physical sciences, and will give his teacher time to learn his tastes, intentions, and abilities, and thus with proper advice, he will be able to make a suitable selection of his final course of studies.

This course should embrace a thorough knowledge of a more limited range of subjects than were included in his elementary course.   He should pursue some of these subjects to the utmost bounds of human knowledge, and all of them as near these limits as his time would admit of.   At these limits he should be taught the method of original research.

Here he should be allowed to graduate, but he should be urged not to close his studies with the receipt of his diploma, but if possible to continue longer in the institution, as a resident graduate, and make original scientific investigations upon such subjects as will most directly bear upon the special industrial operations of life to which he expects to be devoted.

Such being the case, there should be, first, a general course of studies to finish up the English education of the student, and to indoctrinate him with the elementary studies of the sciences.

This course should extend through about two years, after which there should be several distinct courses, any one or more of which, or certain combinations of parts of which, he should be allowed to select.   The number, extent and efficiency of the courses would be dependent upon the resources of the Institution.

The following classification of the students, with the courses proposed, are submitted to the Board, as that best adapted to the organization of an Industrial College :

First.—*A course of Agricultural Science and Practice*, which shall embrace a preliminary training in general Science, and then a careful study of those sciences that relate to Agriculture, together with the details of all parts of agricultural practice, as the raising of crops, stock, &c.

Such a course as that now pursued at the Agricultural College of Pennsylvania, with the addition of the instruction of a special Professor of Agri-

26

cultural Practice, and a Professor of Veterinary and Zöology, aided by the appropriate museums of the foregoing prescribed plan of organization.

The Resident Graduates of this course to make scientific agricultural investigations.

Second.—*A course of Engineering and Architecture*, embracing two grades, one of which should require the study of the higher Mathematics and Mechanics, and the other would require no mathematics higher than the first eight books of Davies Legendre.

The lower course should embrace, in addition to applied Mathematics up to the extent of the Geometrical studies, practical lessons in all the details of ordinary Civil Engineering, Mechanical Drawing, Perspective, Photography, and embrace as much knowledge, Theoretical and Practical, as ordinary engineers have occasion to use in their ordinary duties.

The higher course should, in addition to the lower course, embrace the Fluctional Calculus, the higher Geometry and Mechanics, Astronomy and Navigation. The Resident Graduates of this course should devote themselves to the profound studies of the physical sciences, by means of the fluctional calculus, and to experimentation in these sciences.

To this course it would be easy to add, if desired, a course of Military Engineering and Gunnery.

Third.—*An Industrial Course.* The word industrial is here used in a much more limited signification than elsewhere in this paper, simply to refer to such branches of human industry as are not included in the art and science of Agriculture, or of Engineering. It relates more particularly to a practical and scientific knowledge of those industrial operations which are the offspring of the Natural Sciences, as developed within the present century—as Metallurgy, Technological Chemistry, Pharmacy—giving the student correct knowledge about the intrinsic nature of, and the origin and means of preparing for use, the various articles which contribute to the necessities and luxuries of every day life, thus making him an intelligent manufacturer of such articles as he makes, and an intelligent consumer of such things as are made by others. This course should be varied a little, if the resources of the Institution would admit of it, to suit the peculiar necessities of the person taking it. Resident Graduates of the course would devote themselves to experimental researches into such parts of it as would be of the greatest practical importance to them. Thus, to illustrate with a question of great practical interest to the country, a student who expected to devote himself to the manufacture of sugar from the Sorghum Saccharatum, would apply himself not only to all the methods of analyzing saccharine compounds, but, to estimating the amount of sugar in all plants containing it, to the study of the remarkable transformations in vegetable growth by which sugar is produced and consumed in the growing plant,

27

and to all those purely chemical processes by which sugar is produced modified or destroyed, and to a close study of those organic substances which must be separated from saccharine juices in order to make the best sugar and molasses.   Such a sugar refiner would be an intelligent, scientific man in regard to his profession, and not a mere tradesman, blindly following the empirical rules and recipes he had learned from another without understanding them.

Fourth. *A Purely Practical Course.*—This course should embrace only a popular consideration of science in its relations to industrial operations, such as is embodied in the popular lectures before popular scientific and literary societies, but it should be more extensive and more systematically arranged than these.   The admirable series of popular lectures on Agricultural subjects, delivered at Yale College a few years ago, will give an idea of the kind of instruction referred to in this course.   It is designed for students who are too old, or may not have time, or who are too delicate to stand the close discipline of a more extended course, as also for grown up men, who may not in youth have had the advantages of a scientific education, and who want to get such knowledge of science as will enable them more fully to understand the scientific reading matter and conversation which the progressive spirit of the age is more and more infusing into all the walks of social life.   This course would only extend through a year or part of a year, and would merit no degree on being finished.

Fifth. *A Commercial Course.*—This course should not embrace simply the art of book-keeping, (which should be taught during the first two years to all students,) but it should make the student familiar with the laws of trade and commercial intercourse, and with the business habits and peculiarities of Nations, and with all the channels and sources through which the wealth of the world is moved about and accumulated.   This course could have two grades, in one of which no language but English was studied, and which would extend through one year, and the other of which should embrace the study of at least two modern languages, one of which should be German. This course should extend through two years.   Resident Graduates could devote themselves to additional studies in the modern languages.

Sixth. *A Literary Department.*—It is not designed that this shall dispute with ordinary Colleges the right to teach literary studies, but it should bear some such relation to literary studies as do the Professorships of Natural Sciences in such Colleges to scientific studies.

While the study of Latin and Greek would not be urged upon the student as an indispensable part of mental discipline, or of practical education, means would be provided for his studying these languages, did he desire to do so, in connection with his other studies.   It is not intended by this remark to deny that linguistic studies, and especially the ancient classics are not most

28

potent means of mental culture, but simply to doubt the propriety of students commencing the study of Latin and Greek at so advanced an age, when they expect to devote their time to industrial pursuits. Besides, the ordinary Literary Colleges are open to such as wish to study these, and they are advised to attend to them.

The modern languages would also be taught, and in some cases one or two of them incorporated as part of the course in the foregoing plan of studies, and in all cases where the student's time will permit, he should be recommended to study two modern languages, one of which should be German.

In this Department opportunities should be afforded for the study of such indispensable branches of an English education, as may not have been completed in the first two years of the four year course. They would embrace Logic, Rhetoric, Moral Philosophy, Political Economy and the fundamental principles of human government, including the Constitution of the United States. Associated with this department, and immediately under the charge of its faculty, would be a *primary school* for the purpose of preparing students to enter the College course.

There would be no graduates in this department, but it would have an appropriate mission in helping on the other departments, and students wishing to take a literary degree, could easily do so by afterwards going to a Literary College.

Endowments of Industrial Colleges.

It has already been shown that large sums of money derived from endowments, are requisite to sustain Literary Colleges of high character.

It has been shown that so far as these Colleges have introduced the Natural Sciences, they have required a corresponding degree of expense for museums, apparatus and tuition.

An attempt has been made to make it clear that Industrial Colleges must be large, scientific institutions, in which the entire range of the natural and physical sciences must be taught.

In accordance with this attempt, the organization of such an Industrial College has been given, and the course of instruction commensurate with the organization has been laid out.

In summing up the number of Professors, Assistants and Superintendents, and looking at the extent of the auxiliaries to study, we found an Institution of the magnitude of some of the best Literary Colleges in the country, with fully as extensive a course of instruction as they have, while the students who are expected to attend them are less able to pay for tuition than are the students of Literary Colleges. The obvious inference from all this is, that Industrial Colleges require as large endowments, as do Literary Colleges, if not larger, to enable them to fulfil their mission.

29

Such being the conclusion at which we have arrived, our plan for an Industrial College will be an impracticable ideal if we cannot secure an extensive endowment for its support. For the moment, supposing that it was impossible to do so, our considerations would, at all events, help to explain why it has been that almost all attempts to found Industrial Colleges without endowment have ended in bankruptcy and failure.

But Industrial Education is too important to be left, by our enlightened people, without pecuniary means for its support, and hence we are encouraged to sum up the expenses involved in it.

For this purpose the attention of the Board is invited to the following :

Summary of Annual Income and Expenditure of an Industrial College.

EXPENDITURE.

16 Professors, at $1,500	$24,000 00	
10 Assistants	4,000 00	
A Farm Superintendent	700 00	
Janitor and helps	1,000 00	
		$29,700 00
For additions to Museums, to Scientific Apparatus and to Library		5,000 00
For scientific investigation		5,000 00
For indigent students, orphans of soldiers, free scholarships, &c.,		7,000 00
For repair of buildings		1,000 00
Total expenditure		$47,700 00

INCOME.

400 students, at $50 per annum	$20,000 00
Income required from endowment	27,000 00
	$47,000 00

The annual expenses of such an Industrial College as we have been considering, are stated at $47,700, independent of taxes and interest, or rent of College buildings, grounds and farms, &c.

If any think the sum extravagantly large, they are requested to compare it with the first class Literary Colleges about which we have already said so much, or they are invited to examine the details of expenditure.

The price allowed to each Professor ($1,500) is not as high as is paid by first class Literary Colleges.

And the competition for scientific Professorships is not nearly so great as for those of Literary Colleges.

30

It will be with great difficulty that men of the attainments required, in the plan of organization we have given, can be engaged at these prices.

Harvard University gives $3,000 annually to a Zöological Museum in a Literary College. The sum of $5,000 would not seem extravagant for the entire range of scientific collections in a Scientific College.

When a private individual, Mr. Lawes, of Rothamstead, England, expends $10,000 annually in agricultural scientific investigation, the sum of $5,000 for investigations in *all* of the sciences should not be deemed prodigal.

And when the sons of Pennsylvania's immortal Patriots, who fell upon our country's battle-field, in defence of our National existence, shall ask for an education at our Industrial College, shall any one, who enjoys the liberty they preserved, say that the paltry sum of $7,000 is more than our State can afford them.

Then, if the items of the bill are not over-charged, the sum of them is not unreasonable, and our next question is,

Can an Endowment Fund sufficient to yield $27,700 *annually be secured?*

It was with some such question as this before the minds of the Board of Trustees of the Agricultural College of Pennsylvania that they labored for several years for the passage, by Congress, of the bill donating land to Agricultural Colleges.

It was with this question in his mind that one of the Board turned from the State Legislature, where he had labored successfully to secure funds to complete our College buildings, to his seat in Congress, where he labored no less successfully to secure the means of their endowment.

And this endowment is to be found in the proceeds of the sale of land scrip, donated by Congress to this State for the endowment and support of a College for "Agriculture and the Mechanic Arts."

Owing to the general depreciation of public lands this land scrip will not bring nearly as much as was anticipated at the time the bill was drawn up, and hence the income from it will be less than half what it otherwise would have been, and therefore the income will, it is feared, be considerable less than the amount required to make up the balance sheet in the above account.

But from a careful consideration of the subject, I am led to believe that this income from the scrip will yield the College somewhere between $10,000 and $20,000 annually, which will enable us to enlarge the sphere of our operations, and to gradually throw off the load of debt that now presses heavily upon us and cripples all our efforts. And although this endowment will not enable us to organize the College, upon a plan as extensive as that proposed in this paper for an Industrial College, it will, I doubt not, so far enable us to show what can be done with more extended resources, that some wealthy, public spirited friend of industrial education will, like John Harvard, do

31

himself immortal honor by affording the College the requisite additional means to bring it up to the highest possible standard of excellence.

It therefore now remains for those of us who have the immediate oversight of the Agricultural College of Pennsylvania, to labor with all our powers to make the best possible use of the income from this endowment fund, not only to bring the Institution up to the expectations of those who are interested in its success, but to ultimately secure from private individuals, such additional endowment as will leave nothing further to be desired in its Educational system.

As no income from this endowment will be made available to the College for one or two years yet, it will require the greatest possible economy on the part of the manages of the Institution, and an increased tax upon our already over-taxed Treasurer to meet its expenses.   Since with our present low rates of admission, and with the greatly advanced price of all articles of consumption, notwithstanding our small number of Professors, we are annually sinking deeper in debt.   Hence it is of the utmost importance that this fund be brought into such shape, at the earliest possible moment, that it will yield something to meet the expenses of the College, and enable us to extend its educational resources.

It is only an act of justice to the people of the State, who have directly, or indirectly, through their Representatives in the Legislature, contributed about $200,000 to erect the buildings and purchase and improve the farm of this Institution, that the endowment by which this property only can be efficiently used, should, as soon as possible, be made available.

The grant of Land and Land Scrip from Congress to the several States for the endowment of Agricultural Colleges.

The foregoing considerations, in great part, have had a general character, relating to the whole subject of Industrial Education, rather than to the Agricultural College of Pennsylvania in particular.   This form of considering the subject has been adopted, because all questions involved in the general consideration applied with especial force to this College.

In closing this report I would venture a few remarks upon what would seem to be the legitimate object of the Land Grant by Congress, for the endowment of Colleges for Agriculture and the Mechanic arts.

This Land Grant was the result of the growing intelligence of the agricultural classes of the country, and the modern development of all those sciences which have a practical bearing upon the industrial operations of life.   A necessity for Industrial Colleges was felt throughout the entire country.   Literary Colleges not only failed to supply an education especially adapted to the peculiar necessities of the industrial classes, but through their highest officials they persistently proclaimed that no such special College education was requisite, and that the best education a young man

32

could have to fit him for practical duties in life, was to be found in the study of Latin and Greek. The idea of Industrial Education was turned into ridicule, and Industrial Colleges were denominated visionary ideals of impracticable men. Determined that means should be provided for a general system of Industrial Education, a few prominent friends of such a system of education from other States, in conjunction with the friends of the Agricultural College of Pennsylvania, after about six years of persistent effort, secured the passage, by Congress, of the Land Grant bill. This bill afforded sufficient land, or land scrip to each of the larger States, to enable them, with a reasonable effort from the State, to found one Agricultural College. Smaller States could only use it by establishing Agricultural Chairs in Literary Colleges, as they had not enough to endow an Industrial College. The object of the bill, however, was *most distinctly not simply to found Industrial Chairs* in Literary Colleges, but to *endow Industrial Colleges* such as that, the organization of which, has been discussed in this paper.

No sooner was the bill passed, than in some States the representatives of several Literary Colleges, with singularly bad taste, made a general rush to the State Legislature to secure a portion of the proceeds of the bill, and in the general scramble for a share of the spoils, in some instances, defeated all legislation upon the subject. That Literary Institutions should, with such undignified haste, grasp at resources (secured for the endowment of Industrial Colleges) to which they had not the *slightest legitimate claim*, is a melancholy illustration of the terrible extremities to which they are driven in the struggle for existence. It should warn those States, which would found State Industrial Colleges, to endow them properly, and not cast them into the world to struggle in poverty for existence, guided by a necessity which knows no law and recognizes no right.

For what are the claims of these Literary Colleges upon the Land Grant Fund? Can they afford the kind of education required in an Industrial College? Can they organize the four or five different courses of study required to meet the peculiar necessities of Industrial Education? Can they, with their half dozen Professors, do the work which fourteen first class scientific men are required to do, in addition to teaching all their literary studies? No! They would only degrade Industrial Education to the standard upon which they have heretofore looked with merited contempt. They might well compare the victims of their superficial smattering with the regular students of their classical course, as illustrations of how much better the study of Latin and Greek is for mental discipline than the study of anything else.

Suppose, for illustration, that Ohio were to allow this Land Scrip Fund to be frittered away upon half a dozen Colleges, or even upon two Colleges, while Pennsylvania concentrated the whole upon one College, with some

53

such organization as we have considered; does any one doubt which would have the most desirable plan of Industrial Education—Pennsylvania or Ohio? Would not the ambitious sons of the industrial classes in Ohio despise their own Industrial Colleges, and come to Pennsylvania, just as students now crowd from all States to make up the 800 students of Harvard University.

Ohio would do well to learn a lesson of wisdom from Pennsylvania, New York and Massachusetts, and other States whose Legislatures have been wise enough to keep this great perpetual legacy for the education of her industrial classes together.

In conclusion, it should be remarked, that it is due to the 23 Literary Colleges in Pennsylvania to say, that they made no effort to obstruct legislation, upon the bestowal of the income from the endowment fund upon the Agricultural College of Pennsylvania, doubtless knowing, as they must have known, that the friends of this College had been mainly instrumental in getting the bill, donating the land, through Congress; and hence, *by courtesy*, no less than *by right*, and according to the spirit of the bill, were entitled to the fund for the endowment of the State Institution for which they procured it. Doubtless these Colleges would as likely have thought of asking the Trustees of the Agricultural College of Pennsylvania, to share with them the money they secured by private subscription, as to ask them to divide what was no less obtained by their own efforts to endow this College, and which is no less essential to its prosperity. It would have been fortunate for the interests of industrial education, had Literary Colleges in some other States been guided by the same delicacy of feeling in regard to what they had no legitimate claim upon. But it is not too late to hope that all the States may see the suicidal folly of dividing their respective shares of this fund, and that they will each concentrate it upon one first class State Institution, and that all these Institutions will grow up in one great fraternity of Industrial Colleges, working together in harmony upon one uniform system, adapted to the dissemination of professional knowledge amongst the industrial classes.

All of which is respectfully submitted.

E. PUGH, *President of Faculty.*

NOTE.—Since the above was put into the hands of the printer, it has transpired that the above opinion, as to the willingness of all the Literary Colleges of the State, to allow the Agricultural College of Pennsylvania to reap the full benefit of the funds which its friends had secured from Congress for its endowment, was *too hastily expressed*, as a bill has since been read in place, and referred to a committee, asking for one-third of the land scrip for the Allegheny College at Meadville. It is hoped that the Legislature will

34

give no encouragement whatever to a claim so unreasonable, so unjust, and which will so effectually tend to defeat the object of the land grant bill, while it must cripple, for many years to come, the cause of Industrial Education in our State.

The following are a few of many obvious reasons why this claim should not be encouraged.

1st. As already shown, in this report, the fund will scarcely yield sufficient income to endow one Industrial College properly.

2d. Two or more partially endowed Institutions will be unable to give that character and efficiency to Industrial Education without which the whole system will fall into disgrace.

3d. The Agricultural College of Pennsylvania is a State Institution; the State has appropriated $100,000, and the people of the State have donated nearly an equal sum to bring it into existence. It belongs to the State; its property is held in trust by a Board of Trustees elected by delegates from the County Agricultural Societies of the State.

4th. All this property can only be made available for the purposes designed by it, with the aid of such an endowment as that secured in the land scrip fund. It was part of the plan of the friends of this College, when asking the Legislature to appropriate money to put up its large buildings, to secure an endowment from this source, and to this end they were, at the same time, laboring in Congress for the passage of the Land Grant bill. In view of their being confident of securing an endowment from this source, they promised the Legislature, when asking for money to complete the College buildings, not to ask the State for an endowment.

5th. The friends of the Agricultural College of Pennsylvania secured the passage of the Land Grant bill by Congress.

A member of their Board of Trustees (then, as now, a prominent member of Congress) devoted almost an entire session in Congress to its passage, and other friends of the College visited Washington several times for the same purpose. *Without their aid the bill would not have passed.*

6th. The Agricultural College of Pennsylvania has no other endowment; it has serious pecuniary embarrassments that will oblige it to fall back upon the State Legislature to secure an appropriation to meet, *and these embarrassments will be constantly recurring*, if its managers are thus unjustly deprived of the endowment they have secured from Congress.

7th. The Allegheny College, at Meadville, is *not* a State Institution—it is *not* under the control of the industrial classes of the State—it does *not* belong to the State—it was *not* originated for Industrial Education, nor has it been devoted to it—its friends did nothing for the passage of the Land Grant bill in Congress; and at the time this bill originated they had not conceived the idea of Industrial Education, and even now I am told that their

35

conception of the demand for such education is embraced in what "a Professor of Agricultural Chemistry, who will analyze soils," (the *one thing* which is now discarded by all good Chemists as of no use) can do in their College!!! They seem not to have thought of Industrial Education, and the "Chemist to analyze soils," until to do so afforded a *pretext* for grappling for the Land Grant Fund. The industrial interests of our State and posterity never could pardon an act, fraught with such ruinous consequences to the cause of Industrial education, upon a pretext so flimsy as that upon which it is attempted to divide this fund. The College at Meadville was not originated with the expectation of endowment from this source; and hence it being deprived of it, defeats no expectation entertained and acted upon in calling it into existence. On the contrary, it is a *local denominational literary school*, under the control of a particular sect, and it has other sources of endowment.

It cannot be that the Legislature of Pennsylvania will encourage this claim. There are over 20 other Institutions in the State with claims equally just, or rather *equally preposterous.* In order to promote the interests of this claim, *incorrect* representations have been made as to the price this land scrip will bring in the market, in order to show that it will yield too much for one Institution. The values given on p. 30 are, I think, the limits between which the annual income will be found, and in this opinion I am sustained by a number of prominent gentlemen who have given the subject much attention, and several of whom have been, and some now are, extensive dealers in land scrip.

E. PUGH.

HARRISBURG, *Jan.* 14, 1864.

INDEX.

Preface

1. C. Alfred Smith, "Evan Pugh Ph.D., F.C.S., Memorial Address," June 25, 1890, Box 5, Folder 51, Pugh Papers (hereafter PP) (Pennsylvania State University Archives [PSUA] 1261), 1.
2. Evan Pugh to Samuel W. Johnson, January 6, 1860, Box 5, Folder 12, PP.
3. Charles E. Rosenberg, *No Other Gods: On Science and American Social Thought* (Baltimore: Johns Hopkins University Press, 1997), 135.
4. Alan I. Marcus, *Agricultural Science and the Quest for Legitimacy* (Ames: Iowa State University Press, 1985), 20.
5. Alfred Traverse, "Dr. Pugh's Herbarium," *Journal of the Botanical Research Institute of Texas* 7, 2 (2013: 755.
6. Charles A. Browne, "European Experiences of an Early American Agricultural Chemist—Dr. Evan Pugh (1828–1864)," *Journal of Chemical Education*, March 1930, 499, 517.
7. Earle D. Ross, *Democracy's College: The Land-Grant Movement in the Formative Stage* (Ames: Iowa State College Press, 1942), 55, 29.

Chapter 1

1. Wayland F. Dunaway, *A History of Pennsylvania* (New York: Prentice-Hall, 1935), 89.

2. Jacqueline M. Bloom, "Evan Pugh: The Education of a Scientist, 1828–1859" (M.A. thesis, Pennsylvania State University, 1960), 1–2.
3. Pugh family genealogy, Box 6, Folder 3, PP.
4. Bloom, "Evan Pugh," 2.
5. Jesse Pugh to Achilles Pugh, August 9, 1841, Box 5, Folder 54, PP.
6. Evan Pugh, "Leipsic Journal," October 10, 1853, Box 1, Folder 11, PP, 101.
7. Evan Pugh, autobiographical sketch, "Translation from the Latin of 'A Brief Life of Doctor Evan Pugh,'" 1856, Box 1, Folder 6, PP.
8. Bloom, "Evan Pugh," 5.
9. Jesse Pugh to Achilles Pugh, August 12, 1841, Box 5, Folder 54, PP.
10. Evan Pugh, "Journal of Trip from New York to Hamburg on the Ship George Canning," 1853–55, entry for October 3, 1853, Box 1, Folder 12, PP, 103, 104, 106.
11. Pugh, "Leipsic Journal," 101.
12. Pugh, "Journal of a Trip from New York to Hamburg," 106.
13. Ibid., 88.
14. Pugh, "Translation from the Latin of 'A Brief Life of Doctor Evan Pugh.'"
15. Bloom, "Evan Pugh," 9.
16. Ibid., 10.
17. Excerpt cited in ibid., 11.
18. Evan Pugh, "Osseology," Box 1, Folder 51, PP.

19. George Mason's autograph book, 1852–53, Box 1, Folder 4, PP.

20. *West Chester (Pa.) Register and Examiner*, February 25, 1853, PP.

21. Swithin C. Shortlidge, "Dr. Evan Pugh, Man of Ability; Old Friend Pays Tribute to the First President of Pennsylvania State College," undated, but likely 1928, Box 6, Folder 12, PP. The mothers of Evan Pugh and Swithin Shortlidge were sisters. Shortlidge (b. 1840) graduated from Philips Exeter Academy in 1863 and Harvard University in 1866.

22. Pugh, "Journal of a Trip from New York to Hamburg," 107.

23. "George Thompson's Address at West ·Chester, Delivered on Wednesday afternoon, June 4, 1851. Reported Phonographically for the Freeman, by E. Pugh," Box 1, Folder 9, PP.

24. Evan Pugh, "Trip from Chester County to Newark, N.J.—Educational Convention, Newark, August, 10th, 1852," *West Chester (Pa.) Register and Examiner*, Box 1, Folder 9, PP.

25. Evan Pugh's Parker Girls and Andy Job stories can be found in Box 1, Folder 9, PP.

26. *The Proceedings of the Women's Rights Convention, Held at West Chester, Pa. June 2d and 3d, 1852* (Philadelphia: Merrihew and Thompson, 1852), 18.

27. Rosenberg, *No Other Gods*, 152.

28. W. Wilmer, ed., *Chester County and Its People* (Chicago: Union History Co., 1898), 959–65.

29. Dorothy I. Lansing, "William Darlington, M.D., LL.D, D.Sc., One of the Giants of the Earth," the Dr. William Darlington Commemorative Program Addresses, Chester County Medical Society, January 20, 1965, Box 7, Folder 5, PP.

30. American National Biography Online, "William Darlington."

31. Ancestry.com, "William Darlington."

32. Bloom, "Evan Pugh," 14.

33. J. Eugene Walker to Erwin W. Runkle, January 31, 1928, Box 6, Folder 3, PP.

34. Evan Pugh to the *West Chester (Pa.) Register and Examiner*, September 1853, Box 1, Folder 7, PP.

35. Evan Pugh to Samuel W. Johnson, February 22, 1855, Box 5, Folder 12, PP.

36. Pugh, "Journal of a Trip from New York to Hamburg," 11, 48, 120.

37. Evan Pugh, *The Agricultural College of Pennsylvania, September 1862* (Philadelphia: William S. Young, 1862), PP, 5–9.

38. Roger L. Williams, *The Origins of Federal Support for Higher Education: George W. Atherton and the Land-Grant College Movement* (University Park: Pennsylvania State University Press, 1991), 27.

39. Pugh, *Agricultural College of Pennsylvania*, 8–9.

40. Margaret W. Rossiter, "The Organization of Agricultural Improvement in the United States, 1785–1865," in *The Pursuit of Knowledge in the Early American Republic: American Scientific and Learned Societies from Colonial Times to the Civil War*, ed. Alexandra Oleson and Sanford C. Brown (Baltimore: Johns Hopkins University Press, 1976), 281.

41. J. B. Edmond, *The Magnificent Charter: The Origin and Role of the Morrill Land-Grant Colleges and Universities* (Hicksville, N.Y.: Exposition Press, 1978), 29.

42. A. Hunter Dupree, *Science in the Federal Government: A History of Policies and Activities to 1940* (Cambridge, Mass.: Harvard University Press, 1957), 46.

43. Williams, *Origins of Federal Support for Higher Education*, 23.

44. Roger L. Geiger, *The History of American Higher Education: Learning and Culture from the Founding to World War II* (Princeton: Princeton University Press, 2015), 262.
45. Ibid., 263.
46. Alfred C. True, *History of Agricultural Education in the United States, 1785–1925*, U.S. Department of Agriculture, Misc. Pub. no. 36 (Washington, D.C.: Government Printing Office, 1929), 34.
47. Rosenberg, *No Other Gods*, 136–47.
48. Quoted in William B. Parker, *The Life and Public Services of Justin Smith Morrill* (Boston: Houghton Mifflin, 1924), 263.
49. Williams, *Origins of Federal Support for Higher Education*, 25.
50. Geiger, *History of American Higher Education*, 262.
51. Ibid., 261.

Chapter 2

1. Bloom, "Evan Pugh," 25.
2. Ibid., 26.
3. Laurence R. Veysey, *The Emergence of the American University* (Chicago: University of Chicago Press, 1965), 10.
4. Carl Diehl, "Innocents Abroad: American Students in German Universities, 1810–1870," *History of Education Quarterly* 16, no. 3 (1976): 321–40, passim.
5. Evan Pugh, letter no. 25, "German Universities . . . with statistical evidence," May 2, 1854, Box 1, Folder 10, PP.
6. Evan Pugh to *West Chester (Pa.) Register and Examiner*, October 31, 1853, Box 1, Folder 7, PP.
7. Charles E. Rosenberg, "Science and Social Values in Nineteenth-Century America: A Case Study in the Growth of Scientific Institutions," in Rosenberg, *No Other Gods*, 137.

8. Evan Pugh to *West Chester (Pa.) Register and Examiner*, October 31, 1853, Box 1, Folder 7, PP.
9. Roy Olofson, "Evan Pugh, Professor of Chemistry," memo distributed at Pugh Exhibit in conjunction with the meeting of the Division of Chemical Education of the American Chemical Society, University Park, Pa., August 1974, Box 6, Folder 12, PP.
10. Evan Pugh to *West Chester (Pa.) Register and Examiner*, October 31, 1853, Box 1, Folder 7, PP.
11. Bloom, "Evan Pugh," 20, 31.
12. Evan Pugh to Samuel W. Johnson, December 1, 1854, Box 2, Folder 9, PP.
13. Pugh, letter no. 25, "German Universities . . . with statistical evidence."
14. Evan Pugh, letter no. 1, "Journey from Leipsic to Altenburg in Germany," March 28, 1855, Box 1, Folder 8, PP.
15. Evan Pugh, letter no. 2, "Altenburg and Its Inhabitants—Journey to Ywickau," March 19, 1855, Box 1, Folder 8, PP.
16. Evan Pugh, letter no. 6, "Descent into a silver mine," Freiberg, April 2, 1855, Box 1, Folder 8, PP.
17. Evan Pugh, letter no. 11, "Erfurt—Luther's Cell—Old Cathedral, etc.," April 1855, Box 1, Folder 8, PP.
18. Evan Pugh, letter no. 13, "Old Castle of Wartburg—Luther's Fight with the Devil, etc.," April 1855, Box 1, Folder 8, PP.
19. Evan Pugh, letter no. 17, "Arrival in Gottingen—Impressions—On seeing the Old Town," April 1855, Box 1, Folder 8, PP.
20. Olofson, "Evan Pugh, Professor of Chemistry."
21. Evan Pugh to *West Chester (Pa.) Register and Examiner*, October 31, 1853, Box 1, Folder 7, PP.

22. Evan Pugh, "Gottingen Journal," September 8, 1855, 294, and March 30, 1856, 2, PP.

23. Evan Pugh to *West Chester (Pa.) Register and Examiner,* August 24, 1855, Box 1, Folder 7, PP.

24. Evan Pugh, letter no. 29, "Nicknacks about Student Life in Gottingen," November 29, 1855, Box 1, Folder 8, PP.

25. Evan Pugh to Samuel W. Johnson, July 23, 1855, Box 2, Folder 10, PP.

26. Evan Pugh, "Gottingen and the Harts," August 30, 1855, Box 2, Folders 7 and 8, PP.

27. Ibid., September 27, 1855.

28. Evan Pugh to William Darlington, May 24, 1856, William Darlington Collection, New-York Historical Society.

29. Pugh, "Translation from the Latin of 'A Brief Life of Doctor Evan Pugh.'"

30. George Caldwell to C. Alfred Smith, c. 1890, letter published in *Headlight on Books at Penn State* 19, no. 3 (1949).

31. Quoted in Erwin W. Runkle, "The Pugh Centenary," *Penn State Alumni News* 14, no. 6 (1928): 8.

32. Bloom, "Evan Pugh," 34.

33. Evan Pugh, letter no. 30, "University Life at Heidelberg," August 1856, Box 1, Folder 15, PP.

34. Traverse, "Dr. Pugh's Herbarium," 751–64.

35. Evan Pugh to William Darlington, August 20, 1856, William Darlington Collection, New-York Historical Society.

36. Evan Pugh to *West Chester (Pa.) Register and Examiner*, November 25, 1853, Box 1, Folder 7, PP.

37. Bloom, "Evan Pugh," 35, 36.

38. Ibid., 39.

39. Evan Pugh to *New York Independence Herald and Free American*, October 19, 1856, Box 1, Folder 15, PP.

40. Evan Pugh to *New York Independence Herald and Free American*, October 20, 1856, Box 1, Folder 15, PP.

41. Evan Pugh to *Chester County Times,* January 15, 1857, Box 1, Folder 7, PP.

42. Evan Pugh to Samuel W. Johnson, July 23, 1855, Box 2, Folder 10, PP.

43. Evan Pugh to *Chester County Times*, April 12, 1857, Box 1, Folder 7, PP.

44. Olofson, "Evan Pugh, Professor of Chemistry."

45. Bloom, "Evan Pugh," 51.

46. Olofson, "Evan Pugh, Professor of Chemistry."

47. Evan Pugh to Samuel W. Johnson, June 14, 1856, Box 2, Folder 9, PP.

48. Evan Pugh, "Objections against Ville's book," in *Notebook on Nitrogen*, 1, PP.

49. Bloom, "Evan Pugh," 55.

50. Evan Pugh to Samuel W. Johnson, August 2, 1857, Box 2, Folder 9, PP.

51. E. John Russell, *British Agricultural Research: Rothamsted* (London: British Council, 1942), 2, Box 7, Folder 2, PP.

52. Ibid., 4.

53. Evan Pugh to Frederick O. Watts, June 11, 1859, Box 5, Folder 23, PP.

54. Evan Pugh to Samuel W. Johnson, October 1, 1857, Box 2, Folder 9, PP.

55. George C. Caldwell, as quoted in C. Alfred Smith, "Evan Pugh, Ph.D., F.C.S., Memorial Address," delivered on the occasion of the presentation of a portrait of Dr. Pugh to the Pennsylvania State College, June 25, 1890, Box 5, Folder 51, PP, 4.

56. Bloom, "Evan Pugh," 60–61.

57. Ibid., 61.

58. Evan Pugh to Samuel W. Johnson, March 14, 1858, Box 2, Folder 9, PP.

59. Bloom, "Evan Pugh," 66.

60. A. A. Breneman, "Dr. Evan Pugh, Chemist and Philosopher," an address given June 16, 1908, before the Phi Kappa Phi Society at the Pennsylvania State College, PP, 10–11.

61. J. B. Lawes and J. H. Gilbert, *Rothamsted Memoirs on Agriculture and Chemistry* (1889), quoted in Kristen A. Yarmey, *Labors and Legacies: The Chemists of Penn State, 1855–1947* (University Park: Pennsylvania State University Department of Chemistry, 2006), 20.

62. Yarmey, *Labors and Legacies*, 20.

63. Olofson, "Evan Pugh, Professor of Chemistry."

64. Evan Pugh to Samuel W. Johnson, March 14, 1858, Box 2, Folder 9, PP.

65. Evan Pugh to Samuel W. Johnson, March 15, 1858, Box 2, Folder 9, PP.

66. Yarmey, *Labors and Legacies*, 20.

67. James F. W. Johnston and Charles A. Cameron, *Elements of Agricultural Chemistry and Geology*, 13th ed. (Edinburgh: William Blackwood and Sons, 1883), 239, Box 5, Folder 51, PP.

68. Evan Pugh, "On a New Method for the Quantitative Estimation of Nitric Acid," *Quarterly Journal of the Chemical Society of London* 12 (1860): 35–42, PP.

69. Evan Pugh to Samuel W. Johnson, undated, but probably ca. 1859, Box 2, Folder 10, PP.

Chapter 3

1. Evan Pugh to Alfred W. Elwyn, undated but annotated as being sent "sometime before the summer of 1855," Box 3, Folder 11, PP.

2. Michael Bezilla, *Penn State: An Illustrated History* (University Park: Pennsylvania State University Press, 1985), 4.

3. Frederick O. Watts to Governor William Bigler, January 20, 1854, Box 5, Folder 23, PP.

4. Leon J. Stout, "Penn State's First Trustees," *Town and Gown*, November 2005, 28.

5. Erwin W. Runkle, *The Pennsylvania State College, 1853–1932: Interpretation and Record* (State College, Pa.: Nittany Valley Society, 2013), 51.

6. Ibid., 79.

7. Frederick O. Watts, *Annual Report of the Farmers' High School, 1858*, PSUA.

8. Leon J. Stout, "The Penn State President Who Never Was," *Town and Gown*, April 1996, 23–25.

9. Bezilla, *Penn State*, 7.

10. Runkle, *The Pennsylvania State College*, 55.

11. Evan Pugh to Alfred W. Elwyn, undated but annotated as being sent "sometime before the summer of 1855," Box 3, Folder 11, PP.

12. Ibid.

13. Ibid.

14. Evan Pugh, *A Report upon a Plan for the Organization of Colleges for Agriculture and the Mechanic Arts, with especial reference to the organization of the Agricultural College of Pennsylvania* (Harrisburg: Singerly and Myers, 1864), 15, PP.

15. Evan Pugh to Samuel W. Johnson, October 31, 1855, Box 2, Folder 10, PP.

16. Evan Pugh to Samuel W. Johnson, November 14, 1855, Box 2, Folder 10, PP.

17. Evan Pugh to William Darlington, May 13, 1858, William Darlington Collection, New-York Historical Society.

18. Ibid.

19. George C. Caldwell to William Darlington, May 31, 1858, William Darlington Collection, New-York Historical Society.

20. Evan Pugh to Frederick O. Watts, March 3, 1859, Box 3, Folder 11, PP.

21. Frederick O. Watts to Evan Pugh, April 10, 1859, Box 5, Folder 23, PP.

22. Evan Pugh to Samuel W. Johnson, October 18, 1859, Box 5, Folder 12, PP.

23. True, *A History of Agricultural Education in the United States*, 31.

24. Evan Pugh to Samuel W. Johnson, October 18, 1859, Box 5, Folder 12, PP.

25. Dunaway, *A. History of Pennsylvania*, 269.

26. Margaret A. Rossiter, "The Organization of the Agricultural Sciences," in *The Organization of Knowledge in Modern America, 1860–1920*, ed. Alexandra Oleson and John Voss (Baltimore: Johns Hopkins University Press, 1979), 213.

27. Williams, *Origins of Federal Support for Higher Education*, 27.

28. Ibid., 28.

29. Ibid., 30–31.

30. Keith R. Widder, *Michigan Agricultural College: The Evolution of a Land-Grant Philosophy, 1855–1925* (East Lansing: Michigan State University Press, 2005), 3.

31. Ariel Ron, "Summoning the State: Northern Farmers and the Transformation of American Politics in the Mid-Nineteenth Century," *Journal of American History* 103, no. 2 (2016): 350, 374.

32. Ibid., 352.

33. A. M. Saunders and William Spangler, eds., *Farmer and Gardener* 3 (April 1861): 307.

34. Ron, "Summoning the State," 348.

35. Ibid., 351.

36. Williams, *Origins of Federal Support for Higher Education*, 31.

37. Quoted in Julianna Chaszar, "Leading and Losing in the Agricultural Education Movement: Freeman G. Cary and the Farmers' College, 1846–1884," *History of Higher Education Annual* 18 (1998): 25–46, passim.

38. Williams, *Origins of Federal Support for Higher Education*, 30–32.

39. Roger L. Geiger, "New Themes in the History of Nineteenth-Century Colleges," in *The American College in the Nineteenth Century*, ed. Roger L. Geiger (Nashville: Vanderbilt University Press, 2000), 132–33.

40. Roger L. Geiger, *To Advance Knowledge: The Growth of American Research Universities, 1900–1940* (New York: Oxford University Press, 1986), 6.

41. Frederick O. Watts to Governor William Bigler, January 20, 1854, Box 5, Folder 23, PP.

42. True, *A History of Agricultural Education in the United States*, 60–62.

43. Geiger, *History of American Higher Education*, 194.

Chapter 4

1. Frederick O. Watts to William G. Waring, October 1, 1859, Box 6, GST/AR/1.11, Frederick Watts Letters, 1857–71 (hereafter Watts Letters), Farmers' High School and Agricultural College of Pennsylvania Collection (PSUA 287) (hereafter FHSAC).

2. Minutes, Farmers' High School Board of Trustees, December 5, 1860, PSUA.

3. Runkle, *The Pennsylvania State College*, 57.

4. Bezilla, *Penn State*, 5, 6.

5. Joseph C. G. Kennedy, *Population of the United States in 1860; Compiled from the Original Returns of the Eighth Census* (Washington, D.C.: Government Printing Office, 1864), iv.

6. J. Thomas Mitchell, *Centre County: From Its Earliest Settlement to the Year 1915*, 9, 15, PSUA.

7. John Blair Linn, *History of Centre and Clinton Counties* (Philadelphia: J. B. Lippincott, 1883), 31.

8. Mitchell, *Centre County*, 26.

9. Gerald G. Eggert, *Making Iron on the Bald Eagle: Roland Curtin's Ironworks and Workers' Community* (University

Park: Pennsylvania State University Press, 2000), 2.

10. Mitchell, *Centre County*, 57.
11. Ibid., 34.
12. Bezilla, *Penn State*, 9.
13. Evan Pugh to Hugh N. McAllister, undated, but probably November–December 1859, Box 5, Folder 25, PP.
14. Quoted in Runkle, *The Pennsylvania State College*, 89.
15. Yarmey, *Labors and Legacies*, 22–23.
16. Evan Pugh, *On the Mutual Relations of the Teacher and the Taught*, Inaugural address, 1860 (Philadelphia: William S. Young, 1860), 3–4. PP. Subsequent page numbers appear in the text.
17. Evan Pugh to Hugh N. McAllister, March 2, 1860, Box 5, Folder 25, PP.
18. "An Act to Incorporate the Farmers' High School of Pennsylvania," February 22, 1855, in Runkle, *The Pennsylvania State College*, 397–98.
19. Pugh, *The Agricultural College of Pennsylvania, September 1862*, 45–48, PP.
20. Kennedy, *Population of the United States in 1860*, iv, vii.
21. Evan Pugh, *Catalogue of the Officers and Students for the Second Annual Session of the Farmers' High School of Pennsylvania* (Philadelphia: Bryson's Printing Rooms, 1860), PP, 13.
22. Russell H. Crittendon, *History of the Sheffield Scientific School of Yale University* (New Haven: Yale University Press, 1928), 49–50.
23. Ibid., 52–53.
24. V. Ennis Pilcher, *Early Science and the First Century of Physics at Union College, 1795–1895* (Glens Falls, N.Y.: Coneco Litho Graphics, 1994), 32–33.
25. Pugh, *Catalogue of the Officers and Students for the Second Annual Session of the Farmers' High School*, 31. Subsequent page numbers appear in the text.

26. Minutes, Farmers' High School Board of Trustees, December 5, 1860, PSUA.
27. Evan Pugh to Hugh N. McAllister, December 15, 1859, Box 5, Folder 25, PP.
28. Evan Pugh to Hugh N. McAllister, May 29, 1860, Box 5, Folder 25, PP.
29. Evan Pugh, *Address to the Cumberland County Agricultural Society at their fall meeting, October 1860* (Carlisle, Pa: The Society, 1860), 3, 5. Subsequent page numbers appear in the text.
30. Frederick O. Watts to Hugh N. McAllister, September 2, 1860, Watts Letters.

Chapter 5

1. Runkle, *The Pennsylvania State College*, 99.
2. Wayland F. Dunaway, *History of the Pennsylvania State College* (Lancaster, Pa.: Lancaster Press, 1946), 35.
3. *Old Main: Past, Present, Future*, illustrated booklet, The Pennsylvanian State College, 1929, p. 3, from the private collection of Robert and Jackie Bloom Struble of State College, Pa.
4. Evan Pugh to Samuel W. Johnson, March 13, 1861, Box 5, Folder 12, PP.
5. Runkle, *The Pennsylvania State College*, 99.
6. Dunaway, *History of the Pennsylvania State College*, 36.
7. Pugh, *The Agricultural College of Pennsylvania, September 1862*, 41.
8. Frederick O. Watts to Evan Pugh, April 12, 1861, Box 5, Folder 23, PP.
9. Minutes, Farmers' High School Board of Trustees, May 1, 1861, PSUA.
10. Minutes, Farmers' High School Board of Trustees, October 24, 1861, PSUA.
11. Evan Pugh, *Catalogue of the Officers and Students of the Farmers' High School of Pennsylvania for the Year 1861*

(Philadelphia: William S. Young, 1862), 21.

12. Runkle, *The Pennsylvania State College,* 99.

13. Pugh, *Catalogue . . . for the Year 1861,* 5.

14. Ibid., 8, 9.

15. Pugh, *The Agricultural College of Pennsylvania,* 43.

16. Dunaway, *History of the Pennsylvania State College,* 39.

17. Pugh, *Catalogue . . . for the Year 1861,* 16.

18. Ibid., 17.

19. Ibid., 20.

20. Michael Bezilla, "The Last Word on the First Grad Degree," *Research Matters,* http://researchmatters.psu.edu/tag/c-alfred-smith, September 4, 2013, 1.

21. Evan Pugh to Hugh N. McAllister, February 4, 1862, Box 5, Folder 29, PP.

22. Bezilla, "The Last Word on the First Grad Degree," 3.

23. Pugh, *Catalogue . . . for the year 1861,* 19.

24. Pugh, *The Agricultural College of Pennsylvania,* 43.

25. Ibid., 44.

26. Samuel Foster to Evan Pugh, October 15, 1861, Box 5, Folder 40, PP.

27. J. P. Kimball to Evan Pugh, October 23, 1860, Box 5, Folder 40, PP.

28. J. P. Kimball to Evan Pugh, October 15, 1861, Box 5, Folder 40, PP.

29. Henry Gerich to Evan Pugh, December 6, 1859, Box 5, Folder 40, PP.

30. Charles Davis to Evan Pugh, July 16, 1861, Box 5, Folder 40, PP.

31. Charles Calvert to Evan Pugh, December 14, 1860, Box 5, Folder 40, PP.

32. Evan Pugh to Hugh N. McAllister, February 2, 1860, Box 5, Folder 27, PP.

33. Pugh, *The Agricultural College of Pennsylvania, September 1862,* 11–12, PP.

34. Keith R. Widder, *Michigan Agricultural College: The Evolution of a Land-Grant Philosophy, 1855–1925* (East Lansing:
Michigan State University Press, 2005), x. Subsequent page numbers appear in the text.

35. George C. Callcott, *The University of Maryland at College Park: A History* (Baltimore: Noble House, 2005), 10.

36. Ibid., 16, 23.

37. Harold W. Cary, *The University of Massachusetts: A History of One Hundred Years* (Amherst: University of Massachusetts Press, 1962), 1–38, passim.

38. Dorothy Schweider and Gretchen Van Houten, eds., *A Sesquicentennial History of Iowa State University* (Ames: Iowa State University Press, 2007), xv.

39. James Gray, *The University of Minnesota, 1851–1951* (Minneapolis: University of Minnesota Press, 1951), 23–24.

40. Frederick O. Watts to Evan Pugh, February 26, 1862, Box 6, GST/AR/1.11, Watts Letters.

41. Dunaway, *History of the Pennsylvania State College,* 43.

42. Minutes, Farmers' High School Board of Trustees, May 6, 1862, PSUA.

43. Pugh, *The Agricultural College of Pennsylvania,* 45. Subsequent page numbers appear in the text.

44. Dunaway, *History of the Pennsylvania State College,* 40.

Chapter 6

1. A. J. Angulo, *William Barton Rogers and the Idea of MIT* (Baltimore: Johns Hopkins University Press, 2009), 71, 80.

2. Arthur W. Wright, "Biographical Memoir of Benjamin Silliman, 1816–1885" (1911), http://www.nasonline.org/publications/biographical-memoirs/memoir-pdfs/silliman-benjamin-jr.pdf.

3. Benjamin Silliman Jr. to Evan Pugh, December 3, 1859, on letterhead, Office of Silliman's Journal, New Haven, Connecticut, Box 5, Folder 8, PP.

4. Smith, "Evan Pugh, Ph.D., F.C.S., Memorial Address," 19.

5. "Chemical Society," Wikipedia, https://en.wikipedia.or/wiki/Chemical_Society, December 8, 2015.

6. Evan Pugh to Hugh N. McAllister, August 5, 1860, Box 5, Folder 25, PP.

7. Alfred L. Elwyn, J. Peter Lesley, and another [indecipherable] signatory to the American Philosophical Society, April 18, 1862, Box 3, Folder 18, PP.

8. Evan Pugh to J. Peter Lesley, November 7, 1862, Box 3, Folder 18, PP.

9. Sally Gregory Kohlstedt, *The Formation of the American Scientific Community: The American Association for the Advancement of Science, 1848–1860* (Urbana: University of Illinois Press, 1976), appendix.

10. W. George Waring, "Evan Pugh, Ph.D., F.C.S.," written for the Centennial of Chemistry, under ("American Contributions to Chemistry" by B. Silliman), and published in *American Chemist* 5, nos. 2, 3 (1874): 90–92, Box 3, GST/A/1.26, Waring Family Papers (MGN 107).

11. Evan Pugh, *The Agricultural College of Pennsylvania; Embracing a Succinct History of Agricultural Education in Europe and America, together with the circumstances of the Origin, Rise and Progress of the Agricultural College of Pennsylvania; as also a Statement of the Present Condition, Aims and Prospects of this Institution, its Course of Instruction, Facilities for Study, Terms of Admission, &c. &c. September 1862* (Philadelphia: William S. Young, 1862).

12. Evan Pugh to Samuel W. Johnson, August 16, 1860, Box 5, Folder 12, PP.

13. Evan Pugh to Samuel W. Johnson, June 8, 1861, Box 5, Folder 12, PP.

14. *Dictionary of American Biography*, "Johnson, Samuel W."

15. Evan Pugh to Samuel W. Johnson, October 17, 1861, Box 5, Folder 12, PP.

16. Evan Pugh to Samuel W. Johnson, November 18, 1861, Box 5, Folder 12, PP.

17. R. Adams Dutcher, "Pugh Centenary Radio Address," February 29, 1928, 7, from Dutcher Autobiographical File, PSUA. Dutcher was head of Agricultural and Biological Chemistry at Penn State.

18. Evan Pugh to Hugh N. McAllister, February 4, 1862, Box 5, Folder 29, PP.

19. Evan Pugh to Isaac Newton, U.S. Bureau of Agriculture, March 13, 1862, Box 3, Folder 20, PP.

20. Ibid.

21. Evan Pugh, "A National Agricultural Investigation Station," March 17, 1862, Box 3, Folder 19, PP.

22. Evan Pugh to Samuel W. Johnson, April 7, 1862, Box 5, Folder 12, PP.

23. Runkle, *The Pennsylvania State College*, 68–69.

24. Evan Pugh to David Wilson, September 18, 1863, Box 4, Folder 37, PP.

25. C. Alfred Smith to Evan Pugh, September 21, 1863, Box 4, Folder 16, PP.

26. True, *A History of Agricultural Education in the United States*, 127–28.

27. Williams, *Origins of Federal Support for Higher Education*, 90.

28. Ibid., 92.

29. Ibid., 192.

Chapter 7

1. Pugh, *A Report upon a Plan for the Organization*, 29.

2. Robert V. Bruce, *The Launching of Modern American Science, 1846–1876*

(Ithaca: Cornell University Press, 1987), 302.

3. Williams, *Origins of Federal Support for Higher Education*.

4. Ariel Ron, "The Hidden Development State: Land Grant Policy and the Federal Government in the Nineteenth Century," Working paper, 2010, https://www.academia.edu/4217353.

5. An Act Donating Public Lands to the Several States and Territories which May Provide Colleges for the Benefit of Agriculture and the Mechanic Arts, Pub. L. 37-108, 12 Stat. 503 (1862), § 4.

6. Williams, *Origins of Federal Support for Higher Education*, 46–47.

7. Clark Kerr, *The Uses of the University* (Cambridge, Mass.: Harvard University Press, 1982), 46–48.

8. Nathan M. Sorber and Roger L. Geiger, *The Welding of Opposite Views: Land-Grant Historiography at 150 Years* (Dordrecht: Springer Science+Business Media, 2014), 4, 32.

9. Geiger, *History of American Higher Education*, 281.

10. Ibid., 283.

11. "Agricultural College and a Model Farm," *Pennsylvania Farm Journal* 2, no. 10 (January 1853): 291–92.

12. Edward H. Reisner, *Nationalism and Education since 1789: A Social and Political History of Modern Education* (New York: Macmillan, 1922), 334.

13. Williams, *Origins of Federal Support for Higher Education*, 37–38.

14. Pugh, *An Address to the Cumberland County Agricultural Society*, 35.

15. Williams, *Origins of Federal Support for Higher Education*, 39.

16. Geiger, *History of American Higher Education*, 282.

17. Williams, *Origins of Federal Support for Higher Education*, 39.

18. *Proceedings of the Fourteenth Annual Convention of the Association of American Agricultural Colleges and Experiment Stations, held at Middletown and New Haven, Connecticut, November 13–15, 1900*, U.S. Department of Agriculture, Experiment Station Bulletin no. 93 (Washington, D.C.: Government Printing Office, 1901), 67.

19. Margaret Tschan Riley, "Evan Pugh of Pennsylvania State University and the Morrill Land-Grant Act," *Pennsylvania History* 27, no. 4 (1960): 355.

20. Bruce, *The Launching of Modern American Science*, 302.

21. Ross, *Democracy's College*, 55.

22. Asa E. Martin, "Pennsylvania's Land Grant Under the Morrill Act of 1862," *Pennsylvania History* 9, no. 2 (1942): 93.

23. Evan Pugh to Hugh N. McAllister, February 4, 1862, Box 5, Folder 29, PP.

24. Pugh, *A Report Upon a Plan for the Organization*, 34.

25. *The Legislative Record Containing the Debates and Proceedings of the Pennsylvania Legislature for the Session of 1864*, by George Bergner (Harrisburg: "Telegraph" Steam Book and Job Office, 1864), 771.

26. There is no extant record of correspondence between Pugh and Hale, who served as an elected trustee of the Agricultural College from 1858 until his death in 1865. Most of Pugh's correspondence with trustees was either through the president of the board, Frederick Watts, or, more especially, with Hugh McAllister, on myriad matters pertaining to the operation of the college. Neither do the two local histories, *Commemorative Biographic Record of Central Pennsylvania, including the counties of Centre, Clinton, Union and Snyder* (Chicago: J. H. Beers, 1898), 197–98, and John Blair Linn, *History of Centre and Clinton Counties, Pennsylvania* (Philadelphia:

J. B. Lippincott, 1883), 79–81, describe Hale's legislative work. However, a handful of letters between Hale and Hugh McAllister are in the James T. Hale letters 1860–72, Box 7, GST/AR/1.12, FHSAC.

27. Runkle, *The Pennsylvania State College*, 102.

28. An Act Donating Public Lands to the Several States and Territories which May Provide Colleges for the Benefit of Agriculture and the Mechanic Arts, Pub. L. 37-108, 12 Stat. 503 (1862), § 4.

29. Ibid., § 2.

30. Ibid., §§ 7 and 5.

31. *Legislative Record 1864*, 771.

32. Minutes, Agricultural College of Pennsylvania Board of Trustees, September 2, 1862, PSUA.

33. Evan Pugh to Hugh N. McAllister, January 17, 1863, Box 5, Folder 29, PP.

34. Evan Pugh to Hugh N. McAllister, January 29, 1863, Box 5, Folder 29, PP.

35. An Act to Accept the Grant of Public Lands by the United States to the Several States, for the Endowment of Agricultural Colleges, P.L. 213, no. 227 (passed April 1, 1863).

36. Runkle, *The Pennsylvania State College*, 118.

37. Ibid., 119.

38. *Legislative Record 1864*, 771.

39. Evan Pugh to Hugh N. McAllister, March 23, 1863, Box 5, Folder 29, PP.

40. Ibid.

Chapter 8

1. Evan Pugh, *Catalogue of the Officers and Students of the Agricultural College of Pennsylvania for the year 1863* (Philadelphia: W. S. Young, 1864), 7, 25.

2. Ibid., 3.

3. Evan Pugh to Samuel W. Johnson, February 16, 1864, Box 5, Folder 12, PP.

4. Abbie H. Cromer, curator, the Penn State Room, to A. R. Warnock, dean of men, the Pennsylvania State College, June 1, 1949, Box 5, Folder 53, PP.

5. Dunaway, *History of the Pennsylvania State College*, 53.

6. Thanks are due to Nancy Stover, researcher and archivist for the Pennsylvania Room of the Centre County Library and Historical Museum in Bellefonte. Ms. Stover conducted meticulous research into historical properties and Valentine family genealogy, confirming the location of "Willowbank" (current address of which is 308 South Potter Street, Bellefonte), and using historical maps and documents reconstructed the route Pugh and Valentine would have taken from Willowbank to Forge House on the evening of June 16, 1863.

7. J. Marvin Lee, "Penn State's First Lady," *Town & Gown*, December 1981, 26.

8. "Notes from a Talk with Rebecca Pugh Lyon at West Chester, Pennsylvania, June 17, 1951" (interviewer unidentified, but possibly Abbie Cromer), Box 5, Folder 53, PP.

9. Thomas G. Morton, assisted by Frank Woodbury, *The History of the Pennsylvania Hospital, 1751–1895* (Philadelphia: Times, 1897), 507, https://archive.org/details/historypennsylvo1pagoog.

10. Evan Pugh to Hugh N. McAllister, July 23, 1863, Box 5, Folder 31, PP.

11. Evan Pugh to Hugh M. McAllister, August 11, 1863, Box 5, Folder 31, PP.

12. Evan Pugh to Hugh N. McAllister, August 24, 1863, Box 5, Folder 31, PP.

13. Evan Pugh to Samuel W. Johnson, September 18, 1863, Box 5, Folder 12, PP.

14. Evan Pugh to Samuel W. Johnson, October 16, 1863, Box 5, Folder 12, PP.

15. Evan Pugh to Samuel W. Johnson, December 8, 1863, Box 5, Folder 12, PP.

16. R. S. Caldwell to Evan Pugh, August 6, 1863, Box 5, Folder 13, PP.

17. Evan Pugh to Samuel W. Johnson, October 16, 1863, Box 5, Folder 12, PP.

18. Evan Pugh to Samuel W. Johnson, December 8, 1863, Box 5, Folder 12, PP.

19. John I. Thompson Class of 1862, reminiscence quoted in Runkle, *The Pennsylvania State College*, 384.

20. Evan Pugh to Samuel W. Johnson, October 17, 1861, Box 5, Folder 12, PP.

21. Evan Pugh to Samuel W. Johnson, June 8, 1861, Box 5, Folder 10, PP.

22. Evan Pugh to Samuel W. Johnson, October 17, 1861, Box 5, Folder 12, PP.

23. Evan Pugh to Hugh N. McAllister, September 16, 1862, Box 5, Folder 17, PP.

24. Evan Pugh to Hugh N. McAllister, June 27, 1863, Box 5, Folder 17, PP.

25. Quoted in Runkle, *The Pennsylvania State College*, 385–86.

26. Dunaway, *History of the Pennsylvania State College*, 52.

27. C. Alfred Smith to Evan Pugh, September 14, 1863, Box 4, Folder 16, PP.

28. Evan Pugh to Hugh N. McAllister, September 11, 1863, Box 5, Folder 31, PP.

29. C. Alfred Smith to Evan Pugh, September 21, 1863, Box 4, Folder 16, PP (1261).

30. Ibid.

31. Evan Pugh to Hugh N. McAllister, June 4, 1863, Box 5, Folder 17, PP.

32. Evan Pugh to Hugh N. McAllister, October 7, 1863, Box 5, Folder 17, PP.

33. Evan Pugh to Hugh N. McAllister, December 19, 1863, Box 5, Folder 17, PP.

34. David Wilson to Hugh N. McAllister, May 14, 1859, Box 7, GST/AR/1.12, FHSAC.

35. Evan Pugh to Hugh N. McAllister, July 10, September 24, and October 10, 1861, Box 5, Folder 17, PP.

36. Evan Pugh to Hugh N. McAllister, December 11 and 15, 1863, Box 5, Folder 17, PP.

37. Pugh, *Catalogue . . . for the Year 1863*, 24–25.

38. Minutes, Agricultural College of Pennsylvania Board of Trustees, January 6, 1864, PSUA.

39. Ross, *Democracy's College*, 73, 239.

40. Pugh, *A Report upon a Plan for the Organization*, 5. Subsequent page numbers appear in the text.

Chapter 9

1. Williams, *Origins of Federal Support for Higher Education*, 236.

2. An Act to Accept the Grant of Public Lands by the United States to the Several States for the Endowment of Agricultural Colleges, P.L. 213, No. 227 (passed April 1, 1863), § 4.

3. Runkle, *The Pennsylvania State College*, 120–21.

4. Bezilla, *Penn State*, 12.

5. Saul Sack, *History of Higher Education in Pennsylvania* (Harrisburg: Pennsylvania Historical and Museum Commission, 1963), 479–82.

6. Riley, "Evan Pugh of Pennsylvania State University and the Morrill Land-Grant Act," 357.

7. Evan Pugh to Samuel W. Johnson, February 16, 1864, Box 5, Folder 12, PP.

8. A. O. Hiester to Evan Pugh, November 24, 1863, Box 5, Folder 35, PP.

9. Daniel Kaine to Evan Pugh, November 27, 1863, Box 5, Folder 35, PP.

10. *The Legislative Record Containing The Debates and Proceedings of the Pennsylvania Legislature for the Session of 1864*, 266–67.

11. Runkle, *The Pennsylvania State College*, 125.
12. *Legislative Record 1864*, 748, 776.
13. Evan Pugh, "A Statement made by Dr. E. Pugh, of the Agricultural College of Pennsylvania, at a special meeting of the Judiciary Committee, at Harrisburg, convened March 3rd, 1864, in reference to the proposition to deprive this College of its Endowment," 1–2. Subsequent page numbers appear in the text.
14. Ibid., 9–10.
15. Evan Pugh to Samuel W. Johnson, April 1, 1864, Box 5, Folder 12, PP.
16. *Legislative Record 1864*, 713; Runkle, *The Pennsylvania State College*, 128.
17. James T. Hale to Hugh N. McAllister, April 15, 1864, Box 7, GST/AR/1.12, James T. Hale letters, 1860–72, FHSAC.
18. *Legislative Record 1864*, 744. Subsequent page numbers appear in the text.
19. Pennsylvania State Senate Historical Biographies, http://www.legisl/state/pa/us/cfdocs/legis/BiosHistory/.
20. Evan Pugh's response to HB 809, his last written words, April 22, 1864, with an annotation by C. Alfred Smith, Class of 1861, "student and closest friend of Dr. Pugh," Box 4, Folder 16, PP.
21. Smith, "Evan Pugh, Ph.D., F.C.S., Memorial Address," 14–15.
22. *Legislative Record 1864*, 920.
23. Ibid., 920–21.
24. Pennsylvania State Senate Historical Biographies, http://www.legis.state.pa.us/cfdocs/legis/BiosHistory/MemBio.cfm, and U.S. Government Archives, http://files.usgarchives.net/pa/centre/bios/alexander.
25. *Legislative Record 1864*, 922. Subsequent page numbers appear in the text.

Chapter 10

1. Smith, "Evan Pugh, Ph.D., F.C.S., Memorial Address," 15.
2. John L. Brusch, M.D., and Michael S. Bronze, M.D., "Typhoid Fever," http://www.emedicine@medscape.com, April 22, 2015.
3. Smith, "Evan Pugh, Ph.D., F.C.S., Memorial Address," 13.
4. Evan Pugh, "Gottingen and the Harts."
5. Michael Bezilla, *The College of Agriculture at Penn State: A Tradition of Excellence* (University Park: Pennsylvania State University Press, 1987), 22.
6. "Notes from a Talk with Rebecca Pugh Lyon at West Chester, Pennsylvania, June 17, 1951" (interviewed by Abbie Cromer), Box 5, Folder 53, PP.
7. Lee, "Penn State's First Lady," 48.
8. "Resolution upon the Death of President Pugh," by students of the Agricultural College of Pennsylvania, April 30, 1864, Box 5, Folder 48, PP.
9. Pugh obituary in Bellefonte's *Democratic Watchman*, May 2, 1864, Box 5, Folder 48, PP.
10. Testimonial to Pugh (author and outlet unidentified), Box 5, Folder 48, PP.
11. Thomas P. Knox to Hugh N. McAllister, May 2, 1864, Box 5, Folder 48, PP.
12. Alfred L. Elwyn, Evan Pugh obituary, undated, Box 5, Folder 48, PP.
13. Minutes, Agricultural College of Pennsylvania Board of Trustees, June 15, 1864, PSUA.
14. Pugh obituary in Hertfordshire, England, newspaper, August 2, 1864, Box 5, folder 48, PP.
15. Samuel W. Johnson to Hugh N. McAllister, May 14, 1864, Box 5, Folder 48, PP.

16. Pugh obituary, *American Journal of Science and Arts* 38 (September 1864), Box 5, Folder 48, PP.

17. John Lawes to Rebecca Pugh, cited in Smith, "Evan Pugh, Ph.D., F.C.S., Memorial Address," 19–20.

18. Smith, "Evan Pugh, Ph.D., F.C.S., Memorial Address," 18.

19. Frederick O. Watts to Hugh N. McAllister, May 10, 1864, Box 6, GST/AR/1.11, Watts Letters.

20. Frederick Watts to Samuel W. Johnson, May 10, 1864, Box 6, GST/AR/1.11, Watts Letters.

21. Samuel W. Johnson letter to Hugh N. McAllister, May 12, 1864, Box 5 folder 47, PP.

22. Runkle, *The Pennsylvania State College*, 141; Bezilla, *Penn State*, 14–15.

23. Runkle, *The Pennsylvania State College*, 141.

24. George C. Caldwell to Hugh N. McAllister, June 11, 1864, cited in Yarmey, *Labors and Legacies*, 39.

25. Ibid., 40.

26. Yarmey, *Labors and Legacies,* 44.

27. Bezilla, *Penn State*, 16–17.

28. David Wilson to Hugh N. McAllister, May 25, 1868, Box 7, GST/AR/1.12, FHSAC.

29. J. Lacey Darlington to Hugh McAllister, December 28, 1868, Box 7, GST/AR.1.12, FHSAC.

30. Runkle, *The Pennsylvania State* College, 165–67.

31. Ibid., 175–76.

32. Bezilla, *Penn State*, 21–25.

33. Ibid., 25–27.

34. *The Legislative Record Containing The Debates and Proceedings of the Pennsylvania Legislature for the Session of 1865*, by George Bergner (Harrisburg: "Telegraph" Steam Book and Job Office, 1865), 435.

35. Peter L. Moran and Roger L. Williams, "Saving the Land Grant for the Agricultural College of Pennsylvania," in *The Land-Grant Colleges and the Reshaping of American Higher Education*, ed. Roger L. Geiger and Nathan M. Sorber, Perspectives on the History of Higher Education 30 (New Brunswick, NJ: Transaction, 2013), 117. Subsequent page numbers appear in the text.

36. Bezilla, *Penn State*, 21.

Epilogue

1. Smith, "Evan Pugh, Ph.D., F.C.S., Memorial Address."

2. C. Alfred Smith, "Remembrance of Evan Pugh," Memorial Address, Pennsylvania State College Semi-Centennial, June 1905, p. 70, Box 5, Folder 51, PP.

3. Yarmey, *Labors and Legacies*, 78–79.

4. George Gilbert Pond, "Dr. Pugh's Career as a Chemist," Pennsylvania State University Semi-Centennial, June 1905, passim, Box 5, Folder 51, PP.

5. Runkle, *The Pennsylvania State College*, 405.

6. N. B. Guerrant, D. E. H. Frear, and R. V. Boucher, "R. Adams Dutcher: A Biographical Sketch," *Journal of Nutrition* 81 (1963): 3–4.

7. Erwin W. Runkle, "The Pugh Centenary," *Penn State Alumni News* 14, no. 6 (1928): 3–15.

8. Adams Dutcher, "Pugh Centenary Radio Address," pp. 1, 8, The Pennsylvania State College, February 29, 1928, Box 5, Folder 1, PP.

9. Yarmey, *Chemists of Penn State,* 119.

10. Neil E. Gordon to Erwin W. Runkle, November 18, 1929, Box 5, Folder 49, PP.

11. Browne, "European Laboratory Experiences," 517.

12. *Headlight on Books at Penn State* 19, no. 3 (1949).

13. Margaret Tschan Riley, "Penn State's First President: Scientist, Educator, Administrator," *Penn State Alumni News*, January 1960, 5–11; Riley, "Evan Pugh of Pennsylvania State University and the Morrill Land-Grant Act," *Pennsylvania History* 27, no. 4 (1960), 339–60.

14. Bloom, "Evan Pugh."

15. Riley, "Penn State's First President," 9.

16. David D. Henry, "Evan Pugh and the Land-Grant Centennial," address given at The Pennsylvania State University, February 10, 1862, Box 5, Folder 51, PP.

17. Pugh Historical Markers, Oxford, Pa., Box 8, compact disc, MGN89 GC5/S/5/S04.B0Z.T03, PP.

18. The Pennsylvania State University, Policy HR 87: Evan Pugh Professorships; policy's initial date, December 13, 1971; this version effective February 27, 2015.

Collections

Darlington, William. Collection. New-York Historical Society.
Farmers' High School and Agricultural College of Pennsylvania Collection. Pennsylvania State University Archives 287, Box 6, GST/AR/1.11; Box 7, GST/AR/1.12.
Curtin, Andrew. Letters, 1860–72.
Hale, James T. Letters, 1860–72.
McAllister, Hugh. Letters, 1857–74.
Waring, William G. Papers, 1851–71.
Watts, Frederick. Letters, 1857–74.
Pugh Papers. Evan Pugh Papers, 1822–1864. Pennsylvania State University Archives 1261, Eberly Family Special Collections Library, The Pennsylvania State University.
Waring Family Papers. Eberly Family Special Collections Library, The Pennsylvania State University. MGN 107, Box 3, GST/A/1.26.

Published Sources

An Act Donating Public Lands to the Several States and Territories which May Provide Colleges for the Benefit of Agriculture and the Mechanic Arts. Pub. L. 37-108, 12 Stat. 503 (1862).
An Act to Accept the Grant of Public Lands by the United States to the Several States, for the Endowment of Agricultural Colleges. P.L. 213, No. 227 (passed April 1, 1863).
Angulo, A. J. *William Barton Rogers and the Idea of MIT.* Baltimore: Johns Hopkins University Press, 2009.
Bezilla, Michael. *The College of Agriculture at Penn State: A Tradition of Excellence.* University Park: Pennsylvania State University Press, 1987.
———. "The Last Word on the First Grad Degree." *Research Matters,* September 4, 2013. http://research matters.psu.edu/tag/c-alfred-smith.
———. *Penn State: An Illustrated History.* University Park: Pennsylvania State University Press, 1985.
Bloom, Jacqueline. "Evan Pugh: The Education of a Scientist, 1828–1859." M.A. thesis, Pennsylvania State University, 1960.
———. "The Path of Duty and of Destiny: Evan Pugh's Commitment to a Model for the Land Grant Institutions." Paper for Harvard Department of History class A-450, December 14, 1987. In author's collection.
Breneman, A. A. "Dr. Evan Pugh, Chemist and Philosopher." Address given June 16, 1908, before the Phi Kappa Phi Society at the Pennsylvania State College.

Browne, Charles A. "European Experiences of an Early American Agricultural Chemist—Dr. Evan Pugh (1828–1864)." *Journal of Chemical Education* 7, no. 3 (1930).

Bruce, Robert V. *The Launching of Modern American Science, 1846–1876*. Ithaca: Cornell University Press, 1987.

Brusch, John L., and Michael S. Bronze. "Typhoid Fever." Medscape.com, May 18, 2017. http://emedicine .medscape.com/article/231135 -overview.

Burke, Colin B. *American Collegiate Populations: A Test of the Traditional View*. New York: New York University Press, 1982.

Callcott, George C. *The University of Maryland at College Park: A History*. Baltimore: Noble House, 2005.

Cary, Harold W. *The University of Massachusetts: A History of One Hundred Years*. Amherst: University of Massachusetts Press, 1962.

Chaszar, Julianna. "Leading and Losing in the Agricultural Education Movement: Freeman G. Cary and Farmers' College, 1846–1884." *History of Higher Education Annual* 18 (1998): 25–46.

Cremin, Lawrence A. *American Education: The National Experience, 1873–1876*. New York: Harper and Row, 1980.

Crittendon, Russell H. *History of the Sheffield Scientific School of Yale University*. New Haven: Yale University Press, 1928.

Cross, Coy F., II. *Justin Smith Morrill: Father of the Land-Grant Colleges*. East Lansing: Michigan State University Press, 1999.

Diehl, Carl. "Innocents Abroad: American Students in German Universities, 1810–1870." *History of Education Quarterly* 16, no. 3 (1976): 321–40.

Dunaway, Wayland F. *A History of Pennsylvania*. New York: Prentice-Hall, 1935.

———. *History of the Pennsylvania State College*. Lancaster, Pa.: Lancaster Press, 1946.

Dupree, A. Hunter. *Science in the Federal Government: A History of Policies and Activities to 1940*. Cambridge, Mass.: Harvard University Press, 1957.

Dutcher, R. Adams. "Pugh Centenary Radio Address." February 29, 1928. Pugh Papers.

Edmond, J. B. *The Magnificent Charter: The Origin and Role of the Morrill Land-Grant Colleges and Universities*. Hicksville, N.Y.: Exposition Press, 1978.

Eggert, Gerald G. *Making Iron on the Bald Eagle: Roland Curtin's Ironworks and Workers' Community*. University Park: Pennsylvania State University Press, 2000.

Geiger, Roger L. *The History of American Higher Education: Learning and Culture from the Founding to World War II*. Princeton: Princeton University Press, 2015.

———, ed. "The Land-Grant Act and American Higher Education: Context and Consequences." Special issue, *History of Higher Education Annual* 18 (1998).

———. "New Themes in the History of Nineteenth-Century Colleges." In *The American College in the Nineteenth Century*, ed. Roger L. Geiger, 1–36. Nashville: Vanderbilt University Press, 2000.

———. *To Advance Knowledge: The Growth of American Research Universities, 1900–1940*. New York: Oxford University Press, 1986.

Geiger, Roger L., and Nathan M. Sorber, eds. *The Land-Grant Colleges and the Reshaping of American Higher Education.* Perspectives on the History of Higher Education 30. New Brunswick: Transaction, 2013.

Gray, James, *The University of Minnesota, 1851–1951.* Minneapolis: University of Minnesota Press, 1951.

Henry, David D. "Evan Pugh and the Land-Grant Centennial." Address given at the Pennsylvania State University, February 10, 1862. Box 5, Folder 51, Pugh Papers.

Hofstadter, Richard M. *Academic Freedom in the Age of the College.* New York: Columbia University Press, 1961.

Johnston, James F. W., and Charles A. Cameron. *Elements of Agricultural Chemistry and Geology.* 13th ed. Edinburgh: William Blackwood and Sons, 1883. Box 5, Folder 51, Pugh Papers.

Kennedy, Joseph C. G. *Agriculture of the United States in 1860; Compiled from the Original Returns of the Eighth Census.* Washington, D.C.: Government Printing Office, 1864.

———. *Population of the United States in 1860; Compiled from the Original Returns of the Eighth Census.* Washington, D.C.: Government Printing Office, 1864.

Kerr, Clark. *The Uses of the University.* Cambridge, Mass.: Harvard University Press, 1982.

Kohlstedt, Sally Gregory. *The Formation of the American Scientific Community: The American Association for the Advancement of Science, 1848–1860.* Urbana: University of Illinois Press, 1976.

Lee, J. Marvin. "Penn State's First Lady." *Town and Gown*, December 1981.

The Legislative Record Containing the Debates and Proceedings of the Pennsylvania Legislature for the Session of 1864. By George Bergner. Harrisburg: "Telegraph" Steam Book and Job Office, 1864.

The Legislative Record Containing the Debates and Proceedings of the Pennsylvania Legislature for the Session of 1865. By George Bergner. Harrisburg: "Telegraph" Steam Book and Job Office, 1865.

Linn, John Blair. *History of Centre and Clinton Counties, Pennsylvania.* Philadelphia: J. B. Lippincott, 1883.

Marcus, Alan I. *Agricultural Science and the Quest for Legitimacy.* Ames: Iowa State University Press, 1985.

Martin, Asa E. "Pennsylvania's Land Grant under the Morrill Act of 1862." *Pennsylvania History* 9, no. 2 (1942).

Mitchell, J. Thomas. *Centre County: From Its Earliest Settlement to the Year 1915.* Pennsylvania State University Archives.

Moran, Peter L., and Roger L. Williams. "Saving the Land Grant for the Agricultural College of Pennsylvania." In *The Land-Grant Colleges and the Reshaping of American Higher Education*, ed. Roger L. Geiger and Nathan M. Sorber. Perspectives on the History of Higher Education 30. New Brunswick: Transaction, 2013.

Old Main: Past, Present, Future. The Pennsylvanian State College, 1929. Illustrated booklet from the private collection of Robert and Jackie Bloom Struble of State College, Pa.

Parker, William B. *The Life and Public Services of Justin Smith Morrill.* Boston: Houghton Mifflin, 1924.

Pilcher, V. Ennis. *Early Science and the First Century of Physics at Union College, 1795–1895.* Glens Falls, N.Y.: Coneco Litho Graphics, 1994.

Pond, George Gilbert. "Dr. Pugh's Career as a Chemist." Pennsylvania State

University Semi-Centennial, June 1905. Box 5, Folder 51, Pugh Papers.

Potts, David B. "Curriculum and Enrollments: Some Thoughts on Assessing the Popularity of Ante-Bellum Colleges." *History of Higher Education Annual* 1 (1981): 88–109.

Proceedings of the Fourteenth Annual Convention of the Association of American Agricultural Colleges and Experiment Stations, held in Middletown and New Haven, Connecticut, November 13–15, 1900. U.S. Department of Agriculture, Experiment Station Bulletin No. 93. Washington, D.C.: Government Printing Office, 1901.

Proceedings of the Women's Rights Convention, Held at West Chester, Pa. June 2d and 3d, 1852. Philadelphia: Merrihew and Thompson, 1852.

Pugh, Evan. *An Address to the Cumberland County Agricultural Society at their fall meeting, October 1860.* Carlisle, Pa.: The Society, 1860.

———. *The Agricultural College of Pennsylvania; Embracing a Succinct History of Agricultural Education in Europe and America, together with the circumstances of the Origin, Rise and Progress of the Agricultural College of Pennsylvania and also a Statement of the Present Condition, Aims and Prospects of this Institution, its Course of Instruction, Facilities for Study, Terms of Admission, &c. &c. September 1862.* Philadelphia: William S. Young, 1862.

———. *Catalogue of the Officers and Students for the Second Annual Session of the Farmers' High School of Pennsylvania.* Philadelphia: Bryson's Printing Rooms, 1860.

———. *Catalogue of the Officers and Students of the Agricultural College of Pennsylvania for the Year 1863.* Philadelphia: W. S. Young, 1864.

———. *Catalogue of the Officers and Students of the Farmers' High School of Pennsylvania for the Year 1861.* Philadelphia: William S. Young, 1862.

———. "Gottingen Journal." Pugh Papers.

———. "Leipsic Journal." Pugh Papers.

———. "A National Agricultural Investigation Station." Pugh Papers.

———. "On a new method for the Quantitative Estimation of Nitric Acid." *Quarterly Journal of the Chemical Society of London* 12 (1860): 35–42.

———. *On the Mutual Relations of the Teacher and the Taught.* Inaugural address, 1860. Philadelphia: William S. Young, 1860.

———. *A Report upon A Plan for the Organization of Colleges of Agriculture and the Mechanic Arts, with especial reference to the organization of the Agricultural College of Pennsylvania in view of the endowment of this institution by the land scrip fund donated by Congress to the State of Pennsylvania.* Harrisburg, Pa.: Singerly and Myers, 1864.

———. "A Statement made by Dr. E. Pugh, of the Agricultural College of Pennsylvania, at a special meeting of the Judiciary Committee, at Harrisburg, convened March 3rd, 1864, in reference to the proposition to deprive this College of its Endowment."

Pugh Historical Markers. Oxford, Pa., Box 8, compact disc, MGN89 GC5/S/5/S04.BoZ.T03. Pugh Papers.

Riley, Margaret Tschan. "Evan Pugh of Pennsylvania State University and the Morrill Land-Grant Act." *Pennsylvania History* 27, no. 4 (1960): 339–60.

———. "Penn State's First President: Scientist, Educator, Administrator." *Penn State Alumni News*, January 1960, 5–11.

Ron, Ariel. "The Hidden Development State: Land Grant Policy and the Federal Government in the Nineteenth Century." Working paper, 2010. https://www.academia.edu/4217353.

———. "Summoning the State: Northern Farmers and the Transformation of American Politics in the Mid-Nineteenth Century." *Journal of American History* 103, no. 2 (2016).

Rosenberg, Charles E. *No Other Gods: On Science and American Social Thought.* Rev. and expanded ed. Baltimore: Johns Hopkins University Press, 1997.

Ross, Earle D. *Democracy's College: The Land-Grant Movement in the Formative Stage.* Ames: Iowa State College Press, 1942.

Rossiter, Margaret W. "The Organization of Agricultural Improvement in the United States, 1785–1865." In *The Pursuit of Knowledge in the Early American Republic: American Scientific and Learned Societies from Colonial Times to the Civil War*, ed. Alexandra Oleson and Sanford C. Brown. Baltimore: Johns Hopkins University Press, 1976.

———. "The Organization of the Agricultural Sciences." In *The Organization of Knowledge in Modern America, 1860–1920*, ed. Alexandra Oleson and John Voss, 211–48. Baltimore: Johns Hopkins University Press, 1979.

Runkle, Erwin W. *The Pennsylvania State College, 1853–1932: Interpretation and Record.* State College, Pa.: Nittany Valley Society, 2013. Manuscript copyright 1933.

———. "The Pugh Centenary." *Penn State Alumni News* 14, no. 6 (1928).

Sack, Saul. *History of Higher Education in Pennsylvania.* 2 vols. Harrisburg: Pennsylvania Historical and Museum Commission, 1963.

Schweider, Dorothy, and Gretchen Van Houten, eds. *A Sesquicentennial History of Iowa State University.* Ames: Iowa State University Press, 2007.

Smith, C. Alfred. "Evan Pugh, Ph.D., F.C.S. Memorial Address, June 25, 1890." Delivered on the occasion of the presentation of a portrait of Dr. Pugh to the Pennsylvania State College, June 25, 1890. Box 5, Folder 51, Pugh Papers.

———. "Remembrance of Evan Pugh." Memorial Address, Pennsylvania State College Semi-Centennial, June 1905. Box 5, Folder 51, Pugh Papers.

Sorber, Nathan M. "Farmers, Scientists, and Officers of Industry: The Formation and Reformation of Land-Grant Colleges in the Northeastern United States, 1862–1906." Ph.D. diss., Pennsylvania State University, 2010.

Sorber, Nathan M., and Roger L. Geiger. *The Welding of Opposite Views: Land-Grant Historiography at 150 Years.* Dordrecht: Springer Science+Business Media, 2014.

Stout, Leon J. "The Penn State President Who Never Was." *Town and Gown*, April 1996, 23–25.

———. "Penn State's First Trustees." *Town and Gown*, November 2005.

Traverse, Alfred. "Dr. Pugh's Herbarium." *Journal of the Botanical Research Institute of Texas* 7, no. 2 (2013): 751–64.

True, Alfred C. *A History of Agricultural Education in the United States,*

1785-1925. U.S. Department of Agriculture, Misc. Pub. no. 36. Washington, D.C.: Government Printing Office, July 1929.

U.S. State Department. "Agriculture and the Economy." ThoughtCo., December 19, 2014. Updated March 21, 2017. http://economics.about.com/od /americanagriculture/a/agriculture .htm.

Veysey, Lawrence R. *The Emergence of the American University*. Chicago: University of Chicago Press, 1965.

Waring, W. George. "Evan Pugh, Ph.D., F.C.S." Written for the Centennial of Chemistry, under "American Contributions to Chemistry," by B. Silliman, published in *American Chemist* 5, nos. 2–3 (August–September 1874). Waring Family Papers.

Watts, Frederick. *Annual Report of the Farmers' High School, 1858*. Pennsylvania State University Archives.

Widder, Keith R. *Michigan Agricultural College: The Evolution of a Land-Grant Philosophy, 1855–1925*. East Lansing: Michigan State University Press, 2005.

Williams, Roger L. "Justin S. Morrill and George W. Atherton: A Quarter-Century Collaboration to Advance the Land-Grant Colleges." *History of Higher Education Annual* 18 (1998): 67–80.

———. *The Origins of Federal Support for Higher Education: George W. Atherton and the Land-Grant College Movement*. University Park: Pennsylvania State University Press, 1991.

Wright, Arthur W. "Biographical Memoir of Benjamin Silliman, 1816–1885." 1911. National Academy of Sciences. http://www.nasonline.org/pub lications/biographical-memoirs /memoir-pdfs/silliman-benjamin -jr.pdf.

Yarmey, Kristen A. *Labors and Legacies: The Chemists of Penn State, 1855–1947*. University Park: Pennsylvania State University Department of Chemistry, 2006.